Sasha Kagan's

BIG & LITTLE SWEATERS

Sasha Kagan's

BIG & LITTLE SWEATERS

The Westminster Trading Corporation
Amherst, New Hampshire

CONTENTS

INTRODUCTION   **6**

BEFORE YOU BEGIN   **8**

Editors Melanie Miller, Debra Grayson
Art Editor Michele Walker
Designer Sarah Ponder
Editorial Director Amy Carroll

Text and original knitwear designs
copyright © Sasha Kagan 1987.
Charts and illustrations copyright ©
Dorling Kindersley Limited 1987.

Published in the United States of America by
The Westminster Trading Corporation,
5 Northern Boulevard, Amherst,
New Hampshire 03031.

First published in 1987 in Great Britain by
Dorling Kindersley Limited.

Although every reasonable care has been taken
to ensure that the knitting instructions contained
in this book are accurate and complete, Dorling
Kindersley Publishers Limited cannot accept
responsibility for any errors.

Library of Congress Cataloging-in-Publication
Data

Kagan, Sasha
   Sasha Kagan's Big and Little Sweaters
   1. Knitting – Patterns   I. Title
   TT 825·K328 1987 746·9'2 87-23134
   ISBN 0-938953-03-6

First American Edition: October 1987

10 9 8 7 6 5 4 3 2 1

Printed and bound in Italy

WITTY & WHIMSICAL

POODLE   **14**

COWBOY   **18**

HARLEQUIN   **22**

CHAINSAW   **26**

FLOWER GIRL   **30**

MOUSE   **34**

POSIES & PETALS

LAVENDER   **40**

WELSH POPPY   **44**

BAVARIAN FLOWER   **48**

CHERRY   **52**

ACORN   **56**

ALMOND BLOSSOM   **60**

FLASHES & SPLASHES

SPLASH	66
ODEON	70
LIGHTNING	74
PERSIAN STRIPE	78
CUBE	82
WANDERING LINE	86
OBLOID	90
ZIGZAG	94

BASIC PATTERNS

4 PLY WOOL	99
4 PLY COTTON	104
DOUBLE KNITTING WOOL	108

BASIC TECHNIQUES

BASIC TECHNIQUES	113
GLOSSARY OF TERMS	127
YARN INFORMATION	127

Dear Knitters.

I am pleased to present here my second collection of knitting patterns.

This is not an ordinary knitting book; it is a book of many choices – I have counted over 2,000 possible variations in all! In it you will find patterns for all the family, from toddler to grandmother, teenager to great-grandfather. To this end I have chosen six classic shapes: sweater, jacket, cardigan, slipover, waistcoat and short top, and I have sized them (with a great deal of help from Jeni Morrison) in seven sizes, from a 24″ to a 48″ chest. There are 20 different designs, grouped in three sections: Witty and Whimsical, Posies and Petals, Flashes and Splashes. The wool selected this time is from Rowan, a very creative yarn company in Yorkshire, whose range of colours have been a constant inspiration. I have used their lightweight cotton, Botany 4 ply and Designer Double Knitting yarn. However, you can use your own yarn, but be sure you obtain the tension stated in the pattern instructions.

Handknitting is a very skilled craft, and each piece has its own individuality. With love and care the sweaters should last for years and can be passed on from one child to another. Rowan, my youngest, wears hand-me-downs from Tanya, now 15; rather like teddy bears, the sweaters improve with age. Whatever your family's taste in sweaters, I hope there will be something to please everyone.

For your convenience, Rowan Yarns are providing knitting kits for some of the sweaters shown in the book and these are listed on page 128. The knitting kits will contain enough yarn for the garment you have chosen, buttons (if applicable) and my own label.

My sincere thanks to Jeni Morrison, righthand woman extraordinaire for all her work and enthusiasm on the book, Marlene Richards for sewing and finishing so beautifully, Muriel Jones for knitting swatches in next to no time, and my team of dedicated knitters without whose skills and patience this book would not have been possible.

Happy Knitting!

Sasha Kagan

BEFORE YOU BEGIN

This is not an ordinary knitting pattern book so it is vital that you read these introductory pages before you embark on a pattern.

There are twenty different charted designs in this book, ranging from the figurative, such as "Poodle", to the abstract, such as "Splash". Each charted design can be made into five or six different shapes – a sweater, jacket, cardigan, slipover, waistcoat, or short top. Some of the charted designs are for 4 ply wool, some are for 4 ply cotton, and some are for double knitting wool. All of the garments can be made in a range of seven different sizes, the *actual* chest sizes ranging from 24 inches (*61 centimetres*) to 48 inches (*122 centimetres*).

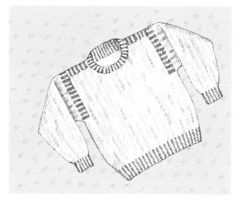
Sweater

Slipover

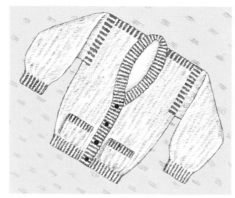
Jacket

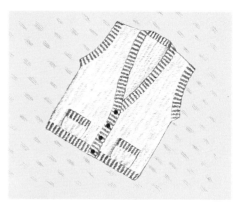
Waistcoat

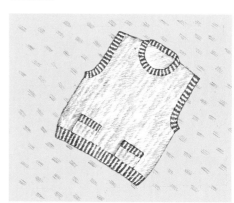
Cardigan

Short top

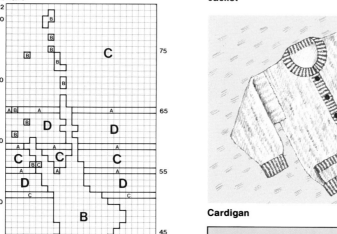

Splash chart

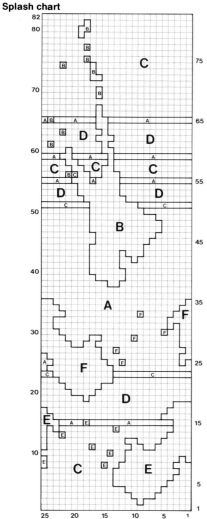

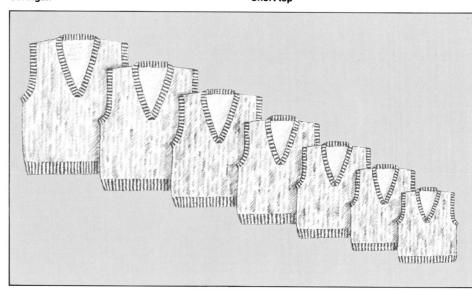

THE PATTERN CHARTS

These fall into three different categories: Witty and Whimsical, Posies and Petals, and Flashes and Splashes. Each pattern chart has been made up into one, two or three garments, in a range of shapes and sizes, and photographed either on models, or flat, or both. Although we might have shown, say, "Poodle" as a slipover and a sweater you can, if you wish, make it up in any of the other garment shapes.

THE BASIC PATTERNS

Basic patterns for each of the garment shapes in the various different yarns are provided at the back of the book, pages 98-112.

YARN

The yarn used throughout the book is by Rowan, details as follows.

4 ply wool patterns

The yarn used is Rowan Botany wool, with the occasional use of Rowan Light Tweed and Fine Fleck Tweed, however any standard 4 ply wool may be used as long as the correct tension is obtained.

4 ply cotton patterns

The yarn is Rowan Sea Breeze cotton, however any standard 4 ply cotton may be used, as long as the correct tension is obtained.

Double knitting wool patterns

The yarn used is Rowan Designer DK, with the occasional use of Rowan Fine Cotton Chenille, however any standard double knitting wool may be used, as long as the correct tension is obtained.

A number of the designs are available in kit form from Rowan stockists. For more information about Rowan yarn and kit stockists turn to page 128.

Child's cotton sweater knitted in the red variation of Splash design.

YARN QUANTITIES

The amount of yarn required to make each garment is given in chart form. Choose the garment shape you wish to make, and then follow the column for your chosen size.

These yarn quantities are based on using Rowan yarn; if you use another yarn you may find you need more, or less, than the quantity stated. Ask your yarn store for advice, if necessary, when substituting yarn.

Quantities of yarn quoted are given in multiples of the quantities in which they can be bought. In some cases, however, only very small quantities of a shade are required, perhaps for working eyes, or a small detail in the pattern. For these you can use scraps of yarn if you have them, so study the pattern before you buy your yarn.

All yarn quantities stated in the book are based on average requirements and are, therefore, approximate.

WORKING WITH COLOURS

There are basically two different ways of working multi-coloured designs, depending on whether isolated blocks of a yarn are worked, or whether a colour is worked repeatedly along a row. For isolated blocks of colour (as used in Harlequin), where the yarn *not* in use is not carried across the back of the work, the intarsia method is used; for an all-over pattern (such as Odeon) the "Fair Isle" method is used. In addition to this, many of my designs are made using a combination of intarsia and "Fair Isle". In these cases yarn is carried across the back of individual motifs, but not across the back of the background. Mouse is an example of this. We have called this method "individual motif" knitting. The "Fair Isle" method makes a double thickness fabric, consequently proportionately more yarn is needed for a garment of the same size. Therefore it is very important, if you are not to run out of yarn or have a great amount left over, to work the pattern in the same way as the garment illustrated. Sometimes it is difficult to tell, just by looking at a pattern, whether intarsia, "Fair Isle" or "individual motif" knitting should be used, so details as to which method should be used are given with each chart pattern. More information about intarsia and "Fair Isle" knitting is provided at the back of the book in the Basic Techniques section, pages 113-127.

SIZING AND MEASUREMENTS

For every garment, pattern instructions are provided for seven sizes. The sizes given are the *actual* chest sizes, not the *to fit* sizes, so you must make your garment larger than your chest measurement, depending on the degree of ease you require. For example, supposing your actual chest size is 33in (*84cm*); if you want a close-fitting garment follow the pattern instructions for the 36in (*91cm*) chest. If you want a loose-fitting garment follow the pattern instructions for the 40in (*102cm*) chest. If you are unsure of the amount of ease you require, measure one of your own sweaters that provides you with the right amount of ease, then follow the chest size nearest to this. Remember that

Harlequin

Odeon

certain garments usually provide more ease than others – a jacket to fit a 33in (*84cm*) chest is larger than a slipover to fit a 33in (*84cm*) chest so take this into account when choosing your size. Full details of finished measurements (actual chest size, length to shoulder, sleeve length) are given at the beginning of the basic patterns. Both imperial and metric measurements are provided throughout the patterns; imperial first and then metric in brackets and/or italics afterwards. Please follow only one set of measurements.

ALTERNATIVE COLOUR VARIATIONS

Up to four different colour variations are provided with each pattern chart. The Rowan shade numbers for the variations are given alongside the pattern chart, so you can choose whichever variation you like or even substitute your own.

THE PATTERN CHARTS

All the designs are presented in chart form. Basically the charts are repeated across a garment and up a garment, starting with stitch one in the right-hand corner. Full instructions for reading the charts are given with each pattern. A motif may be centred on each garment piece, or a complete motif may appear at the edges of jacket, cardigan and waistcoat fronts. If you are not familiar with working from charts please see Basic techniques, pages 113-127.

RIBBING

Most of the garments feature a contrast trim on the edge of the ribbing (apart from the welt), others feature a striped ribbing. Full instructions for the ribbing are given with each chart, along with an indication of the yarn to be used for pocket linings, if applicable. When working a stripe sequence cast-on rows, cast-off rows, and "pick up and knit" rows should be worked as part of the stripe sequence.

SINGLE SHADE GARMENTS

The basic patterns can be used to make garments of a single shade – 4 ply wool and double knitting wool give the best results. Yarn quantities for these are given on page 127.

BASIC TECHNIQUES AND ABBREVIATIONS

All the techniques for knitting the garments are explained on pages 113-126. A list of abbreviations and a glossary of British/American terms are provided on page 127.

SO, TO MAKE A GARMENT FROM THIS BOOK
1. Select your pattern chart.
2. Choose your garment shape.
3. Choose your garment size.
4. Choose your colourway.
5. Follow basic shape pattern instructions at the back of the book.
6. Follow specific pattern instructions alongside your chosen chart.

MODEL SHOT

Shows the pattern chart made up as a garment. May show more than one variation. For example Harlequin, shown here, has been made as two sizes of short tops, however you could knit the pattern chart into any of six different shapes, in any of seven different sizes, in any of the suggested colourways.

YARN QUANTITIES CHART

This provides details of how much of each yarn you need to purchase. Pick the area of the chart that shows your chosen shape (jacket, waistcoat, etc) and then follow the line of the chart that corresponds to your chosen size.

FLAT SHOT

A simple straight-on photograph either of one of the garments shown in the model shot, or another variation.

PATTERN CHART

Given in black and white so it can be used with any colour variation.

COLOUR KEY

Gives details of the different shades used in the colour variations.

PLACING INSTRUCTIONS

Specific instructions explaining how to position the chart on your chosen garment. Follow only the instructions for your chosen shape and your chosen size.

PATTERN INFORMATION

Tells you which basic pattern instructions can be used with this particular pattern chart, the method of knitting (Fair Isle, intarsia or individual motifs), and special instructions for the ribbing and back of waistcoat.

COLOUR VARIATIONS

Close-up photographs of the different colour combinations.

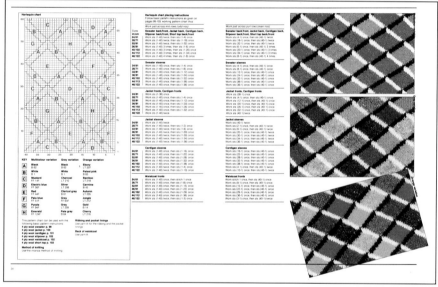

BASIC PATTERN INSTRUCTIONS

These are all given at the back of the book, pages 98-112.

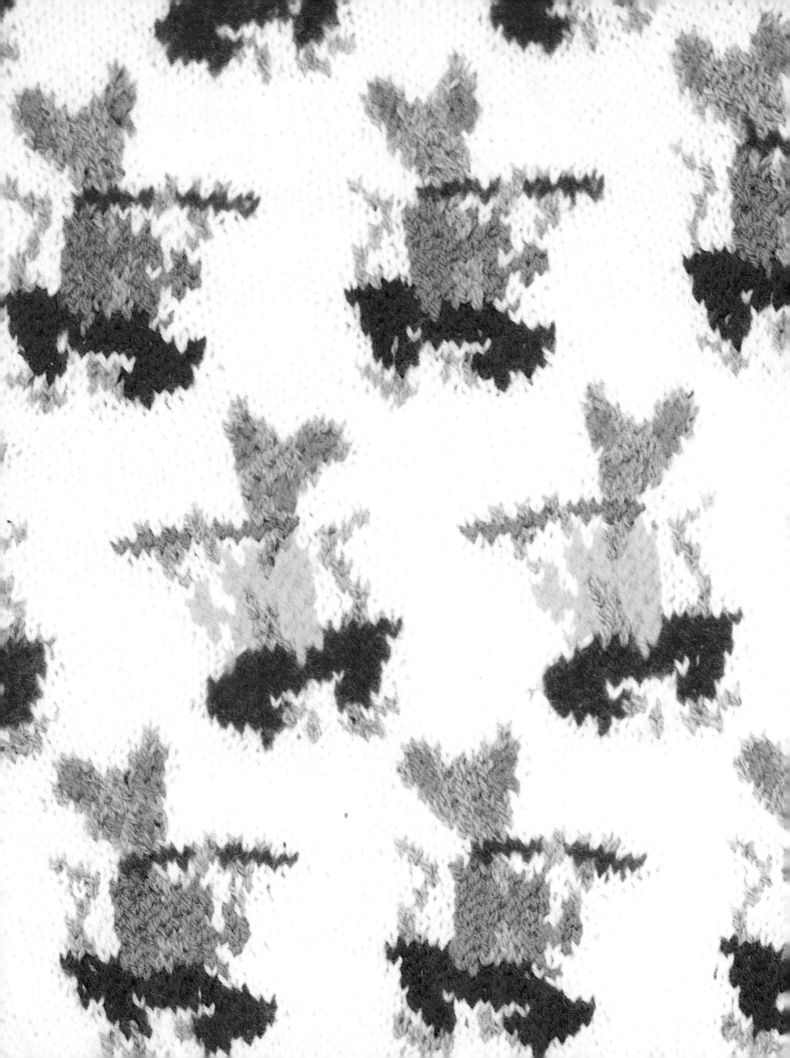

WITTY & WHIMSICAL

POODLE

Oodles of poodles dance across an alternative striped background in this cartoon-inspired garment. The lovable motif is suitable for both the young and young-at-heart.

POODLE YARN QUANTITIES

Each figure represents the number of 25g hanks of Rowan Botany (B), Light Tweed (LT) or Fine Fleck (FF) required.

Sizes in/cm	Sweater A	B	C	D	E	F	G	H	Jacket A	B	C	D	E	F	G	H	Cardigan A	B	C	D	E	F	G	H
24/61	1	1	2	2	1	1	1		2	2	2	2	1	1	1		2	2	2	2	1	1	1	
28/71	2	1	2	2	1	1	1		3	2	2	2	1	1	1		3	2	2	2	1	1	1	
32/81	2	1	3	3	1	1	1		3	2	3	3	1	1	1		3	2	3	3	1	1	1	
36/91	3	2	4	4	1	1	1		4	3	4	4	1	1	1		4	3	4	4	1	1	1	
40/102	3	2	5	4	1	2	1		4	3	5	4	1	2	1		4	3	5	4	1	2	1	
44/112	3	2	7	6	1	2	1		4	3	7	6	1	2	1		4	3	7	6	1	2	1	
48/122	4	3	7	6	1	2	1		5	4	7	6	1	2	1		5	4	7	6	1	2	1	

Sizes in/cm	Slipover A	B	C	D	E	F	G	H	Waistcoat A	B	C	D	E	F	G	H	Short top A	B	C	D	E	F	G	H
24/61	1	1	1	1	1	1	1		2	1	1	1	1	1	1		1	1	1	1	1	1	1	
28/71	1	1	1	1	1	1	1		2	1	1	1	1	1	1		1	1	1	1	1	1	1	
32/81	1	1	2	2	1	1	1		2	1	1	1	1	1	1		1	1	2	2	1	1	1	
36/91	2	1	2	2	1	1	1		3	1	1	1	1	1	1		2	1	2	2	1	1	1	
40/102	2	1	3	2	1	1	1		3	2	2	1	1	1	1		2	1	3	2	1	1	1	
44/112	2	1	4	3	1	1	1		3	2	2	2	1	1	1		2	1	4	3	1	1	1	
48/122	3	2	5	3	1	1	1		4	2	3	2	1	1	1		3	1	5	3	1	1	1	

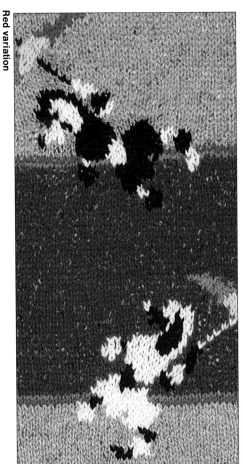

Poodle chart placing instructions

Follow basic pattern instructions as given on pages 99-103, working pattern chart thus:

Sizes in/cm	*Work patt across knit rows (odd nos):*	*Work patt across purl rows (even nos):*
Sweater back/front, Jacket back, Cardigan back, Slipover back/front, Short top back/front		
24/61	Work sts (1-45) once, then sts (1-39) once.	Work sts (39-1) once, then sts (45-1) once.
28/71	Work sts (1-45) twice, then sts (1-8) once.	Work sts (8-1) once, then sts (45-1) twice.
32/81	Work sts (1-45) twice, then sts (1-22) once.	Work sts (22-1) once, then sts (45-1) twice.
36/91	Work sts (1-45) twice, then sts (1-36) once.	Work sts (36-1) once, then sts (45-1) twice.
40/102	Work sts (1-45) 3 times, then sts (1-5) once.	Work sts (5-1) once, then sts (45-1) 3 times.
44/112	Work sts (1-45) 3 times, then sts (1-19) once.	Work sts (19-1) once, then sts (45-1) 3 times.
48/122	Work sts (1-45) 3 times, then sts (1-33) once.	Work sts (33-1) once, then sts (45-1) 3 times.
Sweater sleeves		
24/61	Work sts (1-44) once.	Work sts (44-1) once.
28/71	Work sts (1-45) once, then sts (1-3) once.	Work sts (3-1) once, then sts (45-1) once.
32/81	Work sts (1-45) once, then sts (1-7) once.	Work sts (7-1) once, then sts (45-1) once.
36/91	Work sts (1-45) once, then sts (1-19) once.	Work sts (19-1) once, then sts (45-1) once.
40/102	Work sts (1-45) once, then sts (1-27) once.	Work sts (27-1) once, then sts (45-1) once.
44/112	Work sts (1-45) once, then sts (1-31) once.	Work sts (31-1) once, then sts (45-1) once.
48/122	Work sts (1-45) once, then sts (1-31) once.	Work sts (31-1) once, then sts (45-1) once.
Jacket fronts, Cardigan fronts: left		
24/61	Work sts (5-42) once.	Work sts (42-5) once.
28/71	Work sts (2-45) once.	Work sts (45-2) once.
32/81	Work sts (39-45) once, then sts (1-45) once.	Work sts (45-1) once, then sts (45-39) once.
36/91	Work sts (31-45) once, then sts (1-45) once.	Work sts (45-1) once, then sts (45-31) once.
40/102	Work sts (25-45) once, then sts (1-45) once.	Work sts (45-1) once, then sts (45-25) once.
44/112	Work sts (19-45) once, then sts (1-45) once.	Work sts (45-1) once, then sts (45-19) once.
48/122	Work sts (11-45) once, then sts (1-45) once.	Work sts (45-1) once, then sts (45-11) once.
Jacket fronts, Cardigan fronts: right		
All sizes	Reverse positioning, so right edge of chart runs up centre front. For example, for size 36in/91cm knit rows, work sts (1-45) once, then sts (1-15) once.	
Jacket sleeves		
24/61	Work sts (1-45) once, then sts (1-35) once.	Work sts (35-1) once, then sts (45-1) once.
28/71	Work sts (1-45) once, then sts (1-37) once.	Work sts (37-1) once, then sts (45-1) once.
32/81	Work sts (1-45) once, then sts (1-41) once.	Work sts (41-1) once, then sts (45-1) once.
36/91	Work sts (1-45) twice, then sts (1-10) once.	Work sts (10-1) once, then sts (45-1) twice.
40/102	Work sts (1-45) twice, then sts (1-20) once.	Work sts (20-1) once, then sts (45-1) twice.
44/112	Work sts (1-45) twice, then sts (1-24) once.	Work sts (24-1) once, then sts (45-1) twice.
48/122	Work sts (1-45) twice, then sts (1-26) once.	Work sts (26-1) once, then sts (45-1) twice.
Cardigan sleeves		
24/61	Work sts (1-45) once, then sts (1-11) once.	Work sts (11-1) once, then sts (45-1) once.
28/71	Work sts (1-45) once, then sts (1-17) once.	Work sts (17-1) once, then sts (45-1) once.
32/81	Work sts (1-45) once, then sts (1-23) once.	Work sts (23-1) once, then sts (45-1) once.
36/91	Work sts (1-45) once, then sts (1-27) once.	Work sts (27-1) once, then sts (45-1) once.
40/102	Work sts (1-45) once, then sts (1-33) once.	Work sts (33-1) once, then sts (45-1) once.
44/112	Work sts (1-45) once, then sts (1-39) once.	Work sts (39-1) once, then sts (45-1) once.
48/122	Work sts (1-45) twice.	Work sts (45-1) twice.
Waistcoat fronts: left		
24/61	Work sts (5-45) once.	Work sts (45-5) once.
28/71	Work sts (43-45) once, then sts (1-45) once.	Work sts (45-1) once, then sts (45-43) once.
32/81	Work sts (36-45) once, then sts (1-45) once.	Work sts (45-1) once, then sts (45-36) once.
36/91	Work sts (29-45) once, then sts (1-45) once.	Work sts (45-1) once, then sts (45-29) once.
40/102	Work sts (22-45) once, then sts (1-45) once.	Work sts (45-1) once, then sts (45-22) once.
44/112	Work sts (15-45) once, then sts (1-45) once.	Work sts (45-1) once, then sts (45-15) once.
48/122	Work sts (8-45) once, then sts (1-45) once.	Work sts (45-1) once, then sts (45-8) once.
Waistcoat fronts: right		
All sizes	Reverse positioning, so right edge of chart runs up centre front. For example, for size 36in/91cm knit rows, work sts (1-45) once, then sts (1-17) once.	

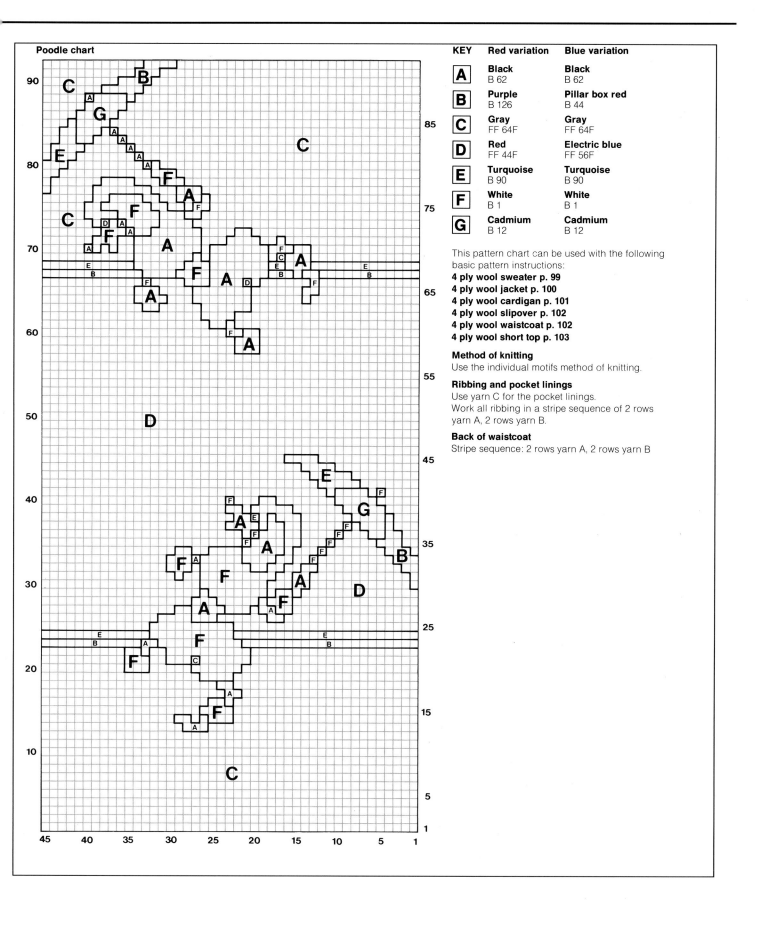

Poodle chart

KEY	Red variation	Blue variation
A	**Black** B 62	**Black** B 62
B	**Purple** B 126	**Pillar box red** B 44
C	**Gray** FF 64F	**Gray** FF 64F
D	**Red** FF 44F	**Electric blue** FF 56F
E	**Turquoise** B 90	**Turquoise** B 90
F	**White** B 1	**White** B 1
G	**Cadmium** B 12	**Cadmium** B 12

This pattern chart can be used with the following
basic pattern instructions:
4 ply wool sweater p. 99
4 ply wool jacket p. 100
4 ply wool cardigan p. 101
4 ply wool slipover p. 102
4 ply wool waistcoat p. 102
4 ply wool short top p. 103

Method of knitting
Use the individual motifs method of knitting.

Ribbing and pocket linings
Use yarn C for the pocket linings.
Work all ribbing in a stripe sequence of 2 rows
yarn A, 2 rows yarn B.

Back of waistcoat
Stripe sequence: 2 rows yarn A, 2 rows yarn B

Rootin', tootin', fast-shooting cowboys at the ready on an exuberant garment trouble-makers of all ages will love. Striped bands accent key shades from the motifs.

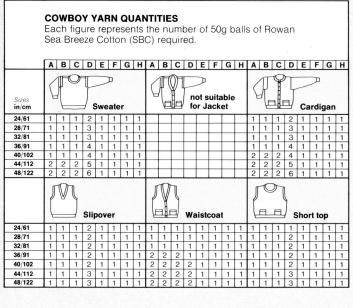

COWBOY YARN QUANTITIES

Each figure represents the number of 50g balls of Rowan Sea Breeze Cotton (SBC) required.

Sizes in/cm	Sweater A	B	C	D	E	F	G	H	Jacket A	B	C	D	E	F	G	H	Cardigan A	B	C	D	E	F	G	H
24/61	1	1	1	2	1	1	1	1				*not suitable for Jacket*					1	1	1	2	1	1	1	1
28/71	1	1	1	3	1	1	1	1									1	1	1	3	1	1	1	1
32/81	1	1	1	3	1	1	1	1									1	1	1	3	1	1	1	1
36/91	1	1	1	4	1	1	1	1									1	1	1	4	1	1	1	1
40/102	1	1	1	4	1	1	1	1									2	2	2	4	1	1	1	1
44/112	2	2	2	5	1	1	1	1									2	2	2	5	1	1	1	1
48/122	2	2	2	6	1	1	1	1									2	2	2	6	1	1	1	1

Sizes in/cm	Slipover A	B	C	D	E	F	G	H	Waistcoat A	B	C	D	E	F	G	H	Short top A	B	C	D	E	F	G	H
24/61	1	1	1	2	1	1	1	1	1	1	1	1	1	1	1	1	1	1	1	1	1	1	1	1
28/71	1	1	1	2	1	1	1	1	1	1	1	1	1	1	1	1	1	1	1	2	1	1	1	1
32/81	1	1	1	2	1	1	1	1	1	1	1	1	1	1	1	1	1	1	1	2	1	1	1	1
36/91	1	1	1	2	1	1	1	1	2	2	2	1	1	1	1	1	1	1	1	2	1	1	1	1
40/102	1	1	1	2	1	1	1	1	2	2	2	2	1	1	1	1	1	1	1	2	1	1	1	1
44/112	1	1	1	3	1	1	1	1	2	2	2	2	1	1	1	1	1	1	1	3	1	1	1	1
48/122	1	1	1	3	1	1	1	1	2	2	2	2	1	1	1	1	1	1	1	3	1	1	1	1

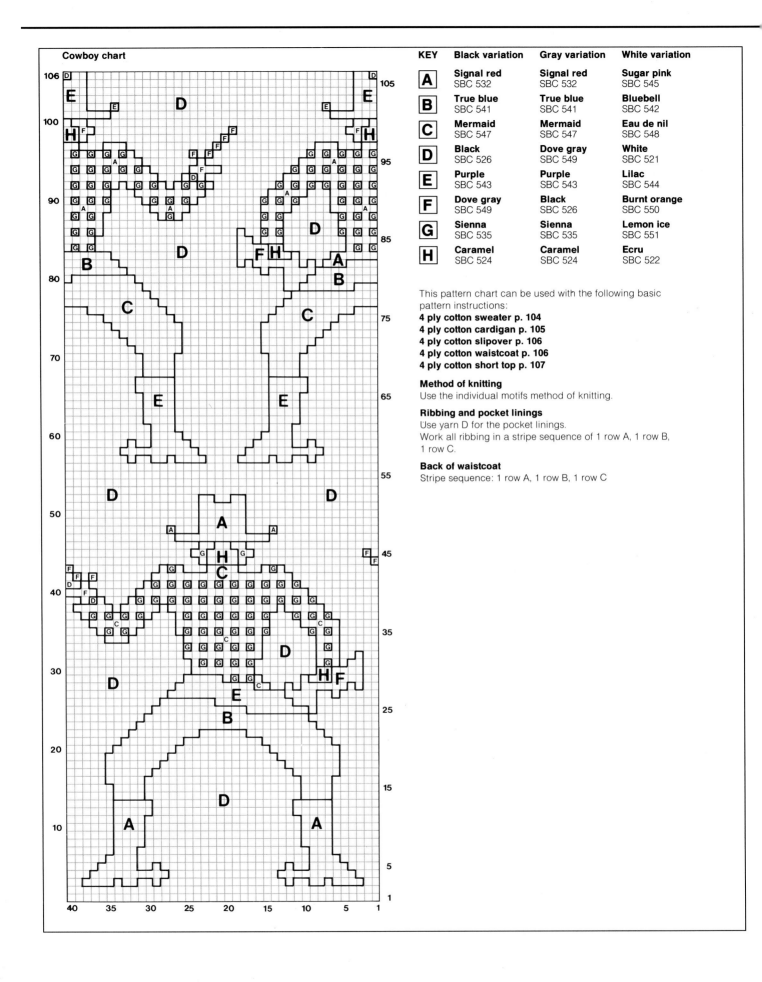

Cowboy chart

This pattern chart can be used with the following basic pattern instructions:
4 ply cotton sweater p. 104
4 ply cotton cardigan p. 105
4 ply cotton slipover p. 106
4 ply cotton waistcoat p. 106
4 ply cotton short top p. 107

Method of knitting
Use the individual motifs method of knitting.

Ribbing and pocket linings
Use yarn D for the pocket linings.
Work all ribbing in a stripe sequence of 1 row A, 1 row B, 1 row C.

Back of waistcoat
Stripe sequence: 1 row A, 1 row B, 1 row C

Cowboy chart placing instructions

Follow basic pattern instructions as given on pages 104-107, working pattern chart thus:

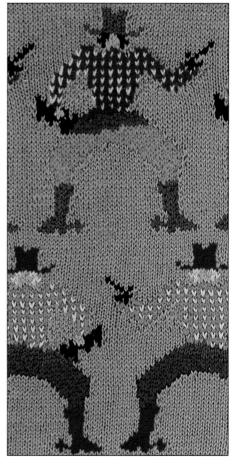

Sizes in/cm	Work patt across knit rows (odd nos):	Work patt across purl rows (even nos):
Sweater back/front, Cardigan back, Slipover back/front, Short top back/front		
24/61	Work sts (11-40) once, then sts (1-40) once, then sts (1-30) once.	Work sts (30-1) once, then sts (40-1) once, then sts (40-11) once.
28/71	Work sts (3-40) once, then sts (1-40) once, then sts (1-38) once.	Work sts (38-1) once, then sts (40-1) once, then sts (40-3) once.
32/81	Work sts (35-40) once, then sts (1-40) 3 times, then sts (1-6) once.	Work sts (6-1) once, then sts (40-1) 3 times, then sts (40-35) once.
36/91	Work sts (27-40) once, then sts (1-40) 3 times, then sts (1-14) once.	Work sts (14-1) once, then sts (40-1) 3 times, then sts (40-27) once.
40/102	Work sts (19-40) once, then sts (1-40) 3 times, then sts (1-22) once.	Work sts (22-1) once, then sts (40-1) 3 times, then sts (40-19) once.
44/112	Work sts (11-40) once, then sts (1-40) 3 times, then sts (1-30) once.	Work sts (30-1) once, then sts (40-1) 3 times, then sts (40-11) once.
48/122	Work sts (3-40) once, then sts (1-30) 3 times, then sts (1-38) once.	Work sts (38-1) once, then sts (40-1) 3 times, then sts (40-3) once.
Sweater sleeves		
24/61	Work sts (1-40) once, then sts (1-18) once.	Work sts (18-1) once, then sts (40-1) once.
28/71	Work sts (1-40) once, then sts (1-26) once.	Work sts (26-1) once, then sts (40-1) once.
32/81	Work sts (1-40) once, then sts (1-28) once.	Work sts (28-1) once, then sts (40-1) once.
36/91	Work sts (1-40) once, then sts (1-36) once.	Work sts (36-1) once, then sts (40-1) once.
40/102	Work sts (1-40) twice.	Work sts (40-1) twice.
44/112	Work sts (1-40) twice, then sts (1-2) once.	Work sts (2-1) once, then sts (40-1) twice.
48/122	Work sts (1-40) twice, then sts (1-6) once.	Work sts (6-1) once, then sts (40-1) twice.
Cardigan fronts		
24/61	Work stitch 40 only, then sts (1-40) once, then stitch 1 once.	Work stitch 1 once, then sts (40-1) once, then stitch 40 only.
28/71	Work sts (35-40) once, then sts (1-40) once, then sts (1-6) once.	Work sts (6-1) once, then sts (40-1) once, then sts (40-35) once.
32/81	Work sts (31-40) once, then sts (1-40) once, then sts (1-10) once.	Work sts (10-1) once, then sts (40-1) once, then sts (40-31) once.
36/91	Work sts (27-40) once, then sts (1-40) once, then sts (1-14) once.	Work sts (14-1) once, then sts (40-1) once, then sts (40-27) once.
40/102	Work sts (23-40) once, then sts (1-40) once, then sts (1-18) once.	Work sts (18-1) once, then sts (40-1) once, then sts (40-23) once.
44/112	Work sts (19-40) once, then sts (1-40) once, then sts (1-22) once.	Work sts (22-1) once, then sts (40-1) once, then sts (40-19) once.
48/122	Work sts (15-40) once, then sts (1-40) once, then sts (1-26) once.	Work sts (26-1) once, then sts (40-1) once, then sts (40-15) once.
Cardigan sleeves		
24/61	Work sts (1-40) once, then sts (1-16) once.	Work sts (16-1) once, then sts (40-1) once.
28/71	Work sts (1-40) once, then sts (1-24) once.	Work sts (24-1) once, then sts (40-1) once.
32/81	Work sts (1-40) once, then sts (1-30) once.	Work sts (30-1) once, then sts (40-1) once.
36/91	Work sts (1-40) once, then sts (1-34) once.	Work sts (34-1) once, then sts (40-1) once.
40/102	Work sts (1-40) once, then sts (1-38) once.	Work sts (38-1) once, then sts (40-1) once.
44/112	Work sts (1-40) twice.	Work sts (40-1) twice.
48/122	Work sts (1-40) twice, then sts (1-4) once.	Work sts (4-1) once, then sts (40-1) twice.
Waistcoat fronts		
24/61	Work sts (38-40) once, then sts (1-40) once, then sts (1-3) once.	Work sts (3-1) once, then sts (40-1) once, then sts (40-38) once.
28/71	Work sts (34-40) once, then sts (1-40) once, then sts (1-7) once.	Work sts (7-1) once, then sts (40-1) once, then sts (40-34) once.
32/81	Work sts (30-40) once, then sts (1-40) once, then sts (1-11) once.	Work sts (11-1) once, then sts (40-1) once, then sts (40-30) once.
36/91	Work sts (26-40) once, then sts (1-40) once, then sts (1-15) once.	Work sts (15-1) once, then sts (40-1) once, then sts (40-26) once.
40/102	Work sts (22-40) once, then sts (1-40) once, then sts (1-19) once.	Work sts (19-1) once, then sts (40-1) once, then sts (40-22) once.
44/112	Work sts (18-40) once, then sts (1-40) once, then sts (1-23) once.	Work sts (23-1) once, then sts (40-1) once, then sts (40-18) once.
48/122	Work sts (14-40) once, then sts (1-40) once, then sts (1-27) once.	Work sts (27-1) once, then sts (40-1) once, then sts (40-14) once.

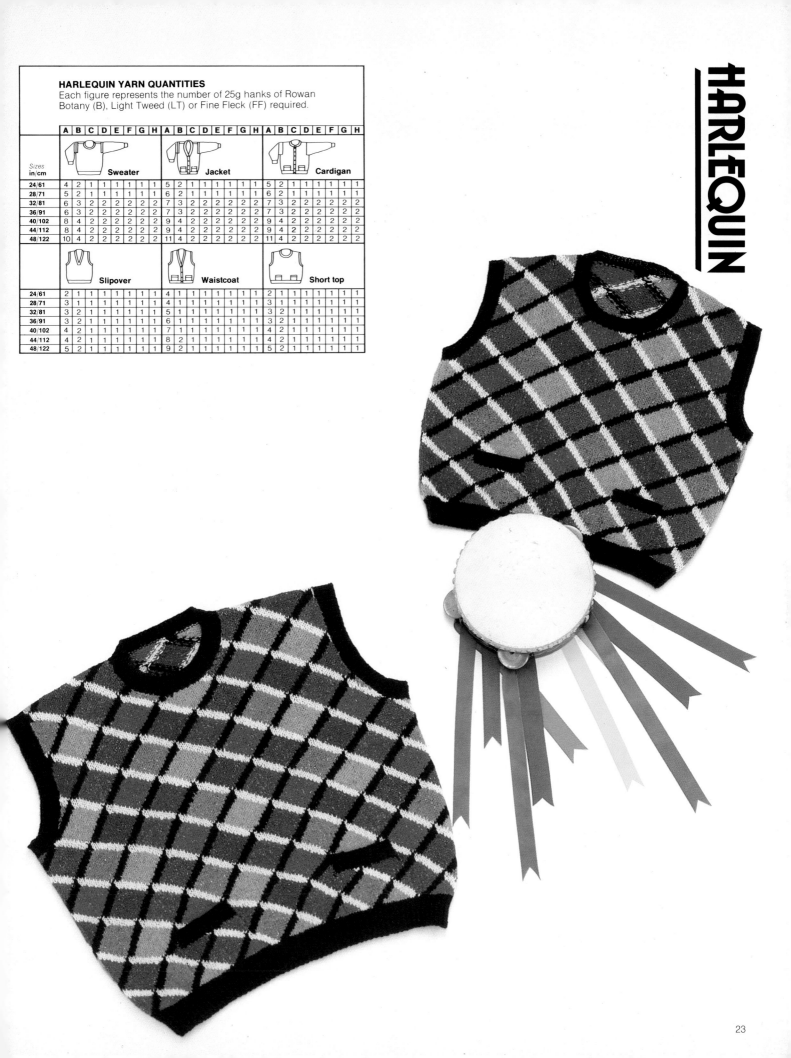

HARLEQUIN YARN QUANTITIES

Each figure represents the number of 25g hanks of Rowan Botany (B), Light Tweed (LT) or Fine Fleck (FF) required.

Sizes in/cm	Sweater A	B	C	D	E	F	G	H	Jacket A	B	C	D	E	F	G	H	Cardigan A	B	C	D	E	F	G	H
24/61	4	2	1	1	1	1	1	1	5	2	1	1	1	1	1	1	5	2	1	1	1	1	1	1
28/71	5	2	1	1	1	1	1	1	6	2	1	1	1	1	1	1	6	2	1	1	1	1	1	1
32/81	6	3	2	2	2	2	2	2	7	3	2	2	2	2	2	2	7	3	2	2	2	2	2	2
36/91	6	3	2	2	2	2	2	2	7	3	2	2	2	2	2	2	7	3	2	2	2	2	2	2
40/102	8	4	2	2	2	2	2	2	9	4	2	2	2	2	2	2	9	4	2	2	2	2	2	2
44/112	8	4	2	2	2	2	2	2	9	4	2	2	2	2	2	2	9	4	2	2	2	2	2	2
48/122	10	4	2	2	2	2	2	2	11	4	2	2	2	2	2	2	11	4	2	2	2	2	2	2

Sizes in/cm	Slipover A	B	C	D	E	F	G	H	Waistcoat A	B	C	D	E	F	G	H	Short top A	B	C	D	E	F	G	H
24/61	2	1	1	1	1	1	1	1	4	1	1	1	1	1	1	1	2	1	1	1	1	1	1	1
28/71	3	1	1	1	1	1	1	1	4	1	1	1	1	1	1	1	3	1	1	1	1	1	1	1
32/81	3	2	1	1	1	1	1	1	5	1	1	1	1	1	1	1	3	2	1	1	1	1	1	1
36/91	3	2	1	1	1	1	1	1	6	1	1	1	1	1	1	1	3	2	1	1	1	1	1	1
40/102	4	2	1	1	1	1	1	1	7	1	1	1	1	1	1	1	4	2	1	1	1	1	1	1
44/112	4	2	1	1	1	1	1	1	8	2	1	1	1	1	1	1	4	2	1	1	1	1	1	1
48/122	5	2	1	1	1	1	1	1	9	2	1	1	1	1	1	1	5	2	1	1	1	1	1	1

HARLEQUIN

Harlequin chart

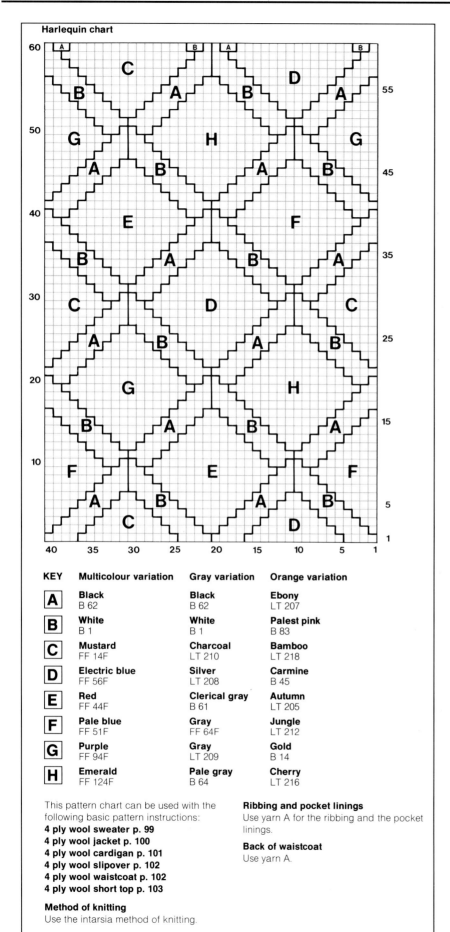

KEY	Multicolour variation	Gray variation	Orange variation
A	**Black** B 62	**Black** B 62	**Ebony** LT 207
B	**White** B 1	**White** B 1	**Palest pink** B 83
C	**Mustard** FF 14F	**Charcoal** LT 210	**Bamboo** LT 218
D	**Electric blue** FF 56F	**Silver** LT 208	**Carmine** B 45
E	**Red** FF 44F	**Clerical gray** B 61	**Autumn** LT 205
F	**Pale blue** FF 51F	**Gray** FF 64F	**Jungle** LT 212
G	**Purple** FF 94F	**Gray** LT 209	**Gold** B 14
H	**Emerald** FF 124F	**Pale gray** B 64	**Cherry** LT 216

This pattern chart can be used with the following basic pattern instructions:
4 ply wool sweater p. 99
4 ply wool jacket p. 100
4 ply wool cardigan p. 101
4 ply wool slipover p. 102
4 ply wool waistcoat p. 102
4 ply wool short top p. 103

Method of knitting
Use the intarsia method of knitting.

Ribbing and pocket linings
Use yarn A for the ribbing and the pocket linings.

Back of waistcoat
Use yarn A.

Harlequin chart placing instructions

Follow basic pattern instructions as given on pages 99-103, working pattern chart thus:

Work patt across knit rows (odd nos):

Sizes in/cm	Sweater back/front, Jacket back, Cardigan back, Slipover back/front, Short top back/front
24/61	Work sts (1-40) twice, then sts (1-4) once.
28/71	Work sts (1-40) twice, then sts (1-18) once.
32/81	Work sts (1-40) twice, then sts (1-32) once.
36/91	Work sts (1-40) 3 times, then sts (1-6) once.
40/102	Work sts (1-40) 3 times, then sts (1-20) once.
44/112	Work sts (1-40) 3 times, then sts (1-34) once.
48/122	Work sts (1-40) 4 times, then sts (1-8) once.

Sweater sleeves

24/61	Work sts (1-40) once, then sts (1-4) once.
28/71	Work sts (1-40) once, then sts (1-8) once.
32/81	Work sts (1-40) once, then sts (1-12) once.
36/91	Work sts (1-40) once, then sts (1-24) once.
40/102	Work sts (1-40) once, then sts (1-32) once.
44/112	Work sts (1-40) once, then sts (1-36) once.
48/122	Work sts (1-40) once, then sts (1-36) once.

Jacket fronts, Cardigan fronts

24/61	Work sts (1-38) once.
28/71	Work sts (1-40) once, then sts (1-4) once.
32/81	Work sts (1-40) once, then sts (1-12) once.
36/91	Work sts (1-40) once, then sts (1-20) once.
40/102	Work sts (1-40) once, then sts (1-26) once.
44/112	Work sts (1-40) once, then sts (1-32) once.
48/122	Work sts (1-40) twice.

Jacket sleeves

24/61	Work sts (1-40) twice.
28/71	Work sts (1-40) twice, then sts (1-2) once.
32/81	Work sts (1-40) twice, then sts (1-6) once.
36/91	Work sts (1-40) twice, then sts (1-20) once.
40/102	Work sts (1-40) twice, then sts (1-30) once.
44/112	Work sts (1-40) twice, then sts (1-34) once.
48/122	Work sts (1-40) twice, then sts (1-36) once.

Cardigan sleeves

24/61	Work sts (1-40) once, then sts (1-16) once.
28/71	Work sts (1-40) once, then sts (1-22) once.
32/81	Work sts (1-40) once, then sts (1-28) once.
36/91	Work sts (1-40) once, then sts (1-32) once.
40/102	Work sts (1-40) once, then sts (1-38) once.
44/112	Work sts (1-40) twice, then sts (1-4) once.
48/122	Work sts (1-40) twice, then sts (1-10) once.

Waistcoat fronts

24/61	Work sts (1-40) once, then stitch 1 once.
28/71	Work sts (1-40) once, then sts (1-8) once.
32/81	Work sts (1-40) once, then sts (1-15) once.
36/91	Work sts (1-40) once, then sts (1-22) once.
40/102	Work sts (1-40) once, then sts (1-29) once.
44/112	Work sts (1-40) once, then sts (1-36) once.
48/122	Work sts (1-40) twice, then sts (1-3) once.

Work patt across purl rows (even nos):

Sweater back/front, Jacket back, Cardigan back, Slipover back/front, Short top back/front
Work sts (4-1) once, then sts (40-1) twice.
Work sts (18-1) once, then sts (40-1) twice.
Work sts (32-1) once, then sts (40-1) twice.
Work sts (6-1) once, then sts (40-1) 3 times.
Work sts (20-1) once, then sts (40-1) 3 times.
Work sts (34-1) once, then sts (40-1) 3 times.
Work sts (8-1) once, then sts (40-1) 4 times.

Sweater sleeves
Work sts (4-1) once, then sts (40-1) once.
Work sts (8-1) once, then sts (40-1) once.
Work sts (12-1) once, then sts (40-1) once.
Work sts (24-1) once, then sts (40-1) once.
Work sts (32-1) once, then sts (40-1) once.
Work sts (36-1) once, then sts (40-1) once.
Work sts (36-1) once, then sts (40-1) once.

Jacket fronts, Cardigan fronts
Work sts (38-1) once.
Work sts (4-1) once, then sts (40-1) once.
Work sts (12-1) once, then sts (40-1) once.
Work sts (20-1) once, then sts (40-1) once.
Work sts (26-1) once, then sts (40-1) once.
Work sts (32-1) once, then sts (40-1) once.
Work sts (40-1) twice.

Jacket sleeves
Work sts (40-1) twice.
Work sts (2-1) once, then sts (40-1) twice.
Work sts (6-1) once, then sts (40-1) twice.
Work sts (20-1) once, then sts (40-1) twice.
Work sts (30-1) once, then sts (40-1) twice.
Work sts (34-1) once, then sts (40-1) twice.
Work sts (36-1) once, then sts (40-1) twice.

Cardigan sleeves
Work sts (16-1) once, then sts (40-1) once.
Work sts (22-1) once, then sts (40-1) once.
Work sts (28-1) once, then sts (40-1) once.
Work sts (32-1) once, then sts (40-1) once.
Work sts (38-1) once, then sts (40-1) once.
Work sts (4-1) once, then sts (40-1) twice.
Work sts (10-1) once, then sts (40-1) twice.

Waistcoat fronts
Work stitch 1 once, then sts (40-1) once.
Work sts (8-1) once, then sts (40-1) once.
Work sts (15-1) once, then sts (40-1) once.
Work sts (22-1) once, then sts (40-1) once.
Work sts (29-1) once, then sts (40-1) once.
Work sts (36-1) once, then sts (40-1) once.
Work sts (3-1) once, then sts (40-1) twice.

CHAINSAW

Paintbox chainsaw
blades slash
across the sweater
in controlled
formation in this
dynamic pattern
designed from my
9-year-old son's
drawing.

CHAINSAW YARN QUANTITIES

Each figure represents the number of 50g balls of Rowan Designer Double Knitting (DDK) or Double Knitting Fleck (DKF) or Fine Cotton Chenille (FCC) required.

Sizes in/cm	Sweater A	B	C	D	E	F	G	H	Jacket A	B	C	D	E	F	G	H	Cardigan A	B	C	D	E	F	G	H
24/61	2	3	1	1	1				3	3	1	1	1				2	3	1	1	1			
28/71	2	4	1	1	1				3	4	1	1	1				2	4	1	1	1			
32/81	2	6	1	1	1				4	6	1	1	1				2	6	1	1	1			
36/91	3	7	1	1	1				4	7	1	1	1				3	7	1	1	1			
40/102	3	8	1	1	1				4	8	1	1	1				3	8	1	1	1			
44/112	4	9	1	1	1				5	9	1	1	1				3	9	1	1	1			
48/122	4	9	1	1	1				5	9	1	1	1				4	9	1	1	1			

Sizes in/cm	Slipover A	B	C	D	E	F	G	H	Waistcoat A	B	C	D	E	F	G	H	Short top A	B	C	D	E	F	G	H
24/61	1	2	1	1	1				2	3	1	1	1				1	2	1	1	1			
28/71	1	2	1	1	1				2	3	1	1	1				1	2	1	1	1			
32/81	2	3	1	1	1				2	4	1	1	1				1	3	1	1	1			
36/91	2	4	1	1	1				3	5	1	1	1				2	3	1	1	1			
40/102	2	5	1	1	1				3	6	1	1	1				2	4	1	1	1			
44/112	3	6	1	1	1				3	7	1	1	1				2	4	1	1	1			
48/122	3	6	1	1	1				4	7	1	1	1				2	5	1	1	1			

27

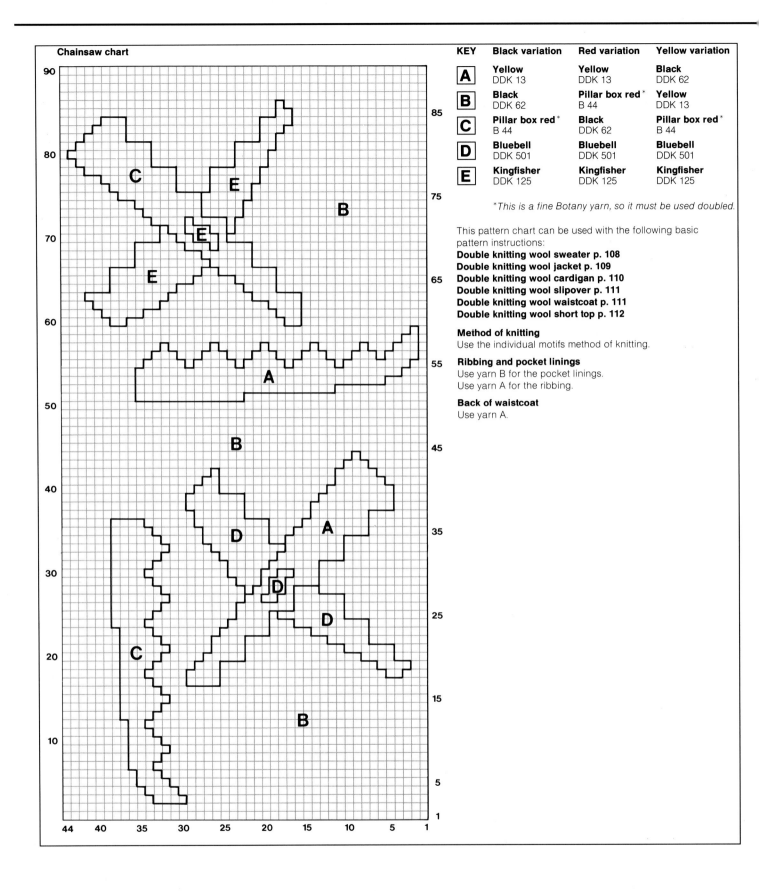

Chainsaw chart

KEY	Black variation	Red variation	Yellow variation
A	**Yellow** DDK 13	**Yellow** DDK 13	**Black** DDK 62
B	**Black** DDK 62	**Pillar box red*** B 44	**Yellow** DDK 13
C	**Pillar box red*** B 44	**Black** DDK 62	**Pillar box red*** B 44
D	**Bluebell** DDK 501	**Bluebell** DDK 501	**Bluebell** DDK 501
E	**Kingfisher** DDK 125	**Kingfisher** DDK 125	**Kingfisher** DDK 125

This is a fine Botany yarn, so it must be used doubled.

This pattern chart can be used with the following basic pattern instructions:

Double knitting wool sweater p. 108
Double knitting wool jacket p. 109
Double knitting wool cardigan p. 110
Double knitting wool slipover p. 111
Double knitting wool waistcoat p. 111
Double knitting wool short top p. 112

Method of knitting
Use the individual motifs method of knitting.

Ribbing and pocket linings
Use yarn B for the pocket linings.
Use yarn A for the ribbing.

Back of waistcoat
Use yarn A.

Chainsaw chart placing instructions

Follow basic pattern instructions as given on pages 108-112, working pattern chart thus:

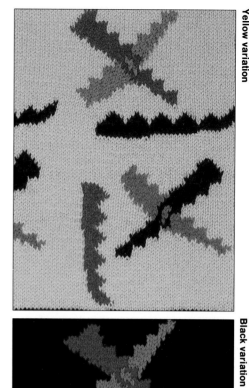

Sizes in/cm	Work patt across knit rows (odd nos):	Work patt across purl rows (even nos):
Sweater back/front, Jacket back, Cardigan back, Slipover back/front, Short top back/front		
24/61	Work sts (1-44) once, then sts (1-26) once.	Work sts (26-1) once, then sts (44-1) once.
28/71	Work sts (1-44) once, then sts (1-37) once.	Work sts (37-1) once, then sts (44-1) once.
32/81	Work sts (1-44) twice, then sts (1-4) once.	Work sts (4-1) once, then sts (44-1) twice.
36/91	Work sts (1-44) twice, then sts (1-15) once.	Work sts (15-1) once, then sts (44-1) twice.
40/102	Work sts (1-44) twice, then sts (1-26) once.	Work sts (26-1) once, then sts (44-1) twice.
44/112	Work sts (1-44) twice, then sts (1-37) once.	Work sts (37-1) once, then sts (44-1) twice.
48/122	Work sts (1-44) 3 times, then sts (1-4) once.	Work sts (4-1) once, then sts (44-1) 3 times.
Sweater sleeves		
24/61	Work sts (1-43).	Work sts (43-1) once.
28/71	Work sts (1-44) once, then stitch 1 once.	Work stitch 1 once, then sts (44-1) once.
32/81	Work sts (1-44) once, then sts (1-5) once.	Work sts (5-1) once, then sts (44-1) once.
36/91	Work sts (1-44) once, then sts (1-11) once.	Work sts (11-1) once, then sts (44-1) once.
40/102	Work sts (1-44) once, then sts (1-17) once.	Work sts (17-1) once, then sts (44-1) once.
44/112	Work sts (1-44) once, then sts (1-21) once.	Work sts (21-1) once, then sts (44-1) once.
48/122	Work sts (1-44) once, then sts (1-19) once.	Work sts (19-1) once, then sts (44-1) once.
Jacket fronts, Cardigan fronts		
24/61	Work sts (1-34) once.	Work sts (34-1) once.
28/71	Work sts (1-40) once.	Work sts (40-1) once.
32/81	Work sts (1-44) once, then sts (1-2) once.	Work sts (2-1) once, then sts (44-1) once.
36/91	Work sts (1-44) once, then sts (1-8) once.	Work sts (8-1) once, then sts (44-1) once.
40/102	Work sts (1-44) once, then sts (1-14) once.	Work sts (14-1) once, then sts (44-1) once.
44/112	Work sts (1-44) once, then sts (1-20) once.	Work sts (20-1) once, then sts (44-1) once.
48/122	Work sts (1-44) once, then sts (1-26) once.	Work sts (26-1) once, then sts (44-1) once.
Jacket sleeves		
24/61	Work sts (1-41) once.	Work sts (41-1) once.
28/71	Work sts (1-43) once.	Work sts (43-1) once.
32/81	Work sts (1-44) once, then sts (1-3) once.	Work sts (3-1) once, then sts (44-1) once.
36/91	Work sts (1-44) once, then sts (1-7) once.	Work sts (7-1) once, then sts (44-1) once.
40/102	Work sts (1-44) once, then sts (1-11) once.	Work sts (11-1) once, then sts (44-1) once.
44/112	Work sts (1-44) once, then sts (1-15) once.	Work sts (15-1) once, then sts (44-1) once.
48/122	Work sts (1-44) once, then sts (1-19) once.	Work sts (19-1) once, then sts (44-1) once.
Cardigan sleeves		
24/61	Work sts (1-37) once.	Work sts (37-1) once.
28/71	Work sts (1-39) once.	Work sts (39-1) once.
32/81	Work sts (1-43) once.	Work sts (43-1) once.
36/91	Work sts (1-44) once, then sts (1-5) once.	Work sts (5-1) once, then sts (44-1) once.
40/102	Work sts (1-44) once, then sts (1-9) once.	Work sts (9-1) once, then sts (44-1) once.
44/112	Work sts (1-44) once, then sts (1-13) once.	Work sts (13-1) once, then sts (44-1) once.
48/122	Work sts (1-44) once, then sts (1-17) once.	Work sts (17-1) once, then sts (44-1) once.
Waistcoat fronts		
24/61	Work sts (1-35) once.	Work sts (35-1) once.
28/71	Work sts (1-41) once.	Work sts (41-1) once.
32/81	Work sts (1-44) once, then sts (1-3) once.	Work sts (3-1) once, then sts (44-1) once.
36/91	Work sts (1-44) once, then sts (1-9) once.	Work sts (9-1) once, then sts (44-1) once.
40/102	Work sts (1-44) once, then sts (1-15) once.	Work sts (15-1) once, then sts (44-1) once.
44/112	Work sts (1-44) once, then sts (1-21) once.	Work sts (21-1) once, then sts (44-1) once.
48/122	Work sts (1-44) once, then sts (1-27) once.	Work sts (27-1) once, then sts (44-1) once.

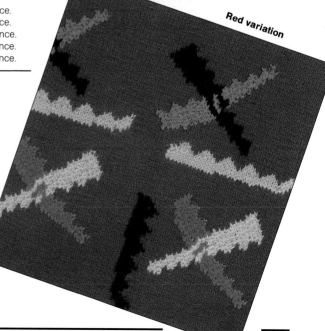

Red variation

ambrse

FLOWER GIRL

Delicate spring blossoms seem the perfect embodiment of flowering feminin- ity. This design was inspired by my daughter and her best friend. It's perfect for knitting a match- ing sisters' set.

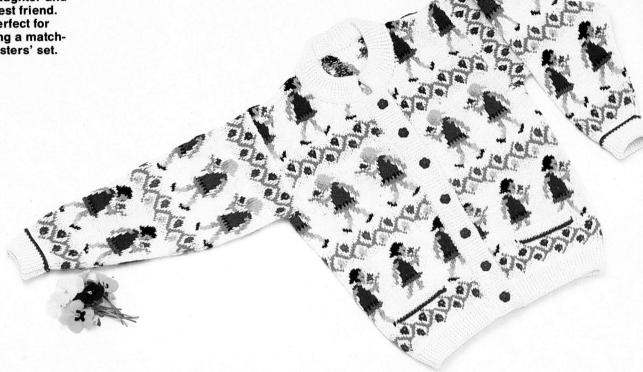

FLOWER GIRL YARN QUANTITIES
Each figure represents the number of 50g balls of Rowan Sea Breeze Cotton (SBC) required.

Sizes in/cm	A	B	C	D	E	F	G	H	A	B	C	D	E	F	G	H	A	B	C	D	E	F	G	H
	Sweater								not suitable for Jacket								Cardigan							
24/61	4	1	1	1	1	1	1	1									4	1	1	1	1	1	1	1
28/71	4	1	1	1	1	1	1	1									5	1	1	1	1	1	1	1
32/81	5	1	1	1	1	1	1	1									6	1	1	1	1	1	1	1
36/91	6	1	1	1	1	1	1	1									7	1	1	1	1	1	1	1
40/102	7	1	2	1	1	1	1	1									8	1	2	1	1	1	1	1
44/112	8	1	2	1	1	1	1	1									9	1	2	1	1	1	1	1
48/122	9	1	2	1	1	1	1	1									10	1	2	1	1	1	1	1
	Slipover								Waistcoat								Short top							
24/61	2	1	1	1	1	1	1	1	3	1	1	1	1	1	1	1	2	1	1	1	1	1	1	1
28/71	3	1	1	1	1	1	1	1	3	1	1	1	1	1	1	1	3	1	1	1	1	1	1	1
32/81	3	1	1	1	1	1	1	1	3	1	1	1	1	1	1	1	3	1	1	1	1	1	1	1
36/91	4	1	1	1	1	1	1	1	4	1	1	1	1	1	1	1	4	1	1	1	1	1	1	1
40/102	5	1	1	1	1	1	1	1	5	1	1	1	1	1	1	1	5	1	1	1	1	1	1	1
44/112	5	1	1	1	1	1	1	1	5	1	1	1	1	1	1	1	5	1	1	1	1	1	1	1
48/122	6	1	1	1	1	1	1	1	6	1	1	1	1	1	1	1	6	1	1	1	1	1	1	1

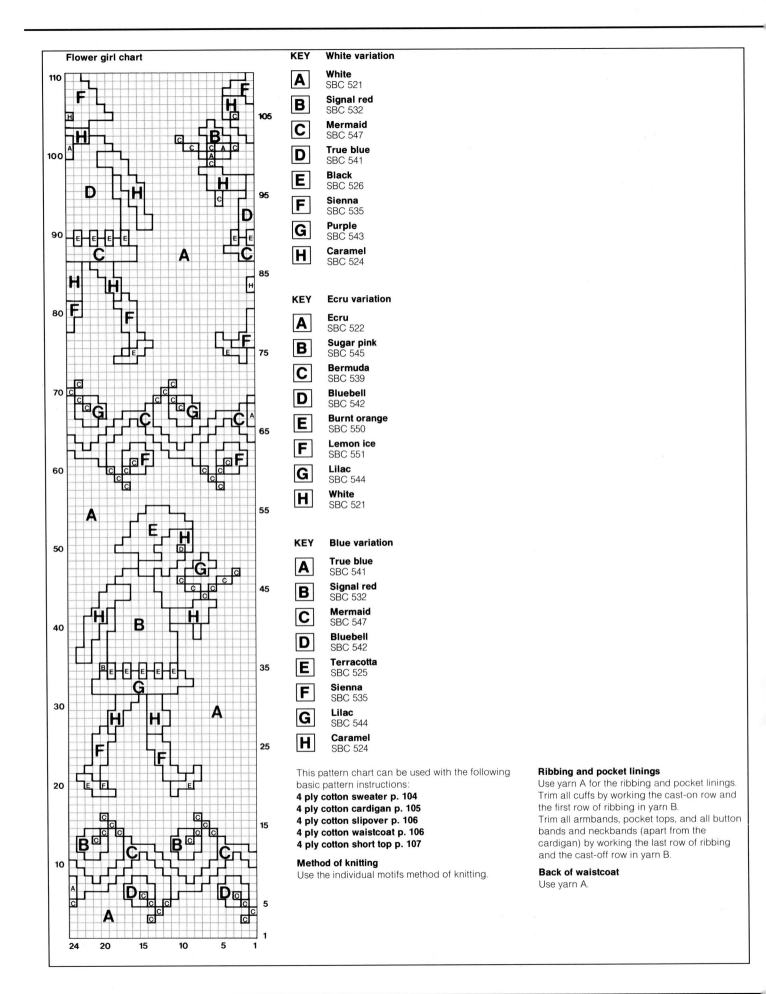

Flower girl chart

This pattern chart can be used with the following basic pattern instructions:
4 ply cotton sweater p. 104
4 ply cotton cardigan p. 105
4 ply cotton slipover p. 106
4 ply cotton waistcoat p. 106
4 ply cotton short top p. 107

Method of knitting
Use the individual motifs method of knitting.

Ribbing and pocket linings
Use yarn A for the ribbing and pocket linings. Trim all cuffs by working the cast-on row and the first row of ribbing in yarn B. Trim all armbands, pocket tops, and all button bands and neckbands (apart from the cardigan) by working the last row of ribbing and the cast-off row in yarn B.

Back of waistcoat
Use yarn A.

Flower girl chart placing instructions

Follow basic pattern instructions as given on pages 104-107, working pattern chart thus:

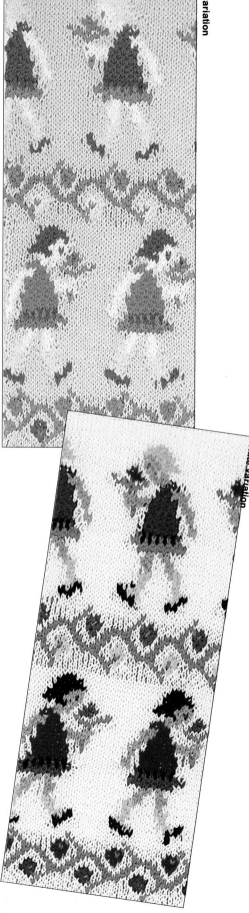

Sizes in/cm	Work patt across knit rows (odd nos):	Work patt across purl rows (even nos):
Sweater back/front, Cardigan back, Slipover back/front, Short top back/front		
24/61	Work sts (1-24) 4 times, then sts (1-4) once.	Work sts (4-1) once, then sts (24-1) 4 times.
28/71	Work sts (1-24) 4 times, then sts (1-20) once.	Work sts (20-1) once, then sts (24-1) 4 times.
32/81	Work sts (1-24) 5 times, then sts (1-12) once.	Work sts (12-1) once, then sts (24-1) 5 times.
36/91	Work sts (1-24) 6 times, then sts (1-4) once.	Work sts (4-1) once, then sts (24-1) 6 times.
40/102	Work sts (1-24) 6 times, then sts (1-20) once.	Work sts (20-1) once, then sts (24-1) 6 times.
44/112	Work sts (1-24) 7 times, then sts (1-12) once.	Work sts (12-1) once, then sts (24-1) 7 times.
48/122	Work sts (1-24) 8 times, then sts (1-4) once.	Work sts (4-1) once, then sts (24-1) 8 times.
Sweater sleeves		
24/61	Work sts (1-24) twice, then sts (1-10) once.	Work sts (10-1) once, then sts (24-1) twice.
28/71	Work sts (1-24) twice, then sts (1-18) once.	Work sts (18-1) once, then sts (24-1) twice.
32/81	Work sts (1-24) twice, then sts (1-20) once.	Work sts (20-1) once, then sts (24-1) twice.
36/91	Work sts (1-24) 3 times, then sts (1-4) once.	Work sts (4-1) once, then sts (24-1) 3 times.
40/102	Work sts (1-24) 3 times, then sts (1-8) once.	Work sts (8-1) once, then sts (24-1) 3 times.
44/112	Work sts (1-24) 3 times, then sts (1-10) once.	Work sts (10-1) once, then sts (24-1) 3 times.
48/122	Work sts (1-24) 3 times, then sts (1-14) once.	Work sts (14-1) once, then sts (24-1) 3 times.
Cardigan fronts		
24/61	Work sts (1-24) once, then sts (1-18) once.	Work sts (18-1) once, then sts (24-1) once.
28/71	Work sts (1-24) twice, then sts (1-4) once.	Work sts (4-1) once, then sts (24-1) twice.
32/81	Work sts (1-24) twice, then sts (1-12) once.	Work sts (12-1) once, then sts (24-1) twice.
36/91	Work sts (1-24) twice, then sts (1-20) once.	Work sts (20-1) once, then sts (24-1) twice.
40/102	Work sts (1-24) 3 times, then sts (1-4) once.	Work sts (4-1) once, then sts (24-1) 3 times.
44/112	Work sts (1-24) 3 times, then sts (1-12) once.	Work sts (12-1) once, then sts (24-1) 3 times.
48/122	Work sts (1-24) 3 times, then sts (1-20) once.	Work sts (20-1) once, then sts (24-1) 3 times.
Cardigan sleeves		
24/61	Work sts (1-24) twice, then sts (1-8) once.	Work sts (8-1) once, then sts (24-1) twice
28/71	Work sts (1-24) twice, then sts (1-16) once.	Work sts (16-1) once, then sts (24-1) twice.
32/81	Work sts (1-24) twice, then sts (1-22) once.	Work sts (22-1) once, then sts (24-1) twice.
36/91	Work sts (1-24) 3 times, then sts (1-2) once.	Work sts (2-1) once, then sts (24-1) 3 times.
40/102	Work sts (1-24) 3 times, then sts (1-6) once.	Work sts (6-1) once, then sts (24-1) 3 times.
44/112	Work sts (1-24) 3 times, then sts (1-8) once.	Work sts (8-1) once, then sts (24-1) 3 times.
48/122	Work sts (1-24) 3 times, then sts (1-12) once.	Work sts (12-1) once, then sts (24-1) 3 times.
Waistcoat fronts		
24/61	Work sts (1-24) once, then sts (1-22) once.	Work sts (22-1) once, then sts (24-1) once.
28/71	Work sts (1-24) twice, then sts (1-6) once.	Work sts (6-1) once, then sts (24-1) twice.
32/81	Work sts (1-24) twice, then sts (1-14) once.	Work sts (14-1) once, then sts (24-1) twice.
36/91	Work sts (1-24) twice, then sts (1-22) once.	Work sts (22-1) once, then sts (24-1) twice.
40/102	Work sts (1-24) 3 times, then sts (1-6) once.	Work sts (6-1) once, then sts (24-1) 3 times.
44/112	Work sts (1-24) 3 times, then sts (1-14) once.	Work sts (14-1) once, then sts (24-1) 3 times.
48/122	Work sts (1-24) 3 times, then sts (1-22) once.	Work sts (22-1) once, then sts (24-1) 3 times.

Riotous rodents romp across this lively sweater. It's meant to be worn by anyone with mischief on the mind.

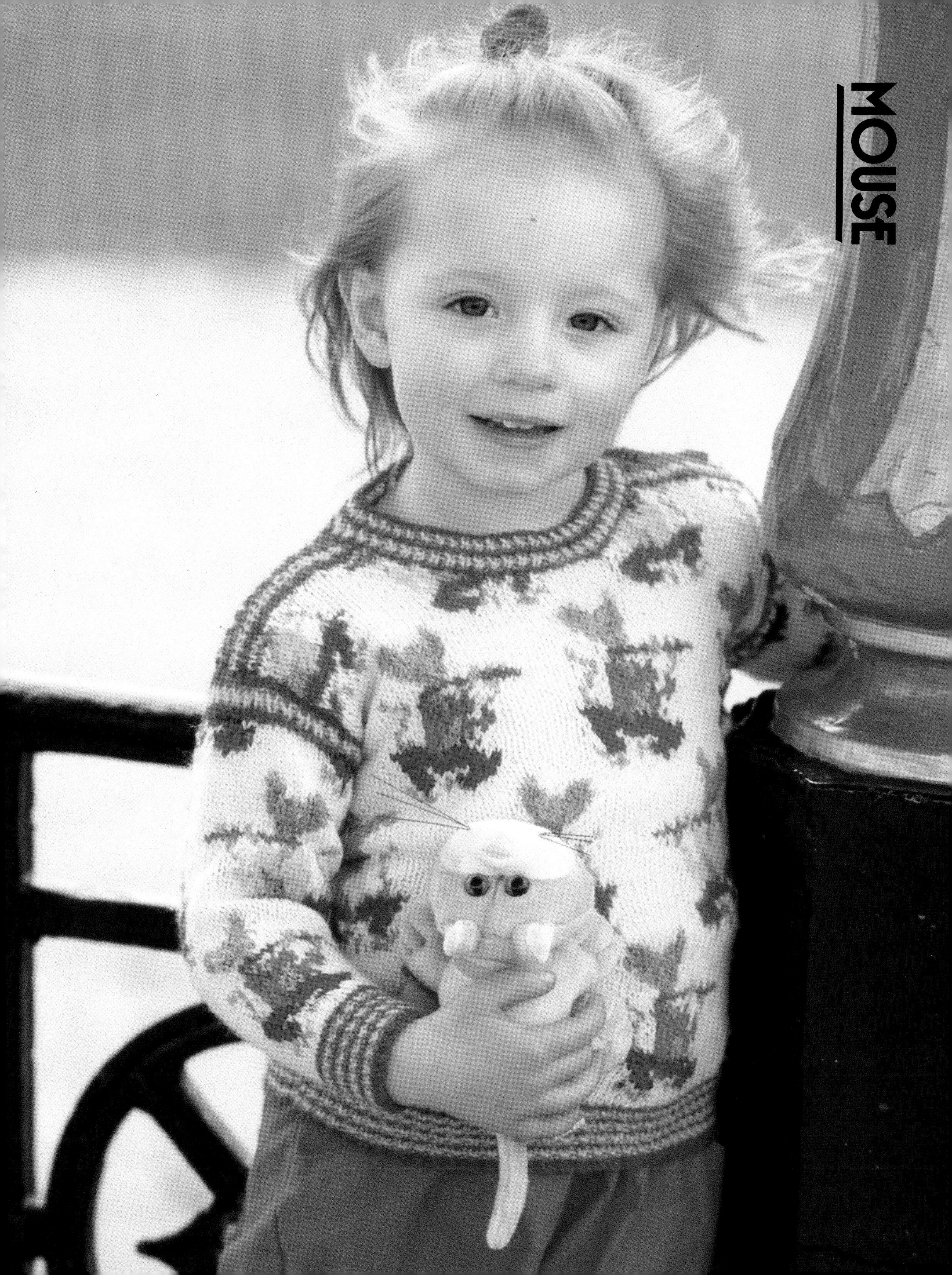

MOUSE

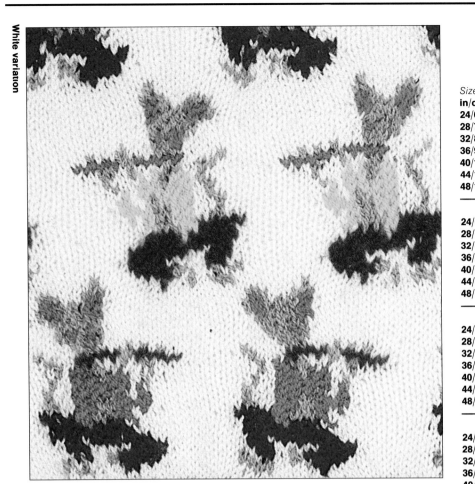

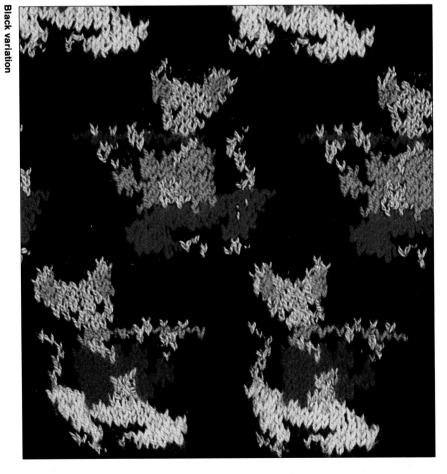

Mouse chart placing instructions

Follow basic pattern instructions as given on pages 99-103, working pattern chart thus:

Work patt across knit rows (odd nos):

Sizes in/cm	Sweater back/front, Jacket back, Cardigan back, Slipover back/front, Short top back/front
24/61	Work sts (1-25) 3 times, then sts (1-9) once.
28/71	Work sts (1-25) 3 times, then sts (1-23) once.
32/81	Work sts (1-25) 4 times, then sts (1-12) once.
36/91	Work sts (1-25) 5 times, then stitch 1 once.
40/102	Work sts (1-25) 5 times, then sts (1-15) once.
44/112	Work sts (1-25) 6 times, then sts (1-4) once.
48/122	Work sts (1-25) 6 times, then sts (1-18) once.

	Sweater sleeves
24/61	Work sts (1-25) once, then sts (1-19) once.
28/71	Work sts (1-25) once, then sts (1-23) once.
32/81	Work sts (1-25) twice, then sts (1-2) once.
36/91	Work sts (1-25) twice, then sts (1-14) once.
40/102	Work sts (1-25) twice, then sts (1-22) once.
44/112	Work sts (1-25) 3 times, then stitch 1 once.
48/122	Work sts (1-25) 3 times, then stitch 1 once.

	Jacket fronts, Cardigan fronts
24/61	Work sts (1-25) once, then sts (1-13) once.
28/71	Work sts (1-25) once, then sts (1-19) once.
32/81	Work sts (1-25) twice, then sts (1-2) once.
36/91	Work sts (1-25) twice, then sts (1-10) once.
40/102	Work sts (1-25) twice, then sts (1-16) once.
44/112	Work sts (1-25) twice, then sts (1-22) once.
48/122	Work sts (1-25) 3 times, then sts (1-5) once.

	Jacket sleeves
24/61	Work sts (1-25) 3 times, then sts (1-5) once.
28/71	Work sts (1-25) 3 times, then sts (1-7) once.
32/81	Work sts (1-25) 3 times, then sts (1-11) once.
36/91	Work sts (1-25) 4 times.
40/102	Work sts (1-25) 4 times, then sts (1-10) once.
44/112	Work sts (1-25) 4 times, then sts (1-14) once.
48/122	Work sts (1-25) 4 times, then sts (1-16) once.

	Cardigan sleeves
24/61	Work sts (1-25) twice, then sts (1-6) once.
28/71	Work sts (1-25) twice, then sts (1-12) once.
32/81	Work sts (1-25) twice, then sts (1-18) once.
36/91	Work sts (1-25) twice, then sts (1-22) once.
40/102	Work sts (1-25) 3 times, then sts (1-3) once.
44/112	Work sts (1-25) 3 times, then sts (1-9) once.
48/122	Work sts (1-25) 3 times, then sts (1-15) once.

	Waistcoat fronts
24/61	Work sts (1-25) once, then sts (1-16) once.
28/71	Work sts (1-25) once, then sts (1-23) once.
32/81	Work sts (1-25) twice, then sts (1-5) once.
36/91	Work sts (1-25) twice, then sts (1-12) once.
40/102	Work sts (1-25) twice, then sts (1-19) once.
44/112	Work sts (1-25) 3 times, then stitch 1 once.
48/122	Work sts (1-25) 3 times, then sts (1-8) once.

Work patt across purl rows (even nos):

Sweater back/front, Jacket back, Cardigan back, Slipover back/front, Short top back/front
Work sts (9-1) once, then sts (25-1) 3 times.
Work sts (23-1) once, then sts (25-1) 3 times.
Work sts (12-1) once, then sts (25-1) 4 times.
Work stitch 1 once, then sts (25-1) 5 times.
Work sts (15-1) once, then sts (25-1) 5 times.
Work sts (4-1) once, then sts (25-1) 6 times.
Work sts (18-1) once, then sts (25-1) 6 times.

Sweater sleeves
Work sts (19-1) once, then sts (25-1) once.
Work sts (23-1) once, then sts (25-1) once.
Work sts (2-1) once, then sts (25-1) twice.
Work sts (14-1) once, then sts (25-1) twice.
Work sts (22-1) once, then sts (25-1) twice.
Work stitch 1 once, then sts (25-1) 3 times.
Work stitch 1 once, then sts (25-1) 3 times.

Jacket fronts, Cardigan fronts
Work sts (13-1) once, then sts (25-1) once.
Work sts (19-1) once, then sts (25-1) once.
Work sts (2-1) once, then sts (25-1) twice.
Work sts (10-1) once, then sts (25-1) twice.
Work sts (16-1) once, then sts (25-1) twice.
Work sts (22-1) once, then sts (25-1) twice.
Work sts (5-1) once, then sts (25-1) 3 times.

Jacket sleeves
Work sts (5-1) once, then sts (25-1) twice.
Work sts (7-1) once, then sts (25-1) 3 times.
Work sts (11-1) once, then sts (25-1) 3 times.
Work sts (25-1) 4 times.
Work sts (10-1) once, then sts (25-1) 4 times.
Work sts (14-1) once, then sts (25-1) 4 times.
Work sts (16-1) once, then sts (25-1) 4 times.

Cardigan sleeves
Work sts (6-1) once, then sts (25-1) twice.
Work sts (12-1) once, then sts (25-1) twice.
Work sts (18-1) once, then sts (25-1) twice.
Work sts (22-1) once, then sts (25-1) twice.
Work sts (3-1) once, then sts (25-1) 3 times.
Work sts (9-1) once, then sts (25-1) 3 times.
Work sts (15-1) once, then sts (25-1) 3 times.

Waistcoat fronts
Work sts (16-1) once, then sts (25-1) once.
Work sts (23-1) once, then sts (25-1) once.
Work sts (5-1) once, then sts (25-1) twice.
Work sts (12-1) once, then sts (25-1) twice.
Work sts (19-1) once, then sts (25-1) twice.
Work stitch 1 once, then sts (25-1) 3 times.
Work sts (8-1) once, then sts (25-1) 3 times.

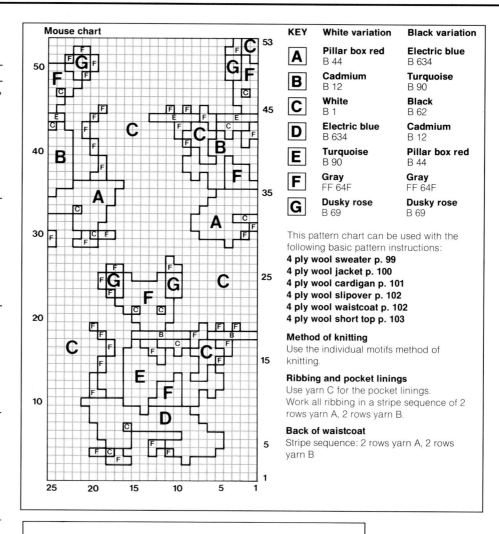

Mouse chart

KEY	White variation	Black variation
A	Pillar box red B 44	Electric blue B 634
B	Cadmium B 12	Turquoise B 90
C	White B 1	Black B 62
D	Electric blue B 634	Cadmium B 12
E	Turquoise B 90	Pillar box red B 44
F	Gray FF 64F	Gray FF 64F
G	Dusky rose B 69	Dusky rose B 69

This pattern chart can be used with the following basic pattern instructions:
4 ply wool sweater p. 99
4 ply wool jacket p. 100
4 ply wool cardigan p. 101
4 ply wool slipover p. 102
4 ply wool waistcoat p. 102
4 ply wool short top p. 103

Method of knitting
Use the individual motifs method of knitting.

Ribbing and pocket linings
Use yarn C for the pocket linings.
Work all ribbing in a stripe sequence of 2 rows yarn A, 2 rows yarn B.

Back of waistcoat
Stripe sequence: 2 rows yarn A, 2 rows yarn B

MOUSE YARN QUANTITIES
Each figure represents the number of 25g hanks of Rowan Botany (B), Light Tweed (LT) or Fine Fleck (FF) required.

Sizes in/cm	Sweater								Jacket								Cardigan							
	A	B	C	D	E	F	G	H	A	B	C	D	E	F	G	H	A	B	C	D	E	F	G	H
24/61	1	1	4	1	1	1	1		2	2	4	1	1	1	1		2	2	4	1	1	1	1	
28/71	2	1	5	1	1	1	1		3	2	5	1	1	1	1		3	2	5	1	1	1	1	
32/81	2	2	6	1	1	2	1		3	3	6	1	1	2	1		3	3	6	1	1	2	1	
36/91	2	2	7	1	1	3	1		3	3	7	1	1	3	1		3	3	7	1	1	3	1	
40/102	2	2	9	2	2	3	1		3	3	9	2	2	3	1		3	3	9	2	2	3	1	
44/112	2	3	10	2	2	4	1		3	4	10	2	2	4	1		3	4	10	2	2	4	1	
48/122	3	3	11	2	2	4	2		4	4	11	2	2	4	2		4	4	11	2	2	4	2	

Sizes in/cm	Slipover								Waistcoat								Short top							
	A	B	C	D	E	F	G	H	A	B	C	D	E	F	G	H	A	B	C	D	E	F	G	H
24/61	1	1	2	1	1	1	1		2	2	1	1	1	1	1		1	1	2	1	1	1	1	
28/71	2	1	3	1	1	1	1		2	2	2	1	1	1	1		2	1	3	1	1	1	1	
32/81	2	2	3	1	1	1	1		3	3	2	1	1	1	1		2	2	3	1	1	1	1	
36/91	2	2	4	1	1	2	1		4	4	2	1	1	1	1		2	2	4	1	1	2	1	
40/102	2	2	5	1	1	2	1		4	4	3	1	1	1	1		2	2	5	1	1	2	1	
44/112	2	3	5	1	1	3	1		5	5	3	1	1	1	1		2	3	5	1	1	3	1	
48/122	3	3	6	1	1	3	1		5	5	3	1	1	1	1		3	3	6	1	1	3	1	

POSIES & PETALS

LAVENDER

Aromatic lavender, found in shades of lilac and purple, is as delightful captured in wool as it is growing wild.

LAVENDER YARN QUANTITIES

Each figure represents the number of 50g balls of Rowan Designer Double Knitting (DDK) or Double Knitting Fleck (DKF) or Fine Cotton Chenille (FCC) required. Yarn A below shows the number of 25g hanks required.

Sizes in/cm	Sweater A	B	C	D	E	F	G	H	Jacket A	B	C	D	E	F	G	H	Cardigan A	B	C	D	E	F	G	H
24/61	7	1		3	1	1	1	1	8	1		3	1	1	1	1	7	1		3	1	1	1	1
28/71	9	1		3	1	1	1	1	10	1		3	1	1	1	1	9	1		3	1	1	1	1
32/81	11	1		4	1	1	1	1	13	1		4	1	1	1	1	11	1		4	1	1	1	1
36/91	13	1		4	1	1	1	1	16	1		4	1	1	1	1	13	1		4	1	1	1	1
40/102	14	1		4	2	1	1	1	18	1		4	2	1	1	1	14	1		4	1	1	1	1
44/112	15	1		5	2	1	1	1	19	1		5	2	1	1	1	15	1		5	2	1	1	1
48/122	16	1		5	2	1	1	1	20	1		5	2	1	1	1	16	1		5	2	1	1	1

Sizes in/cm	Slipover A	B	C	D	E	F	G	H	Waistcoat A	B	C	D	E	F	G	H	Short top A	B	C	D	E	F	G	H
24/61	5	1		2	1	1	1	1	7	1	1	1	1	1	1	1	5	1		2	1	1	1	1
28/71	5	1		2	1	1	1	1	8	1	1	1	1	1	1	1	5	1		2	1	1	1	1
32/81	6	1		2	1	1	1	1	8	1	1	1	1	1	1	1	6	1		2	1	1	1	1
36/91	7	1		3	1	1	1	1	9	1	1	2	1	1	1	1	7	1		2	1	1	1	1
40/102	8	1		3	1	1	1	1	10	1	1	2	1	1	1	1	8	1		3	1	1	1	1
44/112	8	1		3	1	1	1	1	10	1	1	2	1	1	1	1	8	1		3	1	1	1	1
48/122	9	1		3	1	1	1	1	11	1	1	2	1	1	1	1	9	1		3	1	1	1	1

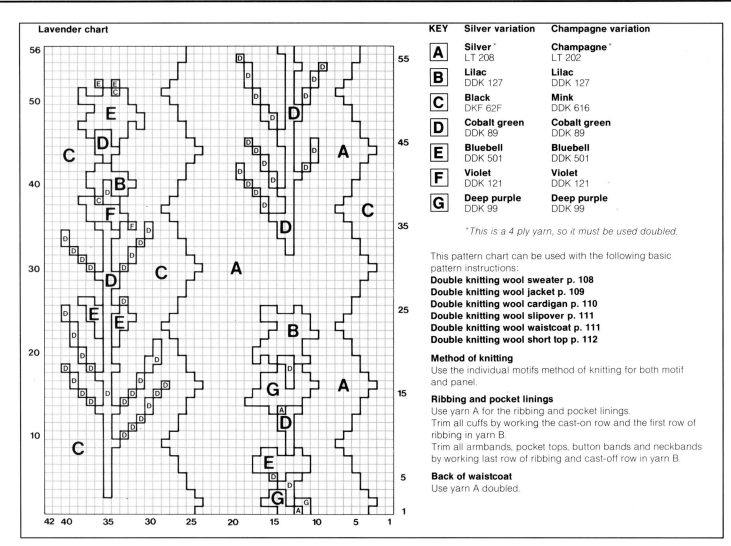

Lavender chart

KEY	Silver variation	Champagne variation
A	**Silver** * LT 208	**Champagne** * LT 202
B	**Lilac** DDK 127	**Lilac** DDK 127
C	**Black** DKF 62F	**Mink** DDK 616
D	**Cobalt green** DDK 89	**Cobalt green** DDK 89
E	**Bluebell** DDK 501	**Bluebell** DDK 501
F	**Violet** DDK 121	**Violet** DDK 121
G	**Deep purple** DDK 99	**Deep purple** DDK 99

This is a 4 ply yarn, so it must be used doubled.

This pattern chart can be used with the following basic pattern instructions:
Double knitting wool sweater p. 108
Double knitting wool jacket p. 109
Double knitting wool cardigan p. 110
Double knitting wool slipover p. 111
Double knitting wool waistcoat p. 111
Double knitting wool short top p. 112

Method of knitting
Use the individual motifs method of knitting for both motif and panel.

Ribbing and pocket linings
Use yarn A for the ribbing and pocket linings.
Trim all cuffs by working the cast-on row and the first row of ribbing in yarn B.
Trim all armbands, pocket tops, button bands and neckbands by working last row of ribbing and cast-off row in yarn B.

Back of waistcoat
Use yarn A doubled.

Champagne variation

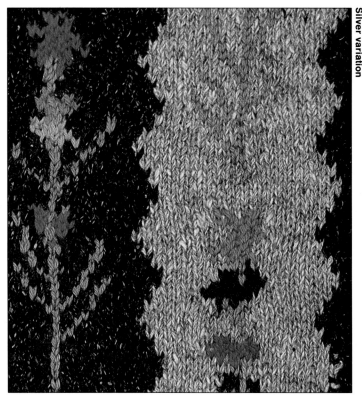

Silver variation

Lavender chart placing instructions

Follow basic pattern instructions as given on pages 108-112, working pattern chart thus:

Sizes in/cm	*Work patt across knit rows (odd nos):*	*Work patt across purl rows (even nos):*
Sweater back/front, Jacket back, Cardigan back, Slipover back/front, Short top back/front		
24/61	Work sts (21-42) once, then sts (1-42) once, then sts (1-6) once.	Work sts (6-1) once, then sts (42-1) once, then sts (42-21) once.
28/71	Work sts (16-42) once, then sts (1-42) once, then sts (1-12) once.	Work sts (12-1) once, then sts (42-1) once, then sts (42-16) once.
32/81	Work sts (10-42) once, then sts (1-42) once, then sts (1-17) once.	Work sts (17-1) once, then sts (42-1) once, then sts (42-10) once.
36/91	Work sts (5-42) once, then sts (1-42) once, then sts (1-23) once.	Work sts (23-1) once, then sts (42-1) once, then sts (42-5) once.
40/102	Work sts (40-42) once, then sts (1-42) twice, then sts (1-27) once.	Work sts (27-1) once, then sts (42-1) twice, then sts (42-40) once.
44/112	Work sts (36-42) once, then sts (1-42) twice, then sts (1-34) once.	Work sts (34-1) once, then sts (42-1) twice, then sts (42-36) once.
48/122	Work sts (30-42) once, then sts (1-42) twice, then sts (1-39) once.	Work sts (39-1) once, then sts (42-1) twice, then sts (42-30) once.
Sweater sleeves		
24/61	Work sts (35-42) once, then sts (1-35) once.	Work sts (35-1) once, then sts (42-35) once.
28/71	Work sts (32-42) once, then sts (1-34) once.	Work sts (34-1) once, then sts (42-32) once.
32/81	Work sts (30-42) once, then sts (1-36) once.	Work sts (36-1) once, then sts (42-30) once.
36/91	Work sts (29-42) once, then sts (1-41) once.	Work sts (41-1) once, then sts (42-29) once.
40/102	Work sts (26-42) once, then sts (1-42) once, then sts (1-2) once.	Work sts (2-1) once, then sts (42-1) once, then sts (42-26) once.
44/112	Work sts (24-42) once, then sts (1-42) once, then sts (1-4) once.	Work sts (4-1) once, then sts (42-1) once, then sts (42-24) once.
48/122	Work sts (25-42) once, then sts (1-42) once, then sts (1-3) once.	Work sts (3-1) once, then sts (42-1) once, then sts (42-25) once.
Jacket fronts, Cardigan fronts		
24/61	Work sts (15-42) once, then sts (1-6) once.	Work sts (6-1) once, then sts (42-15) once.
28/71	Work sts (12-42) once, then sts (1-9) once.	Work sts (9-1) once, then sts (42-12) once.
32/81	Work sts (9-42) once, then sts (1-12) once.	Work sts (12-1) once, then sts (42-9) once.
36/91	Work sts (6-42) once, then sts (1-15) once.	Work sts (15-1) once, then sts (42-6) once.
40/102	Work sts (3-42) once, then sts (1-18) once.	Work sts (18-1) once, then sts (42-3) once.
44/112	Work sts (1-42) once, then sts (1-22) once.	Work sts (22-1) once, then sts (42-1) once.
48/122	Work sts (39-42) once, then sts (1-42) once, then sts (1-24) once.	Work sts (24-1) once, then sts (42-1) once, then sts (42-39) once.
Jacket sleeves		
24/61	Work sts (36-42) once, then sts (1-34) once.	Work sts (34-1) once, then sts (42-36) once.
28/71	Work sts (35-42) once, then sts (1-35) once.	Work sts (35-1) once, then sts (42-35) once.
32/81	Work sts (32-42) once, then sts (1-36) once.	Work sts (36-1) once, then sts (42-32) once.
36/91	Work sts (30-42) once, then sts (1-38) once.	Work sts (38-1) once, then sts (42-30) once.
40/102	Work sts (28-42) once, then sts (1-40) once.	Work sts (40-1) once, then sts (42-28) once.
44/112	Work sts (26-42) once, then sts (1-42) once.	Work sts (42-1) once, then sts (42-26) once.
48/122	Work sts (22-42) once, then sts (1-42) once.	Work sts (42-1) once, then sts (42-22) once.
Cardigan sleeves		
24/61	Work sts (36-42) once, then sts (1-30) once.	Work sts (30-1) once, then sts (42-36) once.
28/71	Work sts (37-42) once, then sts (1-33) once.	Work sts (33-1) once, then sts (42-37) once.
32/81	Work sts (35-42) once, then sts (1-35) once.	Work sts (35-1) once, then sts (42-35) once.
36/91	Work sts (32-42) once, then sts (1-38) once.	Work sts (38-1) once, then sts (42-32) once.
40/102	Work sts (30-42) once, then sts (1-40) once.	Work sts (40-1) once, then sts (42-30) once.
44/112	Work sts (28-42) once, then sts (1-42) once.	Work sts (42-1) once, then sts (42-28) once.
48/122	Work sts (26-42) once, then sts (1-42) once, then sts (1-2) once.	Work sts (2-1) once, then sts (42-1) once, then sts (42-26) once.
Waistcoat fronts		
24/61	Work sts (8-42) once.	Work sts (42-8) once.
28/71	Work sts (6-42) once, then sts (1-4) once.	Work sts (4-1) once, then sts (42-6) once.
32/81	Work sts (3-42) once, then sts (1-7) once.	Work sts (7-1) once, then sts (42-3) once.
36/91	Work stitch 42 once, then sts (1-42) once, then sts (1-10) once.	Work sts (10-1) once, then sts (42-1) once, then stitch 42 once.
40/102	Work sts (39-42) once, then sts (1-42) once, then sts (1-13) once.	Work sts (13-1) once, then sts (42-1) once, then sts (42-39) once.
44/112	Work sts (36-42) once, then sts (42-1) once, then sts (1-16) once.	Work sts (16-1) once, then sts (42-1) once, then sts (42-36) once.
48/122	Work sts (33-42) once, then sts (1-42) once, then sts (1-19) once.	Work sts (19-1) once, then sts (42-1) once, then sts (42-33) once.

The coming of
summer is
heralded by the
blossoming of the
Welsh poppy.
Here on this
winter-weight
jacket, it promises
warmer weather
to come.

44

WELSH POPPY YARN QUANTITIES

Each figure represents the number of 50g balls of Rowan Designer Double Knitting (DDK) or Double Knitting Fleck (DKF) or Fine Cotton Chenille (FCC) required. Fine Fleck comes in 25g hanks; double the number shown below.

Sizes in/cm	Sweater A	B	C	D	E	F	G	H	Jacket A	B	C	D	E	F	G	H	Cardigan A	B	C	D	E	F	G	H
24/61	4	1	1	1	1	1			5	1	1	1	1	1			4	1	1	1	1	1		
28/71	5	1	1	1	1	1			6	1	1	1	1	1			5	1	1	1	1	1		
32/81	7	1	1	1	1	1			8	1	1	1	1	1			7	1	1	1	1	1		
36/91	9	1	1	1	1	1			10	1	1	1	1	1			9	1	1	1	1	1		
40/102	10	1	1	1	1	1			11	1	1	1	1	1			11	1	1	1	1	1		
44/112	11	2	1	1	1	1			12	2	1	1	1	1			12	2	1	1	1	1		
48/122	12	2	1	1	1	1			13	2	1	1	1	1			12	2	1	1	1	1		

Sizes in/cm	Slipover A	B	C	D	E	F	G	H	Waistcoat A	B	C	D	E	F	G	H	Short top A	B	C	D	E	F	G	H
24/61	3	1	1	1	1	1			3	1	1	1	1	1			2	1	1	1	1			
28/71	4	1	1	1	1	1			4	1	1	1	1	1			3	1	1	1	1			
32/81	4	1	1	1	1	1			5	1	1	1	1	1			3	1	1	1	1			
36/91	5	1	1	1	1	1			6	1	1	1	1	1			4	1	1	1	1			
40/102	6	1	1	1	1	1			7	1	1	1	1	1			5	1	1	1	1			
44/112	7	1	1	1	1	1			7	1	1	1	1	1			5	1	1	1	1			
48/122	7	1	1	1	1	1			8	1	1	1	1	1			6	1	1	1	1			

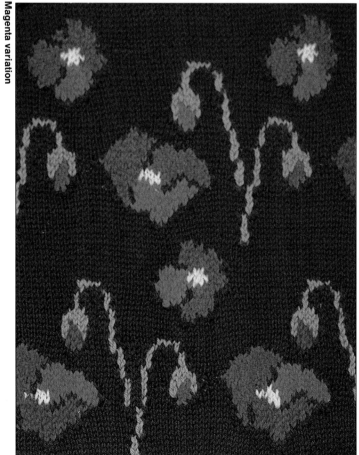

Welsh poppy chart placing instructions

Follow basic pattern instructions as given on pages 108-112, working pattern chart thus:

Work patt across knit rows (odd nos):

Sizes in/cm	Sweater back/front, Jacket back, Cardigan back, Slipover back/front, Short top back/front
24/61	Work sts (1-40) once, then sts (1-30) once.
28/71	Work sts (1-40) twice, then stitch 1 once.
32/81	Work sts (1-40) twice, then sts (1-12) once.
36/91	Work sts (1-40) twice, then sts (1-23) once.
40/102	Work sts (1-40) twice, then sts (1-34) once.
44/112	Work sts (1-40) 3 times, then sts (1-5) once.
48/122	Work sts (1-40) 3 times, then sts (1-16) once.

Sweater sleeves

24/61	Work sts (1-40) once, then sts (1-3) once.
28/71	Work sts (1-40) once, then sts (1-5) once.
32/81	Work sts (1-40) once, then sts (1-9) once.
36/91	Work sts (1-40) once, then sts (1-15) once.
40/102	Work sts (1-40) once, then sts (1-21) once.
44/112	Work sts (1-40) once, then sts (1-25) once.
48/122	Work sts (1-40) once, then sts (1-23) once.

Jacket fronts, Cardigan fronts

24/61	Work sts (1-34) once.
28/71	Work sts (1-40) once.
32/81	Work sts (1-40) once, then sts (1-6) once.
36/91	Work sts (1-40) once, then sts (1-12) once.
40/102	Work sts (1-40) once, then sts (1-18) once.
44/112	Work sts (1-40) once, then sts (1-24) once.
48/122	Work sts (1-40) once, then sts (1-30) once.

Jacket sleeves

24/61	Work sts (1-40) once, then stitch 1 once.
28/71	Work sts (1-40) once, then sts (1-3) once.
32/81	Work sts (1-40) once, then sts (1-7) once.
36/91	Work sts (1-40) once, then sts (1-11) once.
40/102	Work sts (1-40) once, then sts (1-15) once.
44/112	Work sts (1-40) once, then sts (1-19) once.
48/122	Work sts (1-40) once, then sts (1-23) once.

Cardigan sleeves

24/61	Work sts (1-37) once.
28/71	Work sts (1-39) once.
32/81	Work sts (1-40) once, then sts (1-3) once.
36/91	Work sts (1-40) once, then sts (1-9) once.
40/102	Work sts (1-40) once, then sts (1-13) once.
44/112	Work sts (1-40) once, then sts (1-17) once.
48/122	Work sts (1-40) once, then sts (1-21) once.

Waistcoat fronts

24/61	Work sts (1-35) once.
28/71	Work sts (1-40) once, then stitch 1 once.
32/81	Work sts (1-40) once, then sts (1-7) once.
36/91	Work sts (1-40) once, then sts (1-13) once.
40/102	Work sts (1-40) once, then sts (1-19) once.
44/112	Work sts (1-40) once, then sts (1-25) once.
48/122	Work sts (1-40) once, then sts (1-31) once.

Work patt across purl rows (even nos):

Sweater back/front, Jacket back, Cardigan back, Slipover back/front, Short top back/front
Work sts (30-1) once, then sts (40-1) once.
Work stitch 1 once, then sts (40-1) twice.
Work sts (12-1) once, then sts (40-1) twice.
Work sts (23-1) once, then sts (40-1) twice.
Work sts (34-1) once, then sts (40-1) twice.
Work sts (5-1) once, then sts (40-1) 3 times.
Work sts (16-1) once, then sts (40-1) 3 times.

Sweater sleeves
Work sts (3-1) once, then sts (40-1) once.
Work sts (5-1) once, then sts (40-1) once.
Work sts (9-1) once, then sts (40-1) once.
Work sts (15-1) once, then sts (40-1) once.
Work sts (21-1) once, then sts (40-1) once.
Work sts (25-1) once, then sts (40-1) once.
Work sts (23-1) once, then sts (40-1) once.

Jacket fronts, Cardigan fronts
Work sts (34-1) once.
Work sts (40-1) once.
Work sts (6-1) once, then sts (40-1) once.
Work sts (12-1) once, then sts (40-1) once.
Work sts (18-1) once, then sts (40-1) once.
Work sts (24-1) once, then sts (40-1) once.
Work sts (30-1) once, then sts (40-1) once.

Jacket sleeves
Work stitch 1 once, then sts (40-1) once.
Work sts (3-1) once, then sts (40-1) once.
Work sts (7-1) once, then sts (40-1) once.
Work sts (11-1) once, then sts (40-1) once.
Work sts (15-1) once, then sts (40-1) once.
Work sts (19-1) once, then sts (40-1) once.
Work sts (23-1) once, then sts (40-1) once.

Cardigan sleeves
Work sts (37-1) once.
Work sts (39-1) once.
Work sts (3-1) once, then sts (40-1) once.
Work sts (9-1) once, then sts (40-1) once.
Work sts (13-1) once, then sts (40-1) once.
Work sts (17-1) once, then sts (40-1) once.
Work sts (21-1) once, then sts (40-1) once.

Waistcoat fronts
Work sts (35-1) once.
Work stitch 1 once, then sts (40-1) once.
Work sts (7-1) once, then sts (40-1) once.
Work sts (13-1) once, then sts (40-1) once.
Work sts (19-1) once, then sts (40-1) once.
Work sts (25-1) once, then sts (40-1) once.
Work sts (31-1) once, then sts (40-1) once.

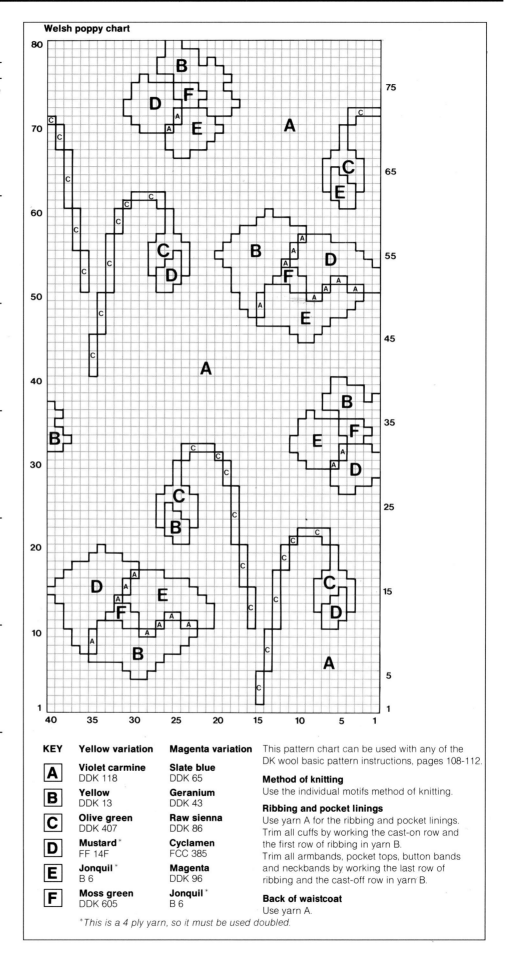

KEY	Yellow variation	Magenta variation
A	**Violet carmine** DDK 118	**Slate blue** DDK 65
B	**Yellow** DDK 13	**Geranium** DDK 43
C	**Olive green** DDK 407	**Raw sienna** DDK 86
D	**Mustard** * FF 14F	**Cyclamen** FCC 385
E	**Jonquil** * B 6	**Magenta** DDK 96
F	**Moss green** DDK 605	**Jonquil** * B 6

This is a 4 ply yarn, so it must be used doubled.

This pattern chart can be used with any of the DK wool basic pattern instructions, pages 108-112.

Method of knitting
Use the individual motifs method of knitting.

Ribbing and pocket linings
Use yarn A for the ribbing and pocket linings.
Trim all cuffs by working the cast-on row and the first row of ribbing in yarn B.
Trim all armbands, pocket tops, button bands and neckbands by working the last row of ribbing and the cast-off row in yarn B.

Back of waistcoat
Use yarn A.

BAVARIAN FLOWER

This pretty flower motif, reminiscent of mid-European decorative design, was inspired by my mother's woven ribbon collection. Wherever I am, when I wear it, it feels like the country.

48

Bavarian flower chart

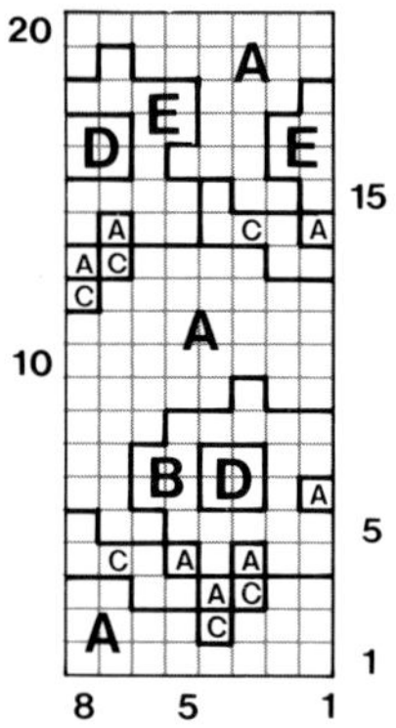

(Bavarian flower chart grid with letters A, B, C, D, E plotted; axis markings 1, 5, 10, 15, 20 on vertical and 8, 5, 1 on horizontal)

KEY   Black variation

 Black
B 62

B **Pillar box red**
B 44

C **Turquoise**
B 90

D **Yellow**
B 629

E **Electric blue**
B 634

KEY   White variation

 White
B 1

B **Gold**
B 14

C **Turquoise**
B 90

D **Purple**
B 126

E **Bright blue**
B 56

KEY   Rust variation

 Carmine
B 45

B **Van Dyke brown**
B 80

C **Gold**
B 14

D **Champagne**
LT 202

E **Lavender**
LT 213

This chart can be used with any 4 ply wool pattern instructions, pages 99-103.

Method of knitting
Use the stranded Fair Isle method.

Ribbing and pocket linings
Use yarn A for the ribbing and pocket linings.
Trim all cuffs by working the cast-on row and the first row of ribbing in yarn B.
Trim all armbands, pocket tops, and all button bands and neckbands (apart from the cardigan) by working the last row of ribbing and the cast-off row in yarn B.

Back of waistcoat
Use yarn A.

Bavarian flower chart placing instructions

Follow basic pattern instructions as given on pages 99-103, working pattern chart thus:

Sizes in/cm	*Work patt across knit rows (odd nos):*	*Work patt across purl rows (even nos):*
Sweater back/front, Jacket back, Cardigan back, Slipover back/front, Short top back/front		
24/61	Work sts (1-8) 10 times, then sts (1-4) once.	Work sts (4-1) once, then sts (8-1) 10 times.
28/71	Work sts (1-8) 12 times, then sts (1-2) once.	Work sts (2-1) once, then sts (8-1) 12 times.
32/81	Work sts (1-8) 14 times.	Work sts (8-1) 14 times.
36/91	Work sts (1-8) 15 times, then sts (1-6) once.	Work sts (6-1) once, then sts (8-1) 15 times.
40/102	Work sts (1-8) 17 times, then sts (1-4) once.	Work sts (4-1) once, then sts (8-1) 17 times.
44/112	Work sts (1-8) 19 times, then sts (1-2) once.	Work sts (2-1) once, then sts (8-1) 19 times.
48/122	Work sts (1-8) 21 times.	Work sts (8-1) 21 times.
Sweater sleeves		
24/61	Work sts (1-8) 5 times, then sts (1-4) once.	Work sts (4-1) once, then sts (8-1) 5 times.
28/71	Work sts (1-8) 6 times.	Work sts (8-1) 6 times.
32/81	Work sts (1-8) 6 times, then sts (1-4) once.	Work sts (4-1) once, then sts (8-1) 6 times.
36/91	Work sts (1-8) 8 times.	Work sts (8-1) 8 times.
40/102	Work sts (1-8) 9 times.	Work sts (8-1) 9 times.
44/112	Work sts (1-8) 9 times, then sts (1-4) once.	Work sts (4-1) once, then sts (8-1) 9 times.
48/122	Work sts (1-8) 9 times, then sts (1-4) once.	Work sts (4-1) once, then sts (8-1) 9 times.
Jacket fronts, Cardigan fronts		
24/61	Work sts (1-8) 4 times, then sts (1-6) once.	Work sts (6-1) once, then sts (8-1) 4 times.
28/71	Work sts (1-8) 5 times, then sts (1-4) once.	Work sts (4-1) once, then sts (8-1) 5 times.
32/81	Work sts (1-8) 6 times, then sts (1-4) once.	Work sts (4-1) once, then sts (8-1) 6 times.
36/91	Work sts (1-8) 7 times, then sts (1-4) once.	Work sts (4-1) once, then sts (8-1) 7 times.
40/102	Work sts (1-8) 8 times, then sts (1-2) once.	Work sts (2-1) once, then sts (8-1) 8 times.
44/112	Work sts (1-8) 9 times.	Work sts (8-1) 9 times.
48/122	Work sts (1-8) 10 times.	Work sts (8-1) 10 times.
Jacket sleeves		
24/61	Work sts (1-8) 10 times.	Work sts (8-1) 10 times.
28/71	Work sts (1-8) 10 times, then sts (1-2) once.	Work sts (2-1) once, then sts (8-1) 10 times.
32/81	Work sts (1-8) 10 times, then sts (1-6) once.	Work sts (6-1) once, then sts (8-1) 10 times.
36/91	Work sts (1-8) 12 times, then sts (1-4) once.	Work sts (4-1) once, then sts (8-1) 12 times.
40/102	Work sts (1-8) 13 times, then sts (1-6) once.	Work sts (6-1) once, then sts (8-1) 13 times.
44/112	Work sts (1-8) 14 times, then sts (1-2) once.	Work sts (2-1) once, then sts (8-1) 14 times.
48/122	Work sts (1-8) 14 times, then sts (1-4) once.	Work sts (4-1) once, then sts (8-1) 14 times.
Cardigan sleeves		
24/61	Work sts (1-8) 7 times.	Work sts (8-1) 7 times.
28/71	Work sts (1-8) 7 times, then sts (1-6) once.	Work sts (6-1) once, then sts (8-1) 7 times.
32/81	Work sts (1-8) 8 times, then sts (1-4) once.	Work sts (4-1) once, then sts (8-1) 8 times.
36/91	Work sts (1-8) 9 times.	Work sts (8-1) 9 times.
40/102	Work sts (1-8) 9 times, then sts (1-6) once.	Work sts (6-1) once, then sts (8-1) 9 times.
44/112	Work sts (1-8) 10 times, then sts (1-4) once.	Work sts (4-1) once, then sts (8-1) 10 times.
48/122	Work sts (1-8) 11 times, then sts (1-2) once.	Work sts (2-1) once, then sts (8-1) 11 times.
Waistcoat fronts		
24/61	Work sts (1-8) 5 times, then stitch 1 once.	Work stitch 1 once, then sts (8-1) 5 times.
28/71	Work sts (1-8) 6 times.	Work sts (8-1) 6 times.
32/81	Work sts (1-8) 6 times, then sts (1-7) once.	Work sts (7-1) once, then sts (8-1) 6 times.
36/91	Work sts (1-8) 7 times, then sts (1-6) once.	Work sts (6-1) once, then sts (8-1) 7 times.
40/102	Work sts (1-8) 8 times, then sts (1-5) once.	Work sts (5-1) once, then sts (8-1) 8 times.
44/112	Work sts (1-8) 9 times, then sts (1-4) once.	Work sts (4-1) once, then sts (8-1) 9 times.
48/122	Work sts (1-8) 10 times, then sts (1-3) once.	Work sts (3-1) once, then sts (8-1) 10 times.

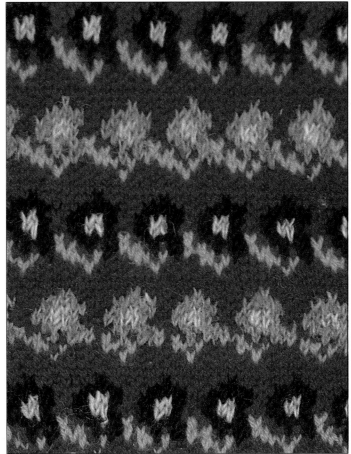

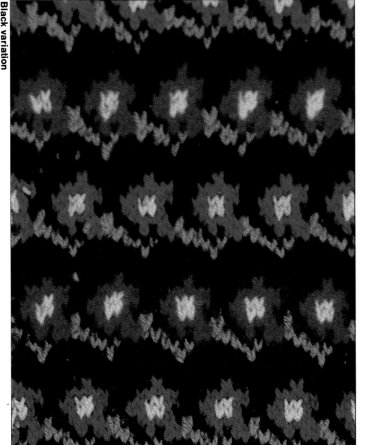

BAVARIAN FLOWER YARN QUANTITIES

Each figure represents the number of 25g hanks of Rowan Botany (B), Light Tweed (LT) or Fine Fleck (FF) required.

Sizes in/cm	A	B	C	D	E	F	G	H	A	B	C	D	E	F	G	H	A	B	C	D	E	F	G	H
			Sweater								Jacket								Cardigan					
24/61	4	1	1	1	1				5	1	1	1	1				5	1	1	1	1			
28/71	6	1	1	1	1				7	1	1	1	1				7	1	1	1	1			
32/81	8	1	1	1	1				9	1	1	1	1				9	1	1	1	1			
36/91	10	1	1	1	1				11	1	1	1	1				11	1	1	1	1			
40/102	12	1	1	1	1				13	1	1	1	1				13	1	1	1	1			
44/112	14	2	1	1	1				15	2	1	1	1				15	2	1	1	1			
48/122	14	2	2	1	2				15	2	2	1	2				15	2	2	1	2			
			Slipover								Waistcoat								Short top					
24/61	3	1	1	1	1				4	1	1	1	1				3	1	1	1	1			
28/71	4	1	1	1	1				4	1	1	1	1				4	1	1	1	1			
32/81	6	1	1	1	1				6	1	1	1	1				6	1	1	1	1			
36/91	7	1	1	1	1				7	1	1	1	1				7	1	1	1	1			
40/102	8	1	1	1	1				8	1	1	1	1				8	1	1	1	1			
44/112	9	1	1	1	1				9	1	1	1	1				9	1	1	1	1			
48/122	10	1	1	1	1				10	1	1	1	1				10	1	1	1	1			

CHERRY

Tiny bunches of cherries that are meant to put you in a carefree mood are strung across in wide bands. This motif was inspired by a cross-stitch embroidery design.

CHERRY YARN QUANTITIES

Each figure represents the number of 25g hanks of Rowan Botany (B), Light Tweed (LT) or Fine Fleck (FF) required.

Sizes in/cm	Sweater A	B	C	D	E	F	G	H	Jacket A	B	C	D	E	F	G	H	Cardigan A	B	C	D	E	F	G	H
24/61	2	2	2	1	1	1			3	3	2	1	1				3	3	2	1	1			
28/71	4	2	4	1	1	1			5	3	4	1	1				5	3	4	1	1			
32/81	4	2	4	1	1	1			5	3	4	1	1				5	3	4	1	1			
36/91	6	2	6	1	1	1			7	3	6	1	1				7	3	6	1	1			
40/102	6	3	6	1	1	1			7	4	6	1	1				7	4	6	1	1			
44/112	7	3	7	1	1	1			8	4	7	1	1				8	4	7	1	1			
48/122	7	4	7	1	1	1			8	5	7	1	1				8	5	7	1	1			

Sizes in/cm	Slipover A	B	C	D	E	F	G	H	Waistcoat A	B	C	D	E	F	G	H	Short top A	B	C	D	E	F	G	H
24/61	1	1	1	1	1				2	2	1	1	1				1	1	1	1	1			
28/71	2	1	2	1	1				3	3	1	1	1				2	1	2	1	1			
32/81	2	1	2	1	1				3	3	1	1	1				2	1	2	1	1			
36/91	3	2	3	1	1				4	4	2	1	1				3	2	3	1	1			
40/102	3	2	3	1	1				4	4	2	1	1				3	2	3	1	1			
44/112	4	2	4	1	1				5	5	2	1	1				4	2	4	1	1			
48/122	4	2	4	1	1				5	5	2	1	1				4	2	4	1	1			

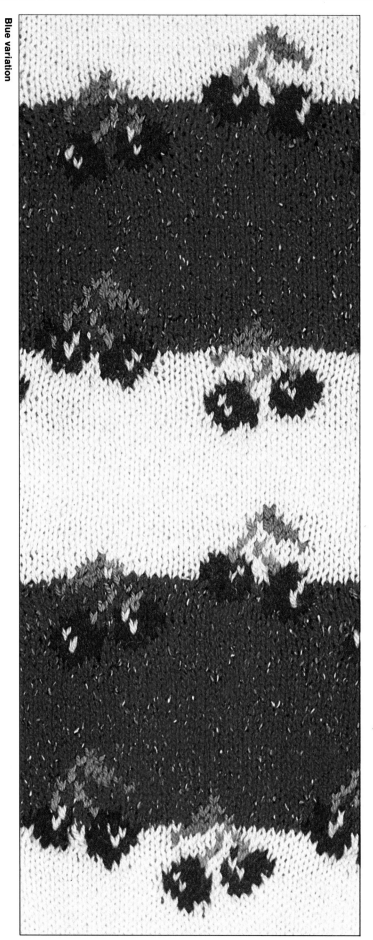

Cherry chart

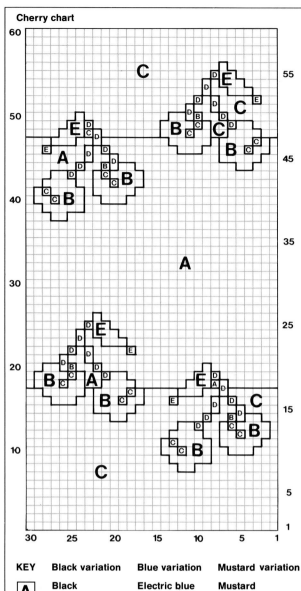

KEY	Black variation	Blue variation	Mustard variation
A	**Black** FF 62F	**Electric blue** FF 56F	**Mustard** FF 14F
B	**Pillar box red** B 44	**Pillar box red** B 44	**Pillar box red** B 44
C	**White** B 1	**White** B 1	**White** B 1
D	**Mouse** B 82	**Mouse** B 82	**Black** B 62
E	**Turquoise** B 90	**Turquoise** B 90	**Turquoise** B 90

This pattern chart can be used with any of the 4 ply wool basic pattern instructions, pages 99-103.

Method of knitting
Use the individual motifs method of knitting.

Ribbing and pocket linings
Use yarn C for the pocket linings.
Work all ribbing in a stripe sequence of 2 rows yarn A, 2 rows yarn B.

Back of waistcoat
Stripe sequence: 2 rows yarn A, 2 rows yarn B

Cherry chart placing instructions

Follow basic pattern instructions as given on pages 99-103, working pattern chart thus:

Sizes in/cm	Work patt across knit rows (odd nos):	Work patt across purl rows (even nos):
	Sweater back/front, Jacket back, Cardigan back, Slipover back/front, Short top back/front	
24/61	Work sts (1-30) twice, then sts (1-24) once.	Work sts (24-1) once, then sts (30-1) twice.
28/71	Work sts (1-30) 3 times, then sts (1-8) once.	Work sts (8-1) once, then sts (30-1) 3 times.
32/81	Work sts (1-30) 3 times, then sts (1-22) once.	Work sts (22-1) once, then sts (30-1) 3 times.
36/91	Work sts (1-30) 4 times, then sts (1-6) once.	Work sts (6-1) once, then sts (30-1) 4 times.
40/102	Work sts (1-30) 4 times, then sts (1-20) once.	Work sts (20-1) once, then sts (30-1) 4 times.
44/112	Work sts (1-30) 5 times, then sts (1-4) once.	Work sts (4-1) once, then sts (30-1) 5 times.
48/122	Work sts (1-30) 5 times, then sts (1-18) once.	Work sts (18-1) once, then sts (30-1) 5 times.
	Sweater sleeves	
24/61	Work sts (1-30) once, then sts (1-14) once.	Work sts (14-1) once, then sts (30-1) once.
28/71	Work sts (1-30) once, then sts (1-18) once.	Work sts (18-1) once, then sts (30-1) once.
32/81	Work sts (1-30) once, then sts (1-22) once.	Work sts (22-1) once, then sts (30-1) once.
36/91	Work sts (1-30) twice, then sts (1-4) once.	Work sts (4-1) once, then sts (30-1) twice.
40/102	Work sts (1-30) twice, then sts (1-12) once.	Work sts (12-1) once, then sts (30-1) twice.
44/112	Work sts (1-30) twice, then sts (1-16) once.	Work sts (16-1) once, then sts (30-1) twice.
48/122	Work sts (1-30) twice, then sts (1-16) once.	Work sts (16-1) once, then sts (30-1) twice.
	Jacket fronts, Cardigan fronts	
24/61	Work sts (1-30) once, then sts (1-8) once.	Work sts (8-1) once, then sts (30-1) once.
28/71	Work sts (1-30) once, then sts (1-14) once.	Work sts (14-1) once, then sts (30-1) once.
32/81	Work sts (1-30) once, then sts (1-22) once.	Work sts (22-1) once, then sts (30-1) once.
36/91	Work sts (1-30) twice.	Work sts (30-1) twice.
40/102	Work sts (1-30) twice, then sts (1-6) once.	Work sts (6-1) once, then sts (30-1) twice.
44/112	Work sts (1-30) twice, then sts (1-12) once.	Work sts (12-1) once, then sts (30-1) twice.
48/122	Work sts (1-30) twice, then sts (1-20) once.	Work sts (20-1) once, then sts (30-1) twice.
	Jacket sleeves	
24/61	Work sts (1-30) twice, then sts (1-20) once.	Work sts (20-1) once, then sts (30-1) twice.
28/71	Work sts (1-30) twice, then sts (1-22) once.	Work sts (22-1) once, then sts (30-1) twice.
32/81	Work sts (1-30) twice, then sts (1-26) once.	Work sts (26-1) once, then sts (30-1) twice.
36/91	Work sts (1-30) 3 times, then sts (1-10) once.	Work sts (10-1) once, then sts (30-1) 3 times.
40/102	Work sts (1-30) 3 times, then sts (1-20) once.	Work sts (20-1) once, then sts (30-1) 3 times.
44/112	Work sts (1-30) 3 times, then sts (1-24) once.	Work sts (24-1) once, then sts (30-1) 3 times.
48/122	Work sts (1-30) 3 times, then sts (1-26) once.	Work sts (26-1) once, then sts (30-1) 3 times.
	Cardigan sleeves	
24/61	Work sts (1-30) once, then sts (1-26) once.	Work sts (26-1) once, then sts (30-1) once.
28/71	Work sts (1-30) twice, then sts (1-2) once.	Work sts (2-1) once, then sts (30-1) twice.
32/81	Work sts (1-30) twice, then sts (1-8) once.	Work sts (8-1) once, then sts (30-1) twice.
36/91	Work sts (1-30) twice, then sts (1-12) once.	Work sts (12-1) once, then sts (30-1) twice.
40/102	Work sts (1-30) twice, then sts (1-18) once.	Work sts (18-1) once, then sts (30-1) twice.
44/112	Work sts (1-30) twice, then sts (1-24) once.	Work sts (24-1) once, then sts (30-1) twice.
48/122	Work sts (1-30) 3 times.	Work sts (30-1) 3 times.
	Waistcoat fronts	
24/61	Work sts (1-30) once, then sts (1-11) once.	Work sts (11-1) once, then sts (30-1) once.
28/71	Work sts (1-30) once, then sts (1-18) once.	Work sts (18-1) once, then sts (30-1) once.
32/81	Work sts (1-30) once, then sts (1-25) once.	Work sts (25-1) once, then sts (30-1) once.
36/91	Work sts (1-30) twice, then sts (1-2) once.	Work sts (2-1) once, then sts (30-1) twice.
40/102	Work sts (1-30) twice, then sts (1-9) once.	Work sts (9-1) once, then sts (30-1) twice.
44/112	Work sts (1-30) twice, then sts (1-16) once.	Work sts (16-1) once, then sts (30-1) twice.
48/122	Work sts (1-30) twice, then sts (1-23) once.	Work sts (23-1) once, then sts (30-1) twice.

Surrounded at home with coppiced woodland, one of its inhabitants, the mighty oak, was the inspiration for this autumnal design.

ACORN YARN QUANTITIES

Each figure represents the number of 25g hanks of Rowan Botany (B), Light Tweed (LT) or Fine Fleck (FF) required.

Sizes in/cm	Sweater A	B	C	D	E	F	G	H	Jacket A	B	C	D	E	F	G	H	Cardigan A	B	C	D	E	F	G	H
24/61	4	1	1	1	1	1	1		5	1	1	1	1	1	1		5	1	1	1	1	1	1	
28/71	6	1	1	1	1	1	1		7	1	1	1	1	1	1		7	1	1	1	1	1	1	
32/81	8	2	2	1	2	1	1		9	2	2	1	2	1	1		9	2	2	1	2	1	1	
36/91	10	2	2	1	2	1	1		11	2	2	1	2	1	1		11	2	2	1	2	1	1	
40/102	12	2	2	1	2	2	1		13	2	2	1	2	2	1		13	2	2	1	2	2	1	
44/112	14	2	2	1	2	2	1		15	2	2	1	2	2	1		15	2	2	1	2	2	1	
48/122	14	2	3	1	2	2	1		15	2	3	1	2	2	1		15	2	3	1	2	2	1	

Sizes in/cm	Slipover A	B	C	D	E	F	G	H	Waistcoat A	B	C	D	E	F	G	H	Short top A	B	C	D	E	F	G	H
24/61	3	1	1	1	1	1	1		4	1	1	1	1	1	1	1	3	1	1	1	1	1	1	1
28/71	4	1	1	1	1	1	1		4	1	1	1	1	1	1	1	4	1	1	1	1	1	1	1
32/81	5	1	1	1	1	1	1		6	1	1	1	1	1	1	1	5	1	1	1	1	1	1	1
36/91	6	1	1	1	1	1	1		7	1	1	1	1	1	1	1	6	1	1	1	1	1	1	1
40/102	7	1	1	1	1	1	1		8	1	1	1	1	1	1	1	7	1	1	1	1	1	1	1
44/112	7	1	2	1	1	1	1		9	1	1	1	1	1	1	1	7	1	2	1	1	1	1	1
48/122	8	2	2	1	2	2	1		10	1	1	1	1	1	1	1	8	2	2	1	2	2	1	

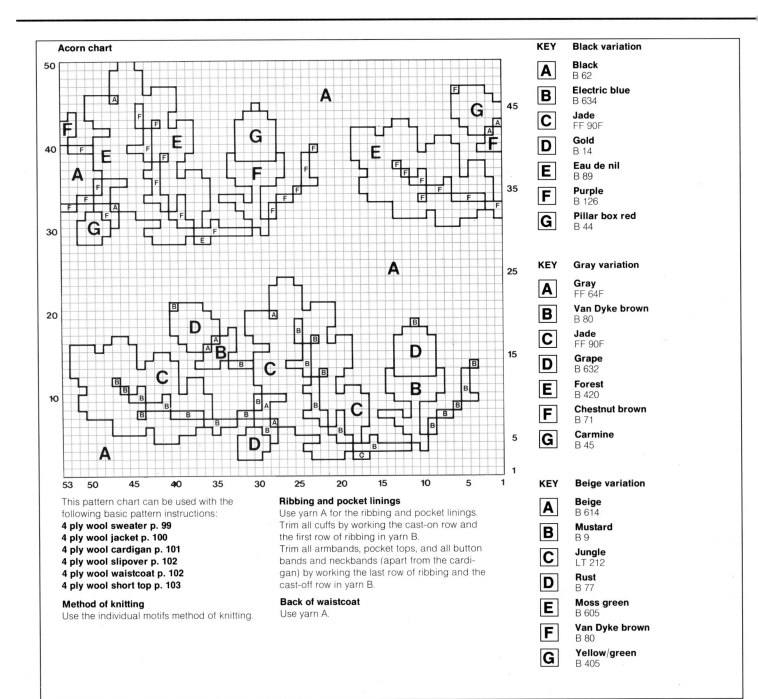

Acorn chart

KEY	Black variation
A	**Black** B 62
B	**Electric blue** B 634
C	**Jade** FF 90F
D	**Gold** B 14
E	**Eau de nil** B 89
F	**Purple** B 126
G	**Pillar box red** B 44

KEY	Gray variation
A	**Gray** FF 64F
B	**Van Dyke brown** B 80
C	**Jade** FF 90F
D	**Grape** B 632
E	**Forest** B 420
F	**Chestnut brown** B 71
G	**Carmine** B 45

KEY	Beige variation
A	**Beige** B 614
B	**Mustard** B 9
C	**Jungle** LT 212
D	**Rust** B 77
E	**Moss green** B 605
F	**Van Dyke brown** B 80
G	**Yellow/green** B 405

This pattern chart can be used with the following basic pattern instructions:
4 ply wool sweater p. 99
4 ply wool jacket p. 100
4 ply wool cardigan p. 101
4 ply wool slipover p. 102
4 ply wool waistcoat p. 102
4 ply wool short top p. 103

Method of knitting
Use the individual motifs method of knitting.

Ribbing and pocket linings
Use yarn A for the ribbing and pocket linings.
Trim all cuffs by working the cast-on row and the first row of ribbing in yarn B.
Trim all armbands, pocket tops, and all button bands and neckbands (apart from the cardigan) by working the last row of ribbing and the cast-off row in yarn B.

Back of waistcoat
Use yarn A.

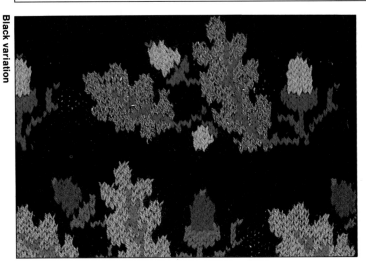

Black variation

Beige variation

Acorn chart placing instructions

Follow basic pattern instructions as given on pages 99-103, working pattern chart thus:

Sizes in/cm	Work patt across knit rows (odd nos):	Work patt across purl rows (even nos):
	Sweater back/front, Jacket back, Cardigan back, Slipover back/front, Short top back/front	
24/61	Work sts (1-53) once, then sts (1-31) once.	Work sts (31-1) once, then sts (53-1) once.
28/71	Work sts (1-53) once, then sts (1-45) once.	Work sts (45-1) once, then sts (53-1) once.
32/81	Work sts (1-53) twice, then sts (1-6) once.	Work sts (6-1) once, then sts (53-1) twice.
36/91	Work sts (1-53) twice, then sts (1-20) once.	Work sts (20-1) once, then sts (53-1) twice.
40/102	Work sts (1-53) twice, then sts (1-34) once.	Work sts (34-1) once, then sts (53-1) twice.
44/112	Work sts (1-53) twice, then sts (1-48) once.	Work sts (48-1) once, then sts (53-1) twice.
48/122	Work sts (1-53) 3 times, then sts (1-9) once.	Work sts (9-1) once, then sts (53-1) 3 times.
	Sweater sleeves	
24/61	Work sts (1-44) once.	Work sts (44-1) once.
28/71	Work sts (1-48) once.	Work sts (48-1) once.
32/81	Work sts (1-52) once.	Work sts (52-1) once.
36/91	Work sts (1-53) once, then sts (1-11) once.	Work sts (11-1) once, then sts (53-1) once.
40/102	Work sts (1-53) once, then sts (1-19) once.	Work sts (19-1) once, then sts (53-1) once.
44/112	Work sts (1-53) once, then sts (1-23) once.	Work sts (23-1) once, then sts (53-1) once.
48/122	Work sts (1-53) once, then sts (1-23) once.	Work sts (23-1) once, then sts (53-1) once.
	Jacket fronts, Cardigan fronts	
24/61	Work sts (1-38) once.	Work sts (38-1) once.
28/71	Work sts (1-44) once.	Work sts (44-1) once.
32/81	Work sts (1-52) once.	Work sts (52-1) once.
36/91	Work sts (1-53) once, then sts (1-7) once.	Work sts (7-1) once, then sts (53-1) once.
40/102	Work sts (1-53) once, then sts (1-13) once.	Work sts (13-1) once, then sts (53-1) once.
44/112	Work sts (1-53) once, then sts (1-19) once.	Work sts (19-1) once, then sts (53-1) once.
48/122	Work sts (1-53) once, then sts (1-27) once.	Work sts (27-1) once, then sts (53-1) once.
	Jacket sleeves	
24/61	Work sts (1-53) once, then sts (1-27) once.	Work sts (27-1) once, then sts (53-1) once.
28/71	Work sts (1-53) once, then sts (1-29) once.	Work sts (29-1) once, then sts (53-1) once.
32/81	Work sts (1-53) once, then sts (1-33) once.	Work sts (33-1) once, then sts (53-1) once.
36/91	Work sts (1-53) once, then sts (1-47) once.	Work sts (47-1) once, then sts (53-1) once.
40/102	Work sts (1-53) twice, then sts (1-4) once.	Work sts (4-1) once, then sts (53-1) twice.
44/112	Work sts (1-53) twice, then sts (1-8) once.	Work sts (8-1) once, then sts (53-1) twice.
48/122	Work sts (1-53) twice, then sts (1-10) once.	Work sts (10-1) once, then sts (53-1) twice.
	Cardigan sleeves	
24/61	Work sts (1-53) once, then sts (1-3) once.	Work sts (3-1) once, then sts (53-1) once.
28/71	Work sts (1-53) once, then sts (1-9) once.	Work sts (9-1) once, then sts (53-1) once.
32/81	Work sts (1-53) once, then sts (1-15) once.	Work sts (15-1) once, then sts (53-1) once.
36/91	Work sts (1-53) once, then sts (1-19) once.	Work sts (19-1) once, then sts (53-1) once.
40/102	Work sts (1-53) once, then sts (1-25) once.	Work sts (25-1) once, then sts (53-1) once.
44/112	Work sts (1-53) once, then sts (1-31) once.	Work sts (31-1) once, then sts (53-1) once.
48/122	Work sts (1-53) once, then sts (1-37) once.	Work sts (37-1) once, then sts (53-1) once.
	Waistcoat fronts	
24/61	Work sts (1-41) once.	Work sts (41-1) once.
28/71	Work sts (1-48) once.	Work sts (48-1) once.
32/81	Work sts (1-53) once, then sts (1-2) once.	Work sts (2-1) once, then sts (53-1) once.
36/91	Work sts (1-53) once, then sts (1-9) once.	Work sts (9-1) once, then sts (53-1) once.
40/102	Work sts (1-53) once, then sts (1-16) once.	Work sts (16-1) once, then sts (53-1) once.
44/112	Work sts (1-53) once, then sts (1-23) once.	Work sts (23-1) once, then sts (53-1) once.
48/122	Work sts (1-53) once, then sts (1-30) once.	Work sts (30-1) once, then sts (53-1) once.

Originally captured in a painting I did of the Alpujarras Mountains, I translated this wonderful mixture of bright sunlight and blossoms on the Spanish hillside to wool.

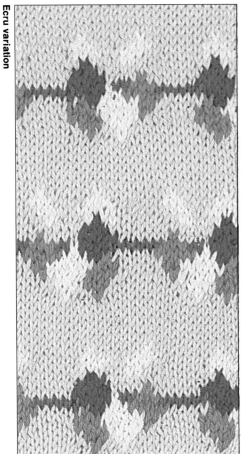

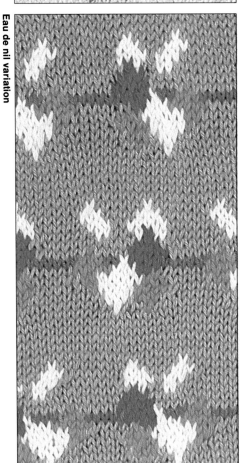

Almond blossom chart

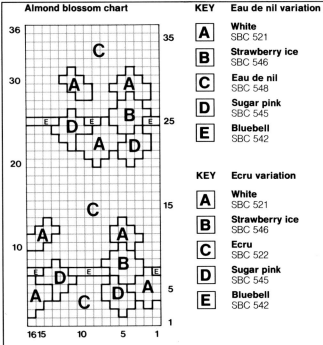

KEY	Eau de nil variation	Bluebell variation
A	**White** SBC 521	**White** SBC 521
B	**Strawberry ice** SBC 546	**Strawberry ice** SBC 546
C	**Eau de nil** SBC 548	**Bluebell** SBC 542
D	**Sugar pink** SBC 545	**Sugar pink** SBC 545
E	**Bluebell** SBC 542	**Ecru** SBC 522

KEY	Ecru variation
A	**White** SBC 521
B	**Strawberry ice** SBC 546
C	**Ecru** SBC 522
D	**Sugar pink** SBC 545
E	**Bluebell** SBC 542

This pattern chart can be used with the following basic pattern instructions:

4 ply cotton sweater p. 104
4 ply cotton cardigan p. 105
4 ply cotton slipover p. 106
4 ply cotton waistcoat p. 106
4 ply cotton short top p. 107

Method of knitting
Use the individual motifs method of knitting.

Ribbing and pocket linings
Use yarn C for the pocket linings.
Use yarn A for the ribbing.
Trim all cuffs by working the cast-on row and the first row of ribbing in yarn D.
Trim all armbands, pocket tops, and all button bands and neckbands (apart from the cardigan) by working the last row of ribbing and the cast-off row in yarn D.

Back of waistcoat
Use yarn A.

ALMOND BLOSSOM YARN QUANTITIES
Each figure represents the number of 50g balls of Rowan Sea Breeze Cotton (SBC) required.

Sizes in/cm	A	B	C	D	E	F	G	H	A	B	C	D	E	F	G	H	A	B	C	D	E	F	G	H
			Sweater								not suitable for Jacket								Cardigan					
24/61	2	1	2	1	1												2	1	2	1	1			
28/71	3	1	3	1	1												3	1	3	1	1			
32/81	4	1	3	1	1												4	1	3	1	1			
36/91	5	1	3	1	1												5	1	3	1	1			
40/102	5	1	4	1	1												5	1	4	1	1			
44/112	6	1	4	1	1												6	1	4	1	1			
48/122	6	1	4	1	1												6	1	4	1	1			
			Slipover								Waistcoat								Short top					
24/61	1	1	2	1	1				2	1	1	1	1				1	1	2	1	1			
28/71	2	1	2	1	1				2	1	1	1	1				2	1	2	1	1			
32/81	2	1	2	1	1				2	1	1	1	1				2	1	2	1	1			
36/91	3	1	3	1	1				3	1	1	1	1				3	1	3	1	1			
40/102	3	1	3	1	1				4	1	2	1	1				3	1	3	1	1			
44/112	4	1	3	1	1				4	1	2	1	1				4	1	3	1	1			
48/122	4	1	3	1	1				5	1	3	1	1				4	1	3	1	1			

Almond blossom chart placing instructions

Follow basic pattern instructions as given on pages 104-107, working pattern chart thus:

Sizes in/cm	*Work patt across knit rows (odd nos):*	*Work patt across purl rows (even nos):*
Sweater back/front, Cardigan back, Slipover back/front, Short top back/front		
24/61	Work sts (1-16) 6 times, then sts (1-4) once.	Work sts (4-1) once, then sts (16-1) 6 times.
28/71	Work sts (1-16) 7 times, then sts (1-4) once.	Work sts (4-1) once, then sts (16-1) 7 times.
32/81	Work sts (1-16) 8 times, then sts (1-4) once.	Work sts (4-1) once, then sts (16-1) 8 times.
36/91	Work sts (1-16) 9 times, then sts (1-4) once.	Work sts (4-1) once, then sts (16-1) 9 times.
40/102	Work sts (1-16) 10 times, then sts (1-4) once.	Work sts (4-1) once, then sts (16-1) 10 times.
44/112	Work sts (1-16) 11 times, then sts (1-4) once.	Work sts (4-1) once, then sts (16-1) 11 times.
48/122	Work sts (1-16) 12 times, then sts (1-4) once.	Work sts (4-1) once, then sts (16-1) 12 times.
Sweater sleeves		
24/61	Work sts (1-16) 3 times, then sts (1-10) once.	Work sts (10-1) once, then sts (16-1) 3 times.
28/71	Work sts (1-16) 4 times, then sts (1-2) once.	Work sts (2-1) once, then sts (16-1) 4 times.
32/81	Work sts (1-16) 4 times, then sts (1-4) once.	Work sts (4-1) once, then sts (16-1) 4 times.
36/91	Work sts (1-16) 4 times, then sts (1-12) once.	Work sts (12-1) once, then sts (16-1) 4 times.
40/102	Work sts (1-16) 5 times.	Work sts (16-1) 5 times.
44/112	Work sts (1-16) 5 times, then sts (1-2) once.	Work sts (2-1) once, then sts (16-1) 5 times.
48/122	Work sts (1-16) 5 times, then sts (1-6) once.	Work sts (6-1) once, then sts (16-1) 5 times.
Cardigan fronts		
24/61	Work sts (1-16) twice, then sts (1-10) once.	Work sts (10-1) once, then sts (16-1) twice.
28/71	Work sts (1-16) 3 times, then sts (1-4) once.	Work sts (4-1) once, then sts (16-1) 3 times.
32/81	Work sts (1-16) 3 times, then sts (1-12) once.	Work sts (12-1) once, then sts (16-1) 3 times.
36/91	Work sts (1-16) 4 times, then sts (1-4) once.	Work sts (4-1) once, then sts (16-1) 4 times.
40/102	Work sts (1-16) 4 times, then sts (1-12) once.	Work sts (12-1) once, then sts (16-1) 4 times.
44/112	Work sts (1-16) 5 times, then sts (1-4) once.	Work sts (4-1) once, then sts (16-1) 5 times.
48/122	Work sts (1-16) 5 times, then sts (1-12) once.	Work sts (12-1) once, then sts (16-1) 5 times.
Cardigan sleeves		
24/61	Work sts (1-16) 3 times, then sts (1-8) once.	Work sts (8-1) once, then sts (16-1) 3 times.
28/71	Work sts (1-16) 4 times.	Work sts (16-1) 4 times.
32/81	Work sts (1-16) 4 times, then sts (1-6) once.	Work sts (6-1) once, then sts (16-1) 4 times.
36/91	Work sts (1-16) 4 times, then sts (1-10) once.	Work sts (10-1) once, then sts (16-1) 4 times.
40/102	Work sts (1-16) 4 times, then sts (1-14) once.	Work sts (14-1) once, then sts (16-1) 4 times.
44/112	Work sts (1-16) 5 times.	Work sts (16-1) 5 times.
48/122	Work sts (1-16) 5 times, then sts (1-4) once.	Work sts (4-1) once, then sts (16-1) 5 times.
Waistcoat fronts		
24/61	Work sts (1-16) twice, then sts (1-14) once.	Work sts (14-1) once, then sts (16-1) twice.
28/71	Work sts (1-16) 3 times, then sts (1-6) once.	Work sts (6-1) once, then sts (16-1) 3 times.
32/81	Work sts (1-16) 3 times, then sts (1-14) once.	Work sts (14-1) once, then sts (16-1) 3 times.
36/91	Work sts (1-16) 4 times, then sts (1-6) once.	Work sts (6-1) once, then sts (16-1) 4 times.
40/102	Work sts (1-16) 4 times, then sts (1-14) once.	Work sts (14-1) once, then sts (16-1) 4 times.
44/112	Work sts (1-16) 5 times, then sts (1-6) once.	Work sts (6-1) once, then sts (16-1) 5 times.
48/122	Work sts (1-16) 5 times, then sts (1-14) once.	Work sts (14-1) once, then sts (16-1) 5 times.

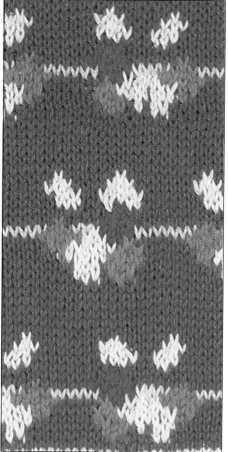

Bluebell variation

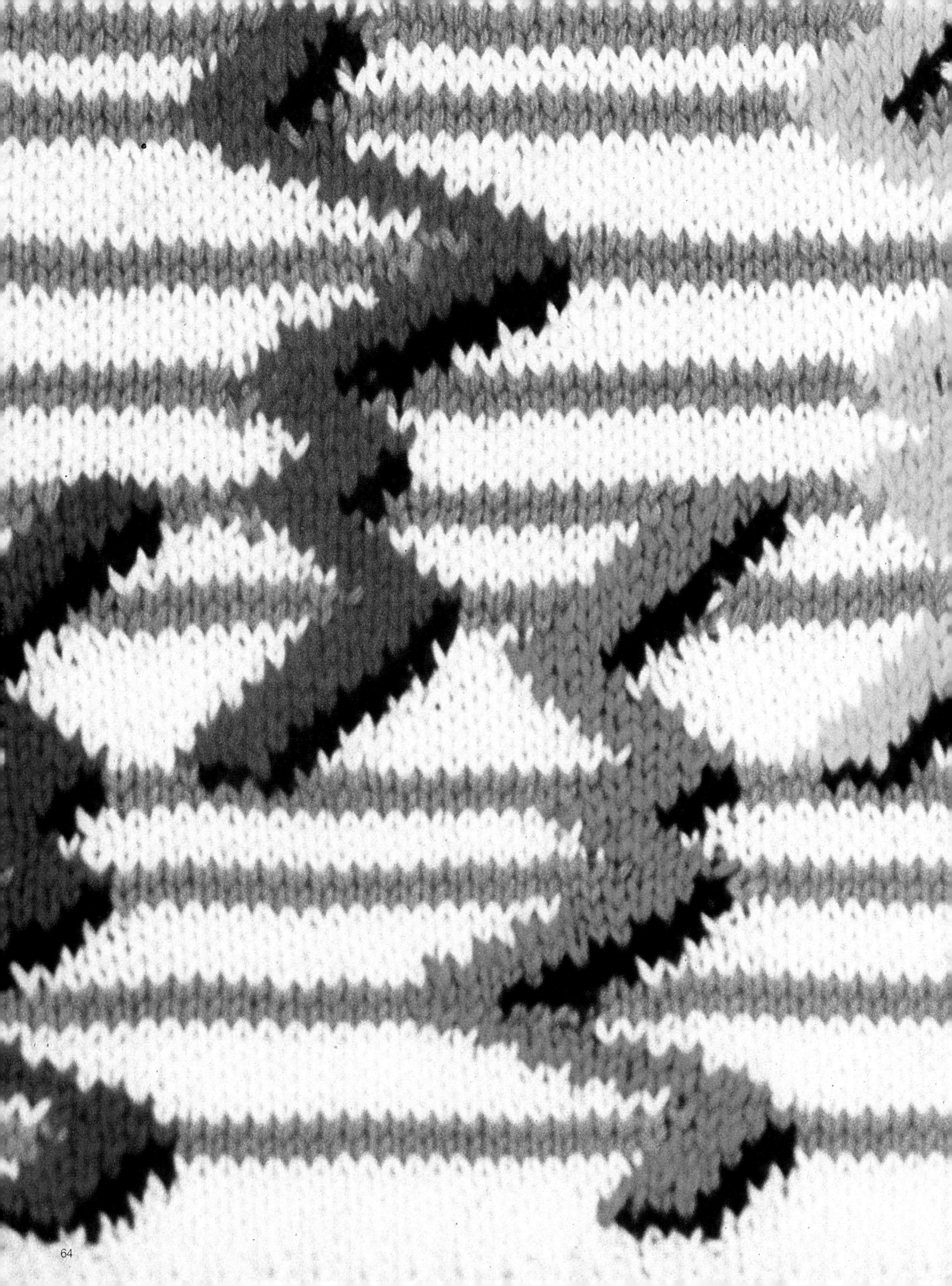

FLASHES & SPLASHES

SPLASH

Carefree splodges of paint give dramatic impact to this casual design. Choose your palette to please all the artists in your family.

66

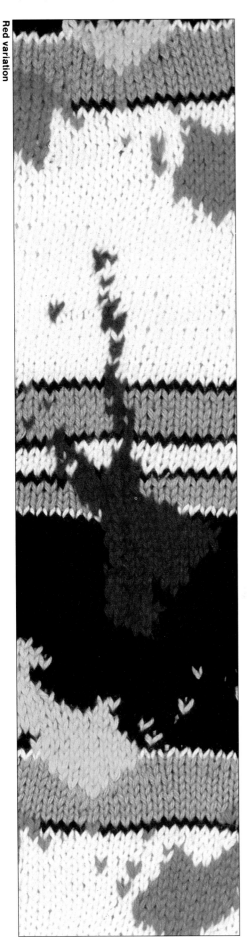

Splash chart

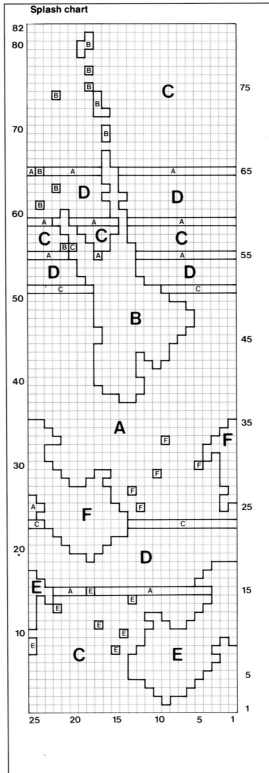

KEY   **Red variation**

A	**Black**	SBC 526
B	**Signal red**	SBC 532
C	**White**	SBC 521
D	**Dove gray**	SBC 549
E	**Burnt orange**	SBC 550
F	**Sienna**	SBC 535

KEY   **Jade variation**

A	**Black**	SBC 526
B	**Mermaid**	SBC 547
C	**White**	SBC 521
D	**Dove gray**	SBC 549
E	**Bluebell**	SBC 542
F	**Purple**	SBC 543

KEY   **Pastel variation**

A	**Black**	SBC 526
B	**Sugar pink**	SBC 546
C	**White**	SBC 521
D	**Dove gray**	SBC 549
E	**Bluebell**	SBC 542
F	**Lemon ice**	SBC 551

This pattern chart can be used with the following basic pattern instructions:
4 ply cotton sweater p. 104
4 ply cotton cardigan p. 105
4 ply cotton slipover p. 106
4 ply cotton waistcoat p. 106
4 ply cotton short top p. 107

Method of knitting
Use the individual motifs method of knitting.

Ribbing and pocket linings
Use yarn C for the pocket linings.
Use yarn A for the ribbing.
Trim all cuffs by working the cast-on row and the first row of ribbing in yarn B.
Trim all armbands, pocket tops, and all button bands and neckbands (apart from the cardigan) by working the last row of ribbing and the cast-off row in yarn B.

Back of waistcoat
Use yarn A.

Splash chart placing instructions

Follow basic pattern instructions as given on pages 104-107, working pattern chart thus:

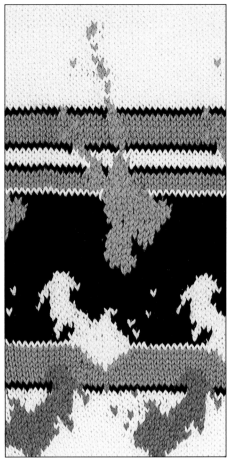

Sizes in/cm	Work patt across knit rows (odd nos):	Work patt across purl rows (even nos):
	Sweater back/front, Cardigan back, Slipover back/front, Short top back/front	
24/61	Work sts (1-25) 4 times.	Work sts (25-1) 4 times.
28/71	Work sts (1-25) 4 times, then sts (1-16) once.	Work sts (16-1) once, then sts (25-1) 4 times.
32/81	Work sts (1-25) 5 times, then sts (1-7) once.	Work sts (7-1) once, then sts (25-1) 5 times.
36/91	Work sts (1-25) 5 times, then sts (1-23) once.	Work sts (23-1) once, then sts (25-1) 5 times.
40/102	Work sts (1-25) 6 times, then sts (1-14) once.	Work sts (14-1) once, then sts (25-1) 6 times.
44/112	Work sts (1-25) 7 times, then sts (1-5) once.	Work sts (5-1) once, then sts (25-1) 7 times.
48/122	Work sts (1-25) 7 times, then sts (1-21) once.	Work sts (21-1) once, then sts (25-1) 7 times.
	Sweater sleeves	
24/61	Work sts (1-25) twice, then sts (1-8) once.	Work sts (8-1) once, then sts (25-1) twice.
28/71	Work sts (1-25) twice, then sts (1-16) once.	Work sts (16-1) once, then sts (25-1) twice.
32/81	Work sts (1-25) twice, then sts (1-18) once.	Work sts (18-1) once, then sts (25-1) twice.
36/91	Work sts (1-25) 3 times, then stitch 1 once.	Work stitch 1 once, then sts (25-1) 3 times.
40/102	Work sts (1-25) 3 times, then sts (1-5) once.	Work sts (5-1) once, then sts (25-1) 3 times.
44/112	Work sts (1-25) 3 times, then sts (1-7) once.	Work sts (7-1) once, then sts (25-1) 3 times.
48/122	Work sts (1-25) 3 times, then sts (1-11) once.	Work sts (11-1) once, then sts (25-1) 3 times.
	Cardigan fronts	
24/61	Work sts (1-25) once, then sts (1-17) once.	Work sts (17-1) once, then sts (25-1) once.
28/71	Work sts (1-25) twice, then sts (1-2) once.	Work sts (2-1) once, then sts (25-1) twice.
32/81	Work sts (1-25) twice, then sts (1-10) once.	Work sts (10-1) once, then sts (25-1) twice.
36/91	Work sts (1-25) twice, then sts (1-18) once.	Work sts (18-1) once, then sts (25-1) twice.
40/102	Work sts (1-25) 3 times, then stitch 1 once.	Work stitch 1 once, then sts (25-1) 3 times.
44/112	Work sts (1-25) 3 times, then sts (1-9) once.	Work sts (9-1) once, then sts (25-1) 3 times.
48/122	Work sts (1-25) 3 times, then sts (1-17) once.	Work sts (17-1) once, then sts (25-1) 3 times.
	Cardigan sleeves	
24/61	Work sts (1-25) twice, then sts (1-6) once.	Work sts (6-1) once, then sts (25-1) twice.
28/71	Work sts (1-25) twice, then sts (1-14) once.	Work sts (14-1) once, then sts (25-1) twice.
32/81	Work sts (1-25) twice, then sts (1-20) once.	Work sts (20-1) once, then sts (25-1) twice.
36/91	Work sts (1-25) twice, then sts (1-24) once.	Work sts (24-1) once, then sts (25-1) twice.
40/102	Work sts (1-25) 3 times, then sts (1-3) once.	Work sts (3-1) once, then sts (25-1) 3 times.
44/112	Work sts (1-25) 3 times, then sts (1-5) once.	Work sts (5-1) once, then sts (25-1) 3 times.
48/122	Work sts (1-25) 3 times, then sts (1-9) once.	Work sts (9-1) once, then sts (25-1) 3 times.
	Waistcoat fronts	
24/61	Work sts (1-25) once, then sts (1-21) once.	Work sts (21-1) once, then sts (25-1) once.
28/71	Work sts (1-25) twice, then sts (1-4) once.	Work sts (4-1) once, then sts (25-1) twice.
32/81	Work sts (1-25) twice, then sts (1-12) once.	Work sts (12-1) once, then sts (25-1) twice.
36/91	Work sts (1-25) twice, then sts (1-20) once.	Work sts (20-1) once, then sts (25-1) twice.
40/102	Work sts (1-25) 3 times, then sts (1-3) once.	Work sts (3-1) once, then sts (25-1) 3 times.
44/112	Work sts (1-25) 3 times, then sts (1-11) once.	Work sts (11-1) once, then sts (25-1) 3 times.
48/122	Work sts (1-25) 3 times, then sts (1-19) once.	Work sts (19-1) once, then sts (25-1) 3 times.

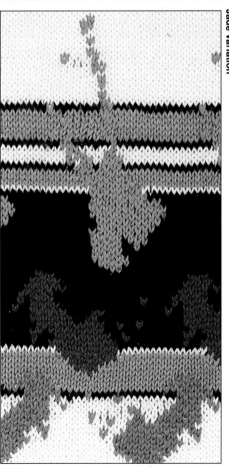

SPLASH YARN QUANTITIES

Each figure represents the number of 50g balls of Rowan Sea Breeze Cotton (SBC) required.

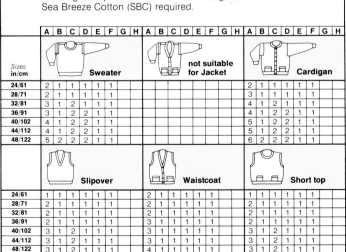

Sizes in/cm	Sweater A	B	C	D	E	F	G	H	Cardigan A	B	C	D	E	F	G	H
24/61	2	1	1	1	1	1			2	1	1	1	1	1		
28/71	2	1	1	1	1	1			3	1	1	1	1	1		
32/81	3	1	2	1	1	1			4	1	2	1	1	1		
36/91	3	1	2	2	1	1			4	1	2	2	1	1		
40/102	4	1	2	2	1	1			5	1	2	2	1	1		
44/112	4	1	2	2	1	1			5	1	2	2	1	1		
48/122	5	2	2	2	1	1			6	2	2	2	1	1		

not suitable for Jacket

Sizes in/cm	Slipover A	B	C	D	E	F	G	H	Waistcoat A	B	C	D	E	F	G	H	Short top A	B	C	D	E	F	G	H
24/61	1	1	1	1	1	1			2	1	1	1	1	1			1	1	1	1	1	1		
28/71	2	1	1	1	1	1			2	1	1	1	1	1			2	1	1	1	1	1		
32/81	2	1	1	1	1	1			2	1	1	1	1	1			2	1	1	1	1	1		
36/91	2	1	1	1	1	1			3	1	1	1	1	1			2	1	1	1	1	1		
40/102	3	1	2	1	1	1			3	1	1	1	1	1			3	1	2	1	1	1		
44/112	3	1	2	1	1	1			3	1	1	1	1	1			3	1	2	1	1	1		
48/122	3	1	2	1	1	1			4	1	1	1	1	1			3	1	2	1	1	1		

ODÉON

A jazzy Art Deco design, Odeon looks elegant in daytime or evening. Blocks of pattern repeat give the illusion of vertical stripes.

ODEON YARN QUANTITIES

Each figure represents the number of 25g hanks of Rowan Botany (B), Light Tweed (LT) or Fine Fleck (FF) required.

Sizes in/cm	A	B	C	D	E	F	G	H	A	B	C	D	E	F	G	H	A	B	C	D	E	F	G	H
				Sweater								Jacket								Cardigan			
24/61	4	1	1	1	1				5	1	1	1	1				5	1	1	1	1			
28/71	6	2	2	1	1				7	2	2	1	1				7	2	2	1	1			
32/81	8	2	2	2	2				9	2	2	2	2				9	2	2	2	2			
36/91	10	2	2	2	2				11	2	2	2	2				11	2	2	2	2			
40/102	12	3	2	2	2				13	3	2	2	2				13	3	2	2	2			
44/112	13	3	3	2	2				14	3	3	2	2				14	3	3	2	2			
48/122	14	3	3	3	3				15	3	3	3	3				15	3	3	3	3			
				Slipover								Waistcoat								Short top			
24/61	2	1	1	1	1				3	1	1	1	1				2	1	1	1	1			
28/71	3	1	1	1	1				4	1	1	1	1				3	1	1	1	1			
32/81	4	1	1	1	1				5	1	1	1	1				4	1	1	1	1			
36/91	4	1	1	1	1				5	1	1	1	1				4	1	1	1	1			
40/102	5	2	2	2	2				6	1	1	1	1				5	1	1	1	1			
44/112	6	2	2	2	2				7	1	1	1	1				6	2	2	2	2			
48/122	6	2	2	2	2				7	1	1	1	1				6	2	2	2	2			

ODEON

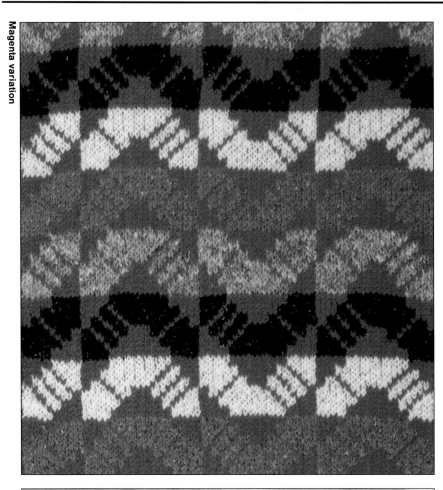

Odeon chart placing instructions

Follow basic pattern instructions as given on pages 99-103, working pattern chart thus:

Work patt across knit rows (odd nos):

Sizes in/cm	Sweater back/front, Jacket back, Cardigan back, Slipover back/front, Short top back/front
24/61	Work sts (1-48) once, then sts (1-36) once.
28/71	Work sts (1-48) twice, then sts (1-2) once.
32/81	Work sts (1-48) twice, then sts (1-16) once.
36/91	Work sts (1-48) twice, then sts (1-30) once.
40/102	Work sts (1-48) twice, then sts (1-44) once.
44/112	Work sts (1-48) 3 times, then sts (1-10) once.
48/122	Work sts (1-48) 3 times, then sts (1-24) once.

	Sweater sleeves
24/61	Work sts (1-44) once.
28/71	Work sts (1-48) once.
32/81	Work sts (1-48) once, then sts (1-4) once.
36/91	Work sts (1-48) once, then sts (1-16) once.
40/102	Work sts (1-48) once, then sts (1-24) once.
44/112	Work sts (1-48) once, then sts (1-28) once.
48/122	Work sts (1-48) once, then sts (1-28) once.

	Jacket fronts, Cardigan fronts
24/61	Work sts (1-38) once.
28/71	Work sts (1-44) once.
32/81	Work sts (1-48) once, then sts (1-4) once.
36/91	Work sts (1-48) once, then sts (1-12) once.
40/102	Work sts (1-48) once, then sts (1-18) once.
44/112	Work sts (1-48) once, then sts (1-24) once.
48/122	Work sts (1-48) once, then sts (1-32) once.

	Jacket sleeves
24/61	Work sts (1-48) once, then sts (1-32) once.
28/71	Work sts (1-48) once, then sts (1-34) once.
32/81	Work sts (1-48) once, then sts (1-38) once.
36/91	Work sts (1-48) twice, then sts (1-4) once.
40/102	Work sts (1-48) twice, then sts (1-14) once.
44/112	Work sts (1-48) twice, then sts (1-18) once.
48/122	Work sts (1-48) twice, then sts (1-20) once.

	Cardigan sleeves
24/61	Work sts (1-48) once, then sts (1-8) once.
28/71	Work sts (1-48) once, then sts (1-14) once.
32/81	Work sts (1-48) once, then sts (1-20) once.
36/91	Work sts (1-48) once, then sts (1-24) once.
40/102	Work sts (1-48) once, then sts (1-30) once.
44/112	Work sts (1-48) once, then sts (1-36) once.
48/122	Work sts (1-48) once, then sts (1-42) once.

	Waistcoat fronts
24/61	Work sts (1-41) once.
28/71	Work sts (1-48) once.
32/81	Work sts (1-48) once, then sts (1-7) once.
36/91	Work sts (1-48) once, then sts (1-14) once.
40/102	Work sts (1-48) once, then sts (1-21) once.
44/112	Work sts (1-48) once, then sts (1-28) once.
48/122	Work sts (1-48) once, then sts (1-35) once.

Sweater back/front, Jacket back, Cardigan back, Slipover back/front, Short top back/front
Work sts (36-1) once, then sts (48-1) once.
Work sts (2-1) once, then sts (48-1) twice.
Work sts (16-1) once, then sts (48-1) twice.
Work sts (30-1) once, then sts (48-1) twice.
Work sts (44-1) once, then sts (48-1) twice.
Work sts (10-1) once, then sts (48-1) 3 times.
Work sts (24-1) once, then sts (48-1) 3 times.

Sweater sleeves
Work sts (44-1) once.
Work sts (48-1) once.
Work sts (4-1) once, then sts (48-1) once.
Work sts (16-1) once, then sts (48-1) once.
Work sts (24-1) once, then sts (48-1) once.
Work sts (28-1) once, then sts (48-1) once.
Work sts (28-1) once, then sts (48-1) once.

Jacket fronts, Cardigan fronts
Work sts (38-1) once.
Work sts (44-1) once.
Work sts (4-1) once, then sts (48-1) once.
Work sts (12-1) once, then sts (48-1) once.
Work sts (18-1) once, then sts (48-1) once.
Work sts (24-1) once, then sts (48-1) once.
Work sts (32-1) once, then sts (48-1) once.

Jacket sleeves
Work sts (32-1) once, then sts (48-1) once.
Work sts (34-1) once, then sts (48-1) once.
Work sts (38-1) once, then sts (48-1) once.
Work sts (4-1) once, then sts (48-1) twice.
Work sts (14-1) once, then sts (48-1) twice.
Work sts (18-1) once, then sts (48-1) twice.
Work sts (20-1) once, then sts (48-1) twice.

Cardigan sleeves
Work sts (8-1) once, then sts (48-1) once.
Work sts (14-1) once, then sts (48-1) once.
Work sts (20-1) once, then sts (48-1) once.
Work sts (24-1) once, then sts (48-1) once.
Work sts (30-1) once, then sts (48-1) once.
Work sts (36-1) once, then sts (48-1) once.
Work sts (42-1) once, then sts (48-1) once.

Waistcoat fronts
Work sts (41-1) once.
Work sts (48-1) once.
Work sts (7-1) once, then sts (48-1) once.
Work sts (14-1) once, then sts (48-1) once.
Work sts (21-1) once, then sts (48-1) once.
Work sts (28-1) once, then sts (48-1) once.
Work sts (35-1) once, then sts (48-1) once.

Odeon chart

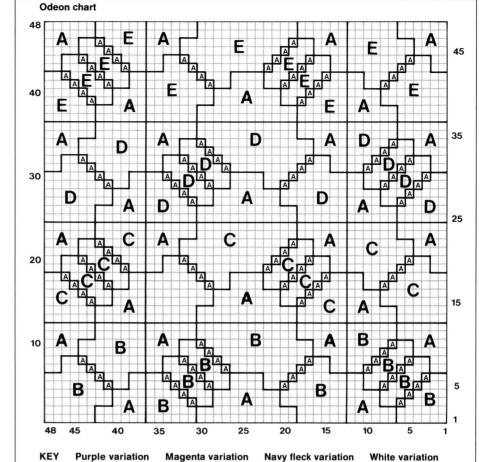

KEY	Purple variation	Magenta variation	Navy fleck variation	White variation
A	**Deep purple** B 99	**Magenta** B 96	**Navy** FF 97F	**White** B 1
B	**Turquoise** B 90	**Lilac** FF 611F	**Lilac** FF 611F	**Mustard** FF 14F
C	**Seville** B 25	**White** B 1	**White** B 1	**Black** FF 62F
D	**Jade** FF 90F	**Navy** FF 97F	**Magenta** B 96	**Salmon** FF 17F
E	**Red** FF 44F	**Silver** LT 208	**Silver** LT 208	**Bluebell** B 501

This pattern chart can be used with the following basic pattern instructions:
4 ply wool sweater p. 99
4 ply wool jacket p. 100
4 ply wool cardigan p. 101
4 ply wool slipover p. 102
4 ply wool waistcoat p. 102
4 ply wool short top p. 103

Method of knitting
Use the woven or stranded Fair Isle method.

Ribbing and pocket linings
Use yarn A for ribbing and pocket linings.

Back of waistcoat
Use yarn A.

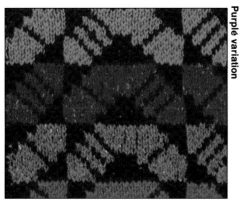

Purple variation

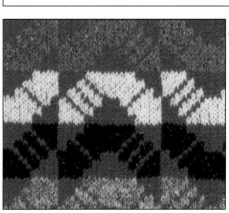

Magenta variation

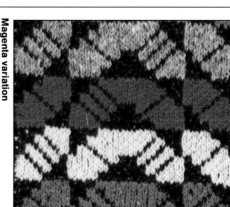

Navy fleck variation

LIGHTNING

Modern art and architecture with their graphic shapes and shadows seem ideal for grafting onto naturally occurring phenomena.

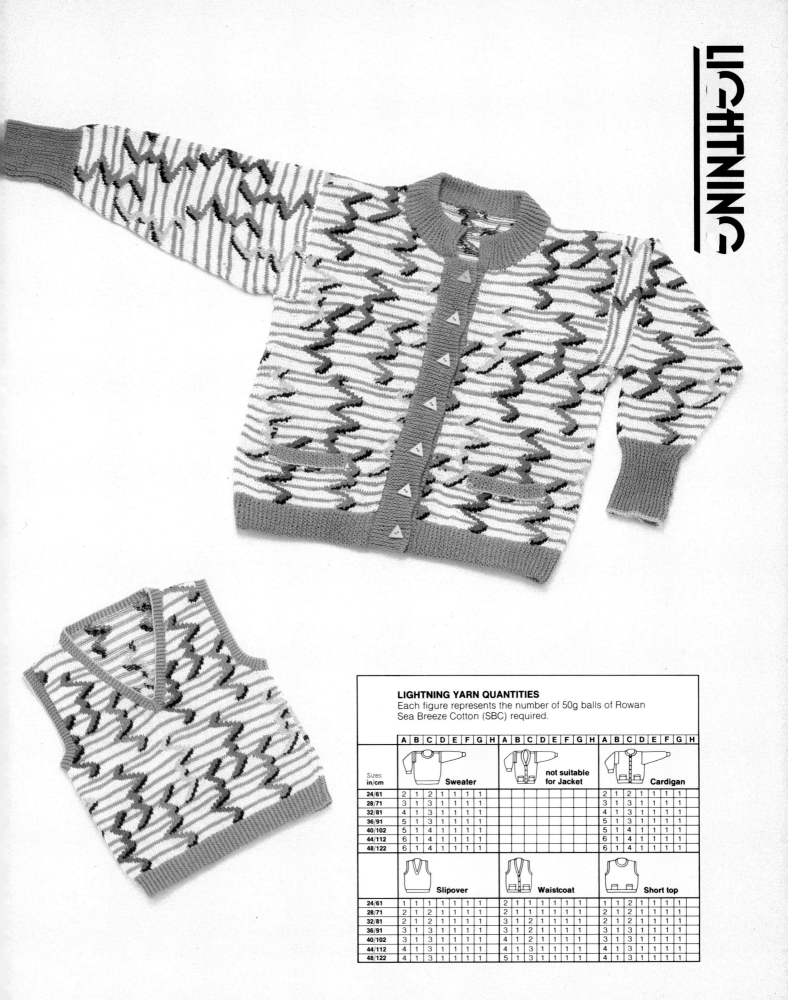

LIGHTNING YARN QUANTITIES

Each figure represents the number of 50g balls of Rowan Sea Breeze Cotton (SBC) required.

Sizes in/cm	A	B	C	D	E	F	G	H	A	B	C	D	E	F	G	H	A	B	C	D	E	F	G	H
	Sweater								not suitable for Jacket								Cardigan							
24/61	2	1	2	1	1	1											2	1	2	1	1	1		
28/71	3	1	3	1	1	1											3	1	3	1	1	1		
32/81	4	1	3	1	1	1											4	1	3	1	1	1		
36/91	5	1	3	1	1	1											5	1	3	1	1	1		
40/102	5	1	4	1	1	1											5	1	4	1	1	1		
44/112	6	1	4	1	1	1											6	1	4	1	1	1		
48/122	6	1	4	1	1	1											6	1	4	1	1	1		
	Slipover								Waistcoat								Short top							
24/61	1	1	1	1	1	1	1		2	1	1	1	1	1	1		1	1	2	1	1	1	1	
28/71	2	1	2	1	1	1	1		2	1	1	1	1	1	1		2	1	2	1	1	1	1	
32/81	2	1	2	1	1	1	1		3	1	2	1	1	1	1		2	1	2	1	1	1	1	
36/91	3	1	3	1	1	1	1		3	1	2	1	1	1	1		3	1	3	1	1	1	1	
40/102	3	1	3	1	1	1	1		4	1	2	1	1	1	1		3	1	3	1	1	1	1	
44/112	4	1	3	1	1	1	1		4	1	3	1	1	1	1		4	1	3	1	1	1	1	
48/122	4	1	3	1	1	1	1		5	1	3	1	1	1	1		4	1	3	1	1	1	1	

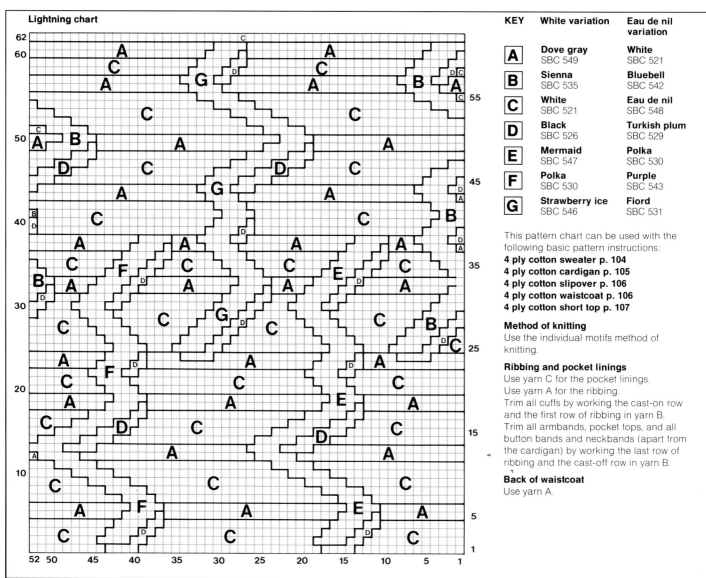

Lightning chart

KEY	White variation	Eau de nil variation
A	**Dove gray** SBC 549	**White** SBC 521
B	**Sienna** SBC 535	**Bluebell** SBC 542
C	**White** SBC 521	**Eau de nil** SBC 548
D	**Black** SBC 526	**Turkish plum** SBC 529
E	**Mermaid** SBC 547	**Polka** SBC 530
F	**Polka** SBC 530	**Purple** SBC 543
G	**Strawberry ice** SBC 546	**Fiord** SBC 531

This pattern chart can be used with the following basic pattern instructions:
4 ply cotton sweater p. 104
4 ply cotton cardigan p. 105
4 ply cotton slipover p. 106
4 ply cotton waistcoat p. 106
4 ply cotton short top p. 107

Method of knitting
Use the individual motifs method of knitting.

Ribbing and pocket linings
Use yarn C for the pocket linings.
Use yarn A for the ribbing.
Trim all cuffs by working the cast-on row and the first row of ribbing in yarn B.
Trim all armbands, pocket tops, and all button bands and neckbands (apart from the cardigan) by working the last row of ribbing and the cast-off row in yarn B.

Back of waistcoat
Use yarn A.

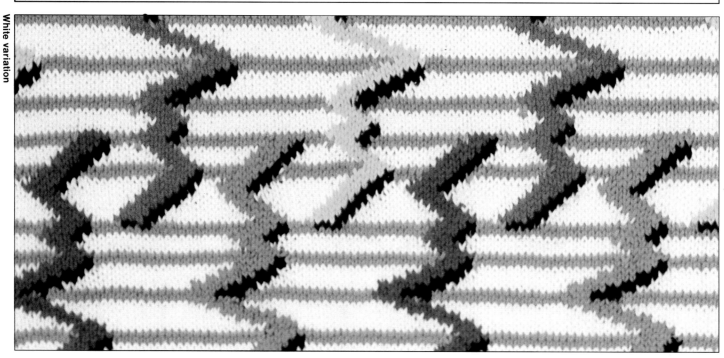

White variation

Lightning chart placing instructions

Follow basic pattern instructions as given on pages 104-107, working pattern chart thus:

Sizes in/cm	Work patt across knit rows (odd nos):	Work patt across purl rows (even nos):
Sweater back/front, Cardigan back, Slipover back/front, Short top back/front		
24/61	Work sts (1-52) once, then sts (1-48) once.	Work sts (48-1) once, then sts (52-1) once.
28/71	Work sts (1-52) twice, then sts (1-12) once.	Work sts (12-1) once, then sts (52-1) twice.
32/81	Work sts (1-52) twice, then sts (1-28) once.	Work sts (28-1) once, then sts (52-1) twice.
36/91	Work sts (1-52) twice, then sts (1-44) once.	Work sts (44-1) once, then sts (52-1) twice.
40/102	Work sts (1-52) 3 times, then sts (1-8) once.	Work sts (8-1) once, then sts (52-1) 3 times.
44/112	Work sts (1-52) 3 times, then sts (1-24) once.	Work sts (24-1) once, then sts (52-1) 3 times.
48/122	Work sts (1-52) 3 times, then sts (1-40) once.	Work sts (40-1) once, then sts (52-1) 3 times.
Sweater sleeves		
24/61	Work sts (1-52) once, then sts (1-6) once.	Work sts (6-1) once, then sts (52-1) once.
28/71	Work sts (1-52) once, then sts (1-14) once.	Work sts (14-1) once, then sts (52-1) once.
32/81	Work sts (1-52) once, then sts (1-16) once.	Work sts (16-1) once, then sts (52-1) once.
36/91	Work sts (1-52) once, then sts (1-24) once.	Work sts (24-1) once, then sts (52-1) once.
40/102	Work sts (1-52) once, then sts (1-28) once.	Work sts (28-1) once, then sts (52-1) once.
44/112	Work sts (1-52) once, then sts (1-30) once.	Work sts (30-1) once, then sts (52-1) once.
48/122	Work sts (1-52) once, then sts (1-34) once.	Work sts (34-1) once, then sts (52-1) once.
Cardigan fronts		
24/61	Work sts (1-42) once.	Work sts (42-1) once.
28/71	Work sts (1-52) once.	Work sts (52-1) once.
32/81	Work sts (1-52) once, then sts (1-8) once.	Work sts (8-1) once, then sts (52-1) once.
36/91	Work sts (1-52) once, then sts (1-16) once.	Work sts (16-1) once, then sts (52-1) once.
40/102	Work sts (1-52) once, then sts (1-24) once.	Work sts (24-1) once, then sts (52-1) once.
44/112	Work sts (1-52) once, then sts (1-32) once.	Work sts (32-1) once, then sts (52-1) once.
48/122	Work sts (1-52) once, then sts (1-40) once.	Work sts (40-1) once, then sts (52-1) once.
Cardigan sleeves		
24/61	Work sts (1-52) once, then sts (1-4) once.	Work sts (4-1) once, then sts (52-1) once.
28/71	Work sts (1-52) once, then sts (1-12) once.	Work sts (12-1) once, then sts (52-1) once.
32/81	Work sts (1-52) once, then sts (1-18) once.	Work sts (18-1) once, then sts (52-1) once.
36/91	Work sts (1-52) once, then sts (1-22) once.	Work sts (22-1) once, then sts (52-1) once.
40/102	Work sts (1-52) once, then sts (1-26) once.	Work sts (26-1) once, then sts (52-1) once.
44/112	Work sts (1-52) once, then sts (1-28) once.	Work sts (28-1) once, then sts (52-1) once.
48/122	Work sts (1-52) once, then sts (1-32) once.	Work sts (32-1) once, then sts (52-1) once.
Waistcoat fronts		
24/61	Work sts (1-46) once.	Work sts (46-1) once.
28/71	Work sts (1-52) once, then sts (1-2) once.	Work sts (2-1) once, then sts (52-1) once.
32/81	Work sts (1-52) once, then sts (1-10) once.	Work sts (10-1) once, then sts (52-1) once.
36/91	Work sts (1-52) once, then sts (1-18) once.	Work sts (18-1) once, then sts (52-1) once.
40/102	Work sts (1-52) once, then sts (1-26) once.	Work sts (26-1) once, then sts (52-1) once.
44/112	Work sts (1-52) once, then sts (1-34) once.	Work sts (34-1) once, then sts (52-1) once.
48/122	Work sts (1-52) once, then sts (1-42) once.	Work sts (42-1) once, then sts (52-1) once.

Eau de nil variation

A Persian border pattern inspired me to play around with hues and textures in order to produce this delicate design.

PERSIAN STRIPE

PERSIAN STRIPE YARN QUANTITIES
Each figure represents the number of 25g hanks of Rowan
Botany (B), Light Tweed (LT) or Fine Fleck (FF) required.

Sizes in/cm	Sweater A	B	C	D	E	F	G	H	Jacket A	B	C	D	E	F	G	H	Cardigan A	B	C	D	E	F	G	H
24/61	4	1	1	1	1	1			5	1	1	1	1	1			5	1	1	1	1	1		
28/71	5	1	1	2	1	1			6	1	1	2	1	1			6	1	1	2	1	1		
32/81	6	2	2	2	1	1			7	2	2	2	1	1			7	2	2	2	1	1		
36/91	8	2	2	3	1	1			9	2	2	3	1	1			9	2	2	3	1	1		
40/102	10	2	2	3	1	1			11	2	2	3	1	1			11	2	2	3	1	1		
44/112	12	2	2	4	2	1			13	2	2	4	2	1			13	2	2	4	2	1		
48/122	13	2	3	5	2	1			15	2	3	5	2	1			15	2	3	5	2	1		

Sizes in/cm	Slipover A	B	C	D	E	F	G	H	Waistcoat A	B	C	D	E	F	G	H	Short top A	B	C	D	E	F	G	H
24/61	2	1	1	1	1	1			4	1	1	1	1	1			2	1	1	1	1	1		
28/71	3	1	1	1	1	1			4	1	1	1	1	1			3	1	1	1	1	1		
32/81	3	1	1	1	1	1			5	1	1	1	1	1			3	1	1	1	1	1		
36/91	3	1	1	1	1	1			6	1	1	1	1	1			3	1	1	1	1	1		
40/102	4	1	1	1	1	1			7	1	1	1	1	1			4	1	1	1	1	1		
44/112	4	2	2	2	1	1			8	1	1	1	1	1			4	2	2	2	1	1		
48/122	5	2	2	2	1	1			9	1	1	1	1	1			5	2	2	2	1	1		

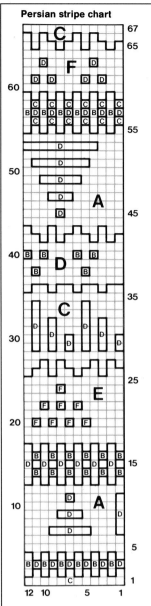

Persian stripe chart

KEY	Pink variation	Blue variation
A	**Silver** LT 208	**Charcoal** LT 210
B	**Lavender** LT 213	**Magenta** B 96
C	**Pale pink** B 68	**Eau de nil** B 89
D	**Rust** B 77	**Electric blue** B 634
E	**White** LT 201	**Lavender** LT 213
F	**Rose mix** LT 215	**Gray** LT 209

This pattern chart can be used with the following basic pattern instructions:

4 ply wool sweater p. 99
4 ply wool jacket p. 100
4 ply wool cardigan p. 101
4 ply wool slipover p. 102
4 ply wool waistcoat p. 102
4 ply wool short top p. 103

Method of knitting
Use the woven or stranded Fair Isle method of knitting.

Ribbing and pocket linings
Use yarn A for the ribbing and pocket linings.
Trim all cuffs by working the cast-on row and the first row of ribbing in yarn B.
Trim all armbands, pocket tops, and all button bands and neckbands (apart from the cardigan) by working the last row of ribbing and the cast-off row in yarn B.

Back of waistcoat
Use yarn A.

Persian stripe chart placing instructions

Follow basic pattern instructions as given on pages 99-103, working pattern chart thus:

Sizes in/cm	*Work patt across knit rows (odd nos):*	*Work patt across purl rows (even nos):*
Sweater back/front, Jacket back, Cardigan back, Slipover back/front, Short top back/front		
24/61	Work sts (1-12) 7 times.	Work sts (12-1) 7 times.
28/71	Work sts (1-12) 8 times, then sts (1-2) once.	Work sts (2-1) once, then sts (12-1) 8 times.
32/81	Work sts (1-12) 9 times, then sts (1-4) once.	Work sts (4-1) once, then sts (12-1) 9 times.
36/91	Work sts (1-12) 10 times, then sts (1-6) once.	Work sts (6-1) once, then sts (12-1) 10 times.
40/102	Work sts (1-12) 11 times, then sts (1-8) once.	Work sts (8-1) once, then sts (12-1) 11 times.
44/112	Work sts (1-12) 12 times, then sts (1-10) once.	Work sts (10-1) once, then sts (12-1) 12 times.
48/122	Work sts (1-12) 14 times.	Work sts (12-1) 14 times.
Sweater sleeves		
24/61	Work sts (1-12) 3 times, then sts (1-8) once.	Work sts (8-1) once, then sts (12-1) 3 times.
28/71	Work sts (1-12) 4 times.	Work sts (12-1) 4 times.
32/81	Work sts (1-12) 4 times, then sts (1-4) once.	Work sts (4-1) once, then sts (12-1) 4 times.
36/91	Work sts (1-12) 5 times, then sts (1-4) once.	Work sts (4-1) once, then sts (12-1) 5 times.
40/102	Work sts (1-12) 6 times.	Work sts (12-1) 6 times.
44/112	Work sts (1-12) 6 times, then sts (1-4) once.	Work sts (4-1) once, then sts (12-1) 6 times.
48/122	Work sts (1-12) 6 times, then sts (1-4) once.	Work sts (4-1) once, then sts (12-1) 6 times.
Jacket fronts, Cardigan fronts		
24/61	Work sts (1-12) 3 times, then sts (1-2) once.	Work sts (2-1) once, then sts (12-1) 3 times.
28/71	Work sts (1-12) 3 times, then sts (1-8) once.	Work sts (8-1) once, then sts (12-1) 3 times.
32/81	Work sts (1-12) 4 times, then sts (1-4) once.	Work sts (4-1) once, then sts (12-1) 4 times.
36/91	Work sts (1-12) 5 times.	Work sts (12-1) 5 times.
40/102	Work sts (1-12) 5 times, then sts (1-6) once.	Work sts (6-1) once, then sts (12-1) 5 times.
44/112	Work sts (1-12) 6 times.	Work sts (12-1) 6 times.
48/122	Work sts (1-12) 6 times, then sts (1-8) once.	Work sts (8-1) once, then sts (12-1) 6 times.
Jacket sleeves		
24/61	Work sts (1-12) 6 times, then sts (1-8) once.	Work sts (8-1) once, then sts (12-1) 6 times.
28/71	Work sts (1-12) 6 times, then sts (1-10) once.	Work sts (10-1) once, then sts (12-1) 6 times.
32/81	Work sts (1-12) 7 times, then sts (1-2) once.	Work sts (2-1) once, then sts (12-1) 7 times.
36/91	Work sts (1-12) 8 times, then sts (1-4) once.	Work sts (4-1) once, then sts (12-1) 8 times.
40/102	Work sts (1-12) 9 times, then sts (1-2) once.	Work sts (2-1) once, then sts (12-1) 9 times.
44/112	Work sts (1-12) 9 times, then sts (1-6) once.	Work sts (6-1) once, then sts (12-1) 9 times.
48/122	Work sts (1-12) 9 times, then sts (1-8) once.	Work sts (8-1) once, then sts (12-1) 9 times.
Cardigan sleeves		
24/61	Work sts (1-12) 4 times, then sts (1-8) once.	Work sts (8-1) once, then sts (12-1) 4 times.
28/71	Work sts (1-12) 5 times, then sts (1-2) once.	Work sts (2-1) once, then sts (12-1) 5 times.
32/81	Work sts (1-12) 5 times, then sts (1-8) once.	Work sts (8-1) once, then sts (12-1) 5 times.
36/91	Work sts (1-12) 6 times.	Work sts (12-1) 6 times.
40/102	Work sts (1-12) 6 times, then sts (1-6) once.	Work sts (6-1) once, then sts (12-1) 6 times.
44/112	Work sts (1-12) 7 times.	Work sts (12-1) 7 times.
48/122	Work sts (1-12) 7 times, then sts (1-6) once.	Work sts (6-1) once, then sts (12-1) 7 times.
Waistcoat fronts		
24/61	Work sts (1-12) 3 times, then sts (1-5) once.	Work sts (5-1) once, then sts (12-1) 3 times.
28/71	Work sts (1-12) 4 times.	Work sts (12-1) 4 times.
32/81	Work sts (1-12) 4 times, then sts (1-7) once.	Work sts (7-1) once, then sts (12-1) 4 times.
36/91	Work sts (1-12) 5 times, then sts (1-2) once.	Work sts (2-1) once, then sts (12-1) 5 times.
40/102	Work sts (1-12) 5 times, then sts (1-9) once.	Work sts (9-1) once, then sts (12-1) 5 times.
44/112	Work sts (1-12) 6 times, then sts (1-4) once.	Work sts (4-1) once, then sts (12-1) 6 times.
48/122	Work sts (1-12) 6 times, then sts (1-11) once.	Work sts (11-1) once, then sts (12-1) 6 times.

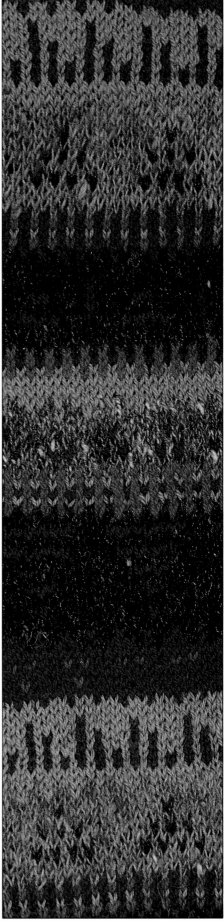

CUBE

Building blocks, optical illusions, or crazy cubes — however you look at it, this fun design is suitable for any age.

CUBE YARN QUANTITIES

Each figure represents the number of 50g balls of Rowan Sea Breeze Cotton (SBC) required.

Sizes in/cm	Sweater A	B	C	D	E	F	G	H	not suitable for Jacket A	B	C	D	E	F	G	H	Cardigan A	B	C	D	E	F	G	H
24/61	2	1	2	1	1	1	1	1									2	1	2	1	1	1	1	1
28/71	3	1	3	1	1	1	1	1									3	1	3	1	1	1	1	1
32/81	4	1	3	1	1	1	1	1									4	1	3	1	1	1	1	1
36/91	5	1	3	1	1	1	1	1									5	1	3	1	1	1	1	1
40/102	5	1	4	1	1	1	1	1									5	1	4	1	1	1	1	1
44/112	6	1	4	1	1	1	1	1									6	1	4	1	1	1	1	1
48/122	6	1	4	1	1	1	1	1									6	1	4	1	1	1	1	1

Sizes in/cm	Slipover A	B	C	D	E	F	G	H	Waistcoat A	B	C	D	E	F	G	H	Short top A	B	C	D	E	F	G	H
24/61	1	1	2	1	1	1	1	1	2	1	1	1	1	1	1	1	1	1	2	1	1	1	1	1
28/71	1	1	2	1	1	1	1	1	2	1	1	1	1	1	1	1	1	1	2	1	1	1	1	1
32/81	2	1	2	1	1	1	1	1	3	1	1	1	1	1	1	1	2	1	2	1	1	1	1	1
36/91	3	1	3	1	1	1	1	1	3	1	2	1	1	1	1	1	3	1	3	1	1	1	1	1
40/102	3	1	3	1	1	1	1	1	4	1	2	1	1	1	1	1	3	1	3	1	1	1	1	1
44/112	4	1	3	1	1	1	1	1	4	1	3	1	1	1	1	1	4	1	3	1	1	1	1	1
48/122	4	1	3	1	1	1	1	1	5	1	3	1	1	1	1	1	4	1	3	1	1	1	1	1

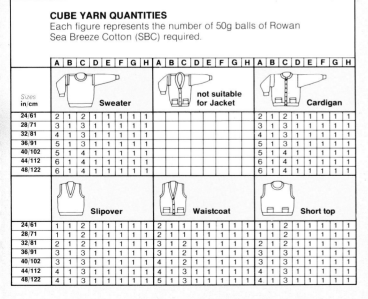

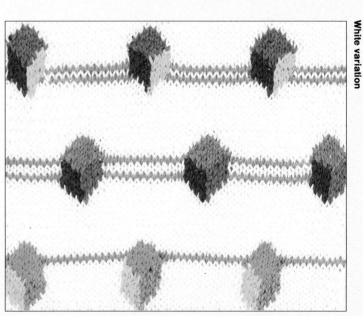

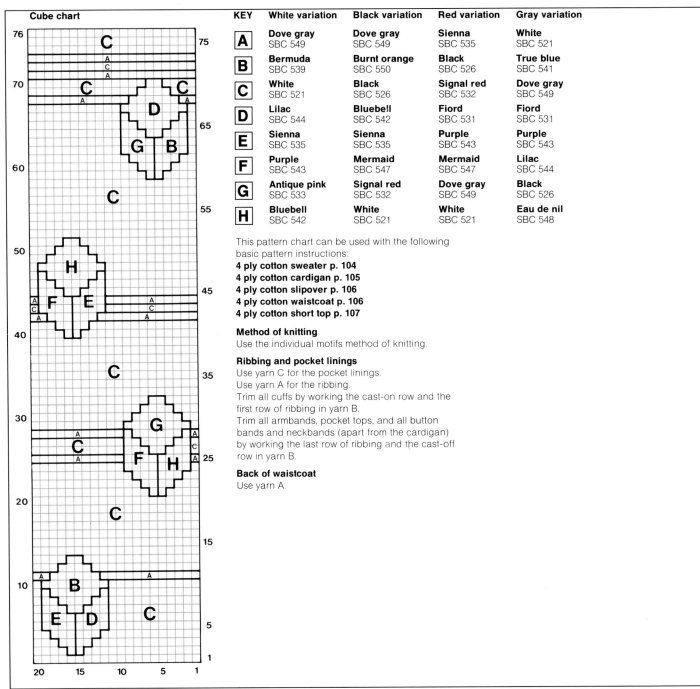

Cube chart

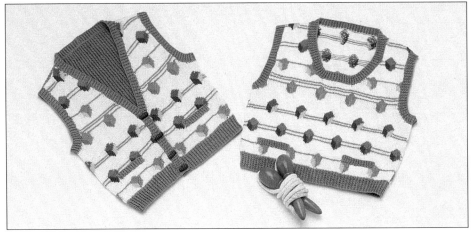

KEY	White variation	Black variation	Red variation	Gray variation
A	Dove gray SBC 549	Dove gray SBC 549	Sienna SBC 535	White SBC 521
B	Bermuda SBC 539	Burnt orange SBC 550	Black SBC 526	True blue SBC 541
C	White SBC 521	Black SBC 526	Signal red SBC 532	Dove gray SBC 549
D	Lilac SBC 544	Bluebell SBC 542	Fiord SBC 531	Fiord SBC 531
E	Sienna SBC 535	Sienna SBC 535	Purple SBC 543	Purple SBC 543
F	Purple SBC 543	Mermaid SBC 547	Mermaid SBC 547	Lilac SBC 544
G	Antique pink SBC 533	Signal red SBC 532	Dove gray SBC 549	Black SBC 526
H	Bluebell SBC 542	White SBC 521	White SBC 521	Eau de nil SBC 548

This pattern chart can be used with the following
basic pattern instructions:
4 ply cotton sweater p. 104
4 ply cotton cardigan p. 105
4 ply cotton slipover p. 106
4 ply cotton waistcoat p. 106
4 ply cotton short top p. 107

Method of knitting
Use the individual motifs method of knitting.

Ribbing and pocket linings
Use yarn C for the pocket linings.
Use yarn A for the ribbing.
Trim all cuffs by working the cast-on row and the
first row of ribbing in yarn B.
Trim all armbands, pocket tops, and all button
bands and neckbands (apart from the cardigan)
by working the last row of ribbing and the cast-off
row in yarn B.

Back of waistcoat
Use yarn A.

Cube chart placing instructions

Follow basic pattern instructions as given on pages 104-107, working pattern chart thus:

Sizes in/cm	Work patt across knit rows (odd nos):	Work patt across purl rows (even nos):

Sweater back/front, Cardigan back, Slipover back/front, Short top back/front

Sizes in/cm	Work patt across knit rows (odd nos):	Work patt across purl rows (even nos):
24/61	Work sts (1-20) 5 times.	Work sts (20-1) 5 times.
28/71	Work sts (1-20) 5 times, then sts (1-16) once.	Work sts (16-1) once, then sts (20-1) 5 times.
32/81	Work sts (1-20) 6 times, then sts (1-12) once.	Work sts (12-1) once, then sts (20-1) 6 times.
36/91	Work sts (1-20) 7 times, then sts (1-8) once.	Work sts (8-1) once, then sts (20-1) 7 times.
40/102	Work sts (1-20) 8 times, then sts (1-4) once.	Work sts (4-1) once, then sts (20-1) 8 times.
44/112	Work sts (1-20) 9 times.	Work sts (20-1) 9 times.
48/122	Work sts (1-20) 9 times, then sts (1-16) once.	Work sts (16-1) once, then sts (20-1) 9 times.

Sweater sleeves

Sizes in/cm	Work patt across knit rows (odd nos):	Work patt across purl rows (even nos):
24/61	Work sts (1-20) twice, then sts (1-18) once.	Work sts (18-1) once, then sts (20-1) twice.
28/71	Work sts (1-20) 3 times, then sts (1-6) once.	Work sts (6-1) once, then sts (20-1) 3 times.
32/81	Work sts (1-20) 3 times, then sts (1-8) once.	Work sts (8-1) once, then sts (20-1) 3 times.
36/91	Work sts (1-20) 3 times, then sts (1-16) once.	Work sts (16-1) once, then sts (20-1) 3 times.
40/102	Work sts (1-20) 4 times.	Work sts (20-1) 4 times.
44/112	Work sts (1-20) 4 times, then sts (1-2) once.	Work sts (2-1) once, then sts (20-1) 4 times.
48/122	Work sts (1-20) 4 times, then sts (1-6) once.	Work sts (6-1) once, then sts (20-1) 4 times.

Cardigan sleeves

Sizes in/cm	Work patt across knit rows (odd nos):	Work patt across purl rows (even nos):
24/61	Work sts (1-20) twice, then sts (1-16) once.	Work sts (16-1) once, then sts (20-1) twice.
28/71	Work sts (1-20) 3 times, then sts (1-4) once.	Work sts (4-1) once, then sts (20-1) 3 times.
32/81	Work sts (1-20) 3 times, then sts (1-10) once.	Work sts (10-1) once, then sts (20-1) 3 times.
36/91	Work sts (1-20) 3 times, then sts (1-14) once.	Work sts (14-1) once, then sts (20-1) 3 times.
40/102	Work sts (1-20) 3 times, then sts (1-18) once.	Work sts (18-1) once, then sts (20-1) 3 times.
44/112	Work sts (1-20) 4 times.	Work sts (20-1) 4 times.
48/122	Work sts (1-20) 4 times, then sts (1-4) once.	Work sts (4-1) once, then sts (20-1) 4 times.

Cardigan fronts

Sizes in/cm	Work patt across knit rows (odd nos):	Work patt across purl rows (even nos):
24/61	Work sts (1-20) twice, then sts (1-2) once.	Work sts (2-1) once, then sts (20-1) twice.
28/71	Work sts (1-20) twice, then sts (1-12) once.	Work sts (12-1) once, then sts (20-1) twice.
32/81	Work sts (1-20) 3 times.	Work sts (20-1) 3 times.
36/91	Work sts (1-20) 3 times, then sts (1-8) once.	Work sts (8-1) once, then sts (20-1) 3 times.
40/102	Work sts (1-20) 3 times, then sts (1-16) once.	Work sts (16-1) once, then sts (20-1) 3 times.
44/112	Work sts (1-20) 4 times, then sts (1-4) once.	Work sts (4-1) once, then sts (20-1) 4 times.
48/122	Work sts (1-20) 4 times, then sts (1-12) once.	Work sts (12-1) once, then sts (20-1) 4 times.

Waistcoat fronts

Sizes in/cm	Work patt across knit rows (odd nos):	Work patt across purl rows (even nos):
24/61	Work sts (1-20) twice, then sts (1-6) once.	Work sts (6-1) once, then sts (20-1) twice.
28/71	Work sts (1-20) twice, then sts (1-14) once.	Work sts (14-1) once, then sts (20-1) twice.
32/81	Work sts (1-20) 3 times, then sts (1-2) once.	Work sts (2-1) once, then sts (20-1) 3 times.
36/91	Work sts (1-20) 3 times, then sts (1-10) once.	Work sts (10-1) once, then sts (20-1) 3 times.
40/102	Work sts (1-20) 3 times, then sts (1-18) once.	Work sts (18-1) once, then sts (20-1) 3 times.
44/112	Work sts (1-20) 4 times, then sts (1-6) once.	Work sts (6-1) once, then sts (20-1) 4 times.
48/122	Work sts (1-20) 4 times, then sts (1-14) once.	Work sts (14-1) once, then sts (20-1) 4 times.

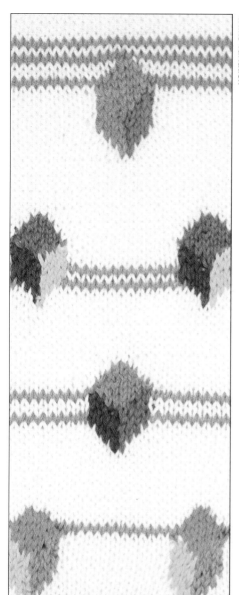

White variation

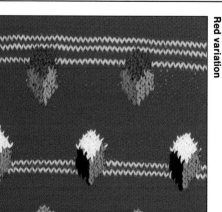

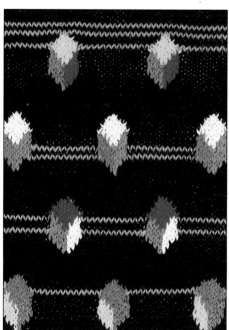

Red variation

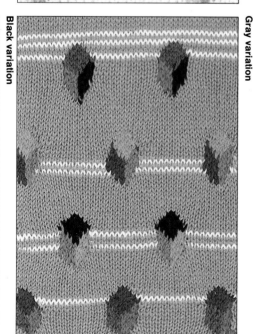

Black variation

Gray variation

WANDERING LINE

Influenced by African tribal art, and inspired by a quote from Paul Klee, I have "taken a line for a walk" across a piece of knitting and arrived at this fluid design.

WANDERING LINE

WANDERING LINE YARN QUANTITIES

Each figure represents the number of 50g balls of Rowan Designer Double Knitting (DDK) or Double Knitting Fleck (DKF) or Fine Cotton Chenille (FCC) required.

Sizes in/cm	Sweater A	B	C	D	E	F	G	H	Jacket A	B	C	D	E	F	G	H	Cardigan A	B	C	D	E	F	G	H
24/61	4	2							5	2							4	2						
28/71	5	3							6	3							5	3						
32/81	7	3							8	3							7	3						
36/91	9	4							10	4							9	4						
40/102	10	4							11	4							11	4						
44/112	11	5							12	5							12	5						
48/122	12	5							13	5							12	5						

Sizes in/cm	Slipover A	B	C	D	E	F	G	H	Waistcoat A	B	C	D	E	F	G	H	Short top A	B	C	D	E	F	G	H
24/61	3	1							3	1							2	1						
28/71	4	1							4	1							3	1						
32/81	4	2							5	2							3	2						
36/91	5	2							6	2							4	2						
40/102	6	2							7	2							5	3						
44/112	6	3							7	2							5	3						
48/122	7	3							8	2							6	3						

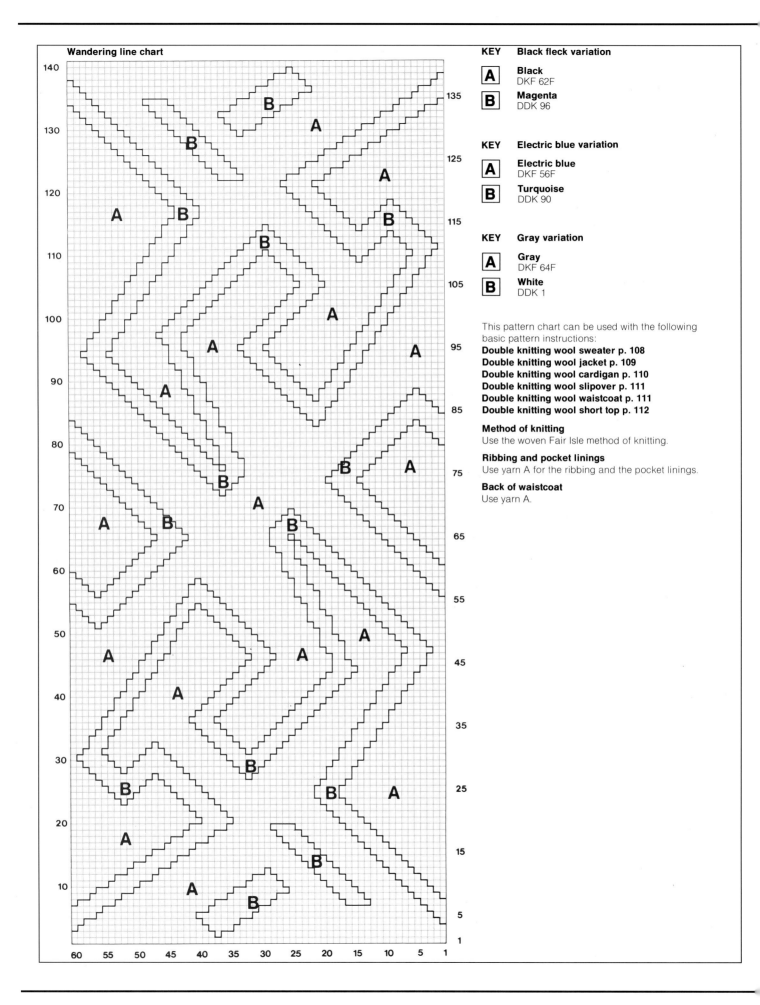

Wandering line chart

KEY **Black fleck variation**

A   **Black**
DKF 62F

B   **Magenta**
DDK 96

KEY **Electric blue variation**

A   **Electric blue**
DKF 56F

B   **Turquoise**
DDK 90

KEY **Gray variation**

A   **Gray**
DKF 64F

B   **White**
DDK 1

This pattern chart can be used with the following basic pattern instructions:
Double knitting wool sweater p. 108
Double knitting wool jacket p. 109
Double knitting wool cardigan p. 110
Double knitting wool slipover p. 111
Double knitting wool waistcoat p. 111
Double knitting wool short top p. 112

Method of knitting
Use the woven Fair Isle method of knitting.

Ribbing and pocket linings
Use yarn A for the ribbing and the pocket linings.

Back of waistcoat
Use yarn A.

Wandering line chart placing instructions

Follow basic pattern instructions as given on pages 108-112, working pattern chart thus:

Sizes in/cm	Work patt across knit rows (odd nos):	Work patt across purl rows (even nos):
	Sweater back/front, Jacket back, Cardigan back, Slipover back/front, Short top back/front	
24/61	Work sts (26-60) once, then sts (1-35) once.	Work sts (35-1) once, then sts (60-26) once.
28/71	Work sts (20-60) once, then sts (1-40) once.	Work sts (40-1) once, then sts (60-20) once.
32/81	Work sts (15-60) once, then sts (1-46) once.	Work sts (46-1) once, then sts (60-15) once.
36/91	Work sts (9-60) once, then sts (1-51) once.	Work sts (51-1) once, then sts (60-9) once.
40/102	Work sts (4-60) once, then sts (1-57) once.	Work sts (57-1) once, then sts (60-4) once.
44/112	Work sts (59-60) once, then sts (1-60) twice, then sts (1-3) once.	Work sts (3-1) once, then sts (60-1) twice, then sts (60-59) once.
48/122	Work sts (53-60) once, then sts (1-60) twice, then sts (1-8) once.	Work sts (8-1) once, then sts (60-1) twice, then sts (60-53) once.
	Sweater sleeves	
24/61	Work sts (1-43) once.	Work sts (43-1) once.
28/71	Work sts (1-45) once.	Work sts (45-1) once.
32/81	Work sts (1-49) once.	Work sts (49-1) once.
36/91	Work sts (1-55) once.	Work sts (55-1) once.
40/102	Work sts (1-60) once, then stitch 1 once.	Work stitch 1 once, then sts (60-1) once.
44/112	Work sts (1-60) once, then sts (1-5) once.	Work sts (5-1) once, then sts (60-1) once.
48/122	Work sts (1-60) once, then sts (1-3) once.	Work sts (3-1) once, then sts (60-1) once.
	Jacket fronts, Cardigan fronts	
24/61	Work sts (44-60) once, then sts (1-17) once.	Work sts (17-1) once, then sts (60-44) once.
28/71	Work sts (41-60) once, then sts (1-20) once.	Work sts (20-1) once, then sts (60-41) once.
32/81	Work sts (38-60) once, then sts (1-23) once.	Work sts (23-1) once, then sts (60-38) once.
36/91	Work sts (35-60) once, then sts (1-26) once.	Work sts (26-1) once, then sts (60-35) once.
40/102	Work sts (32-60) once, then sts (1-29) once.	Work sts (29-1) once, then sts (60-32) once.
44/112	Work sts (29-60) once, then sts (1-32) once.	Work sts (32-1) once, then sts (60-29) once.
48/122	Work sts (26-60) once, then sts (1-35) once.	Work sts (35-1) once, then sts (60-26) once.
	Jacket sleeves	
24/61	Work sts (1-41) once.	Work sts (41-1) once.
28/71	Work sts (1-43) once.	Work sts (43-1) once.
32/81	Work sts (1-47) once.	Work sts (47-1) once.
36/91	Work sts (1-51) once.	Work sts (51-1) once.
40/102	Work sts (1-55) once.	Work sts (55-1) once.
44/112	Work sts (1-59) once.	Work sts (59-1) once.
48/122	Work sts (1-60) once, then sts (1-3) once.	Work sts (3-1) once, then sts (60-1) once.
	Cardigan sleeves	
24/61	Work sts (1-37) once.	Work sts (37-1) once.
28/71	Work sts (1-39) once.	Work sts (39-1) once.
32/81	Work sts (1-43) once.	Work sts (43-1) once.
36/91	Work sts (1-49) once.	Work sts (49-1) once.
40/102	Work sts (1-53) once.	Work sts (53-1) once.
44/112	Work sts (1-57) once.	Work sts (57-1) once.
48/122	Work sts (1-60) once, then stitch 1 once.	Work stitch 1 once, then sts (60-1) once.
	Waistcoat fronts	
24/61	Work sts (43-60) once, then sts (1-17) once.	Work sts (17-1) once, then sts (60-43) once.
28/71	Work sts (40-60) once, then sts (1-20) once.	Work sts (20-1) once, then sts (60-40) once.
32/81	Work sts (37-60) once, then sts (1-23) once.	Work sts (23-1) once, then sts (60-37) once.
36/91	Work sts (34-60) once, then sts (1-26) once.	Work sts (26-1) once, then sts (60-34) once.
40/102	Work sts (31-60) once, then sts (1-29) once.	Work sts (29-1) once, then sts (60-31) once.
44/112	Work sts (28-60) once, then sts (1-32) once.	Work sts (32-1) once, then sts (60-28) once.
48/122	Work sts (25-60) once, then sts (1-35) once.	Work sts (35-1) once, then sts (60-25) once.

OBLOID

Experiments with shapes, shadows and space led to the creation of this ultra-modern design. Choose cheery shades to be flamboyant, or subtler tones for a conservative effect.

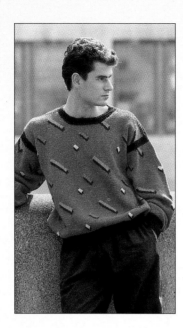

OBLOID YARN QUANTITIES

Each figure represents the number of 50g balls of Rowan Designer Double Knitting (DDK) or Double Knitting Fleck (DKF) or Fine Cotton Chenille (FCC) required.

Sizes in/cm	A	B	C	D	E	F	G	H	A	B	C	D	E	F	G	H	A	B	C	D	E	F	G	H
			Sweater								Jacket								Cardigan					
24/61	2	3	1	1	1				3	3	1	1	1				2	3	1	1	1			
28/71	2	4	1	1	1				3	4	1	1	1				2	4	1	1	1			
32/81	2	6	1	1	1				4	6	1	1	1				2	6	1	1	1			
36/91	3	8	1	1	1				4	8	1	1	1				3	8	1	1	1			
40/102	3	10	1	1	1				5	10	1	1	1				3	10	1	1	1			
44/112	3	11	1	1	1				5	11	1	1	1				3	11	1	1	1			
48/122	4	11	1	1	1				5	11	1	1	1				4	11	1	1	1			
			Slipover								Waistcoat								Short top					
24/61	1	2	1	1	1				2	3	1	1	1				1	2	1	1	1			
28/71	1	2	1	1	1				2	3	1	1	1				1	2	1	1	1			
32/81	2	3	1	1	1				2	4	1	1	1				1	3	1	1	1			
36/91	2	4	1	1	1				3	5	1	1	1				2	3	1	1	1			
40/102	2	5	1	1	1				3	6	1	1	1				2	4	1	1	1			
44/112	3	6	1	1	1				3	7	1	1	1				2	4	1	1	1			
48/122	3	6	1	1	1				4	7	1	1	1				2	5	1	1	1			

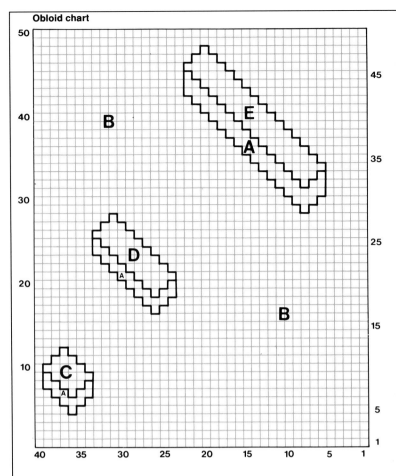

Obloid chart

KEY

	Blue variation	Gray variation	Black variation
A	**Black** DDK 62	**Black** DDK 62	**Lilac** DDK 127
B	**Electric blue** DKF 56F	**Gray** DKF 64F	**Black** DKF 62F
C	**Yellow** DDK 13	**Yellow** DDK 13	**Yellow** DDK 13
D	**Magenta** DDK 96	**Magenta** DDK 96	**Magenta** DDK 96
E	**Turquoise** DDK 90	**Turquoise** DDK 90	**Turquoise** DDK 90

This pattern chart can be used with the following basic pattern instructions:
Double knitting wool sweater p. 108
Double knitting wool jacket p. 109
Double knitting wool cardigan p. 110
Double knitting wool slipover p. 111
Double knitting wool waistcoat p. 111
Double knitting wool short top p. 112

Method of knitting
Use the individual motifs method of knitting.

Ribbing and pocket linings
Use yarn B for the pocket linings.
Use yarn A for the ribbing.

Back of waistcoat
Use yarn A.

Obloid chart placing instructions
Follow basic pattern instructions as given on pages 108-112, working pattern chart thus:

Work patt across knit rows (odd nos):

Sizes in/cm	Sweater back/front, Jacket back, Cardigan back, Slipover back/front, Short top back/front
24/61	Work sts (1-40) once, then sts (1-30) once.
28/71	Work sts (1-40) twice, then stitch 1 once.
32/81	Work sts (1-40) twice, then sts (1-12) once.
36/91	Work sts (1-40) twice, then sts (1-23) once.
40/102	Work sts (1-40) twice, then sts (1-34) once.
44/112	Work sts (1-40) 3 times, then sts (1-5) once.
48/122	Work sts (1-40) 3 times, then sts (1-16) once.

	Sweater sleeves
24/61	Work sts (1-40) once, then sts (1-3) once.
28/71	Work sts (1-40) once, then sts (1-5) once.
32/81	Work sts (1-40) once, then sts (1-9) once.
36/91	Work sts (1-40) once, then sts (1-15) once.
40/102	Work sts (1-40) once, then sts (1-21) once.
44/112	Work sts (1-40) once, then sts (1-25) once.
48/122	Work sts (1-40) once, then sts (1-23) once.

	Jacket fronts, Cardigan fronts
24/61	Work sts (1-34) once.
28/71	Work sts (1-40) once.
32/81	Work sts (1-40) once, then sts (1-6) once.
36/91	Work sts (1-40) once, then sts (1-12) once.
40/102	Work sts (1-40) once, then sts (1-18) once.
44/112	Work sts (1-40) once, then sts (1-24) once.
48/122	Work sts (1-40) once, then sts (1-30) once.

	Jacket sleeves
24/61	Work sts (1-40) once, then stitch 1 once.
28/71	Work sts (1-40) once, then sts (1-3) once.
32/81	Work sts (1-40) once, then sts (1-7) once.
36/91	Work sts (1-40) once, then sts (1-11) once.
40/102	Work sts (1-40) once, then sts (1-15) once.
44/112	Work sts (1-40) once, then sts (1-19) once.
48/122	Work sts (1-40) once, then sts (1-23) once.

	Cardigan sleeves
24/61	Work sts (1-37) once.
28/71	Work sts (1-39) once.
32/81	Work sts (1-40) once, then sts (1-3) once.
36/91	Work sts (1-40) once, then sts (1-9) once.
40/102	Work sts (1-40) once, then sts (1-13) once.
44/112	Work sts (1-40) once, then sts (1-17) once.
48/122	Work sts (1-40) once, then sts (1-21) once.

	Waistcoat fronts
24/61	Work sts (1-35) once.
28/71	Work sts (1-40) once, then stitch 1 once.
32/81	Work sts (1-40) once, then sts (1-7) once.
36/91	Work sts (1-40) once, then sts (1-13) once.
40/102	Work sts (1-40) once, then sts (1-19) once.
44/112	Work sts (1-40) once, then sts (1-25) once.
48/122	Work sts (1-40) once, then sts (1-31) once.

Work patt across purl rows (even nos):

Sweater back/front, Jacket back, Cardigan back,
Slipover back/front, Short top back/front
Work sts (30-1) once, then sts (40-1) once.
Work stitch 1 once, then sts (40-1) twice.
Work sts (12-1) once, then sts (40-1) twice.
Work sts (23-1) once, then sts (40-1) twice.
Work sts (34-1) once, then sts (40-1) twice.
Work sts (5-1) once, then sts (40-1) 3 times.
Work sts (16-1) once, then sts (40-1) 3 times.

Sweater sleeves
Work sts (3-1) once, then sts (40-1) once.
Work sts (5-1) once, then sts (40-1) once.
Work sts (9-1) once, then sts (40-1) once.
Work sts (15-1) once, then sts (40-1) once.
Work sts (21-1) once, then sts (40-1) once.
Work sts (25-1) once, then sts (40-1) once.
Work sts (23-1) once, then sts (40-1) once.

Jacket fronts, Cardigan fronts
Work sts (34-1) once.
Work sts (40-1) once.
Work sts (6-1) once, then sts (40-1) once.
Work sts (12-1) once, then sts (40-1) once.
Work sts (18-1) once, then sts (40-1) once.
Work sts (24-1) once, then sts (40-1) once.
Work sts (30-1) once, then sts (40-1) once.

Jacket sleeves
Work stitch 1 once, then sts (40-1) once.
Work sts (3-1) once, then sts (40-1) once.
Work sts (7-1) once, then sts (40-1) once.
Work sts (11-1) once, then sts (40-1) once.
Work sts (15-1) once, then sts (40-1) once.
Work sts (19-1) once, then sts (40-1) once.
Work sts (23-1) once, then sts (40-1) once.

Cardigan sleeves
Work sts (37-1) once.
Work sts (39-1) once.
Work sts (3-1) once, then sts (40-1) once.
Work sts (9-1) once, then sts (40-1) once.
Work sts (13-1) once, then sts (40-1) once.
Work sts (17-1) once, then sts (40-1) once.
Work sts (21-1) once, then sts (40-1) once.

Waistcoat fronts
Work sts (35-1) once.
Work stitch 1 once, then sts (40-1) once.
Work sts (7-1) once, then sts (40-1) once.
Work sts (13-1) once, then sts (40-1) once.
Work sts (19-1) once, then sts (40-1) once.
Work sts (25-1) once, then sts (40-1) once.
Work sts (31-1) once, then sts (40-1) once.

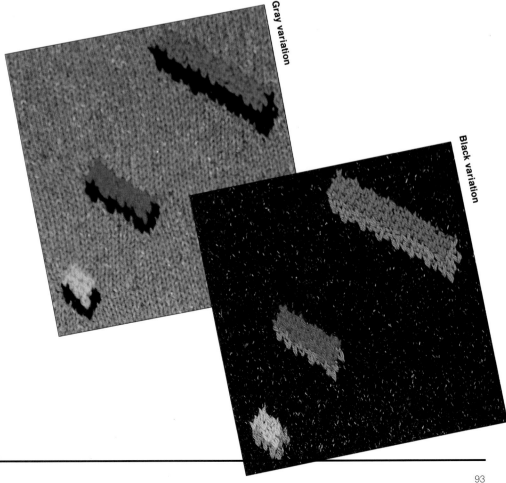

Gray variation

Black variation

ZIGZAG

Flashy zigzags
march across
horizontal lines in
this stylish pattern
suitable for both
sexes.

Zigzag chart

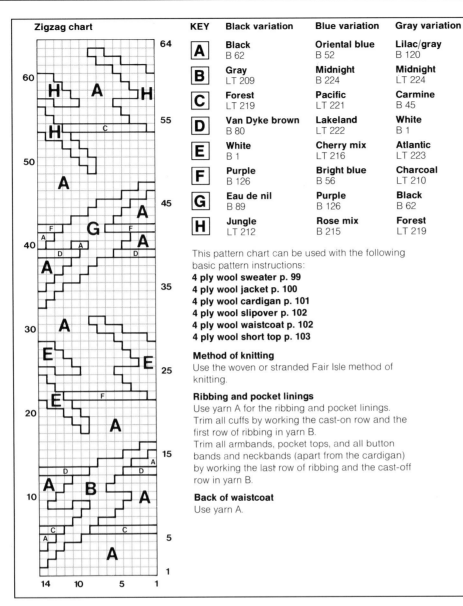

This pattern chart can be used with the following basic pattern instructions:

4 ply wool sweater p. 99
4 ply wool jacket p. 100
4 ply wool cardigan p. 101
4 ply wool slipover p. 102
4 ply wool waistcoat p. 102
4 ply wool short top p. 103

Method of knitting
Use the woven or stranded Fair Isle method of knitting.

Ribbing and pocket linings
Use yarn A for the ribbing and pocket linings.
Trim all cuffs by working the cast-on row and the first row of ribbing in yarn B.
Trim all armbands, pocket tops, and all button bands and neckbands (apart from the cardigan) by working the last row of ribbing and the cast-off row in yarn B.

Back of waistcoat
Use yarn A.

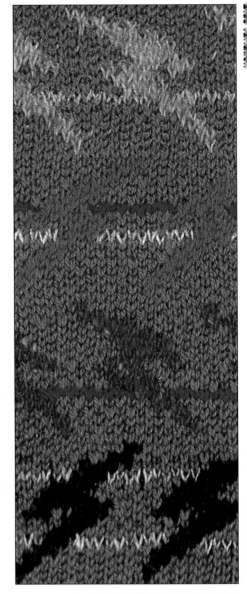

ZIGZAG YARN QUANTITIES
Each figure represents the number of 25g hanks of Rowan Botany (B), Light Tweed (LT) or Fine Fleck (FF) required.

Sizes in/cm	A	B	C	D	E	F	G	H	A	B	C	D	E	F	G	H	A	B	C	D	E	F	G	H
					Sweater								Jacket								Cardigan			
24/61	4	1	1	1	1	1	1	1	5	1	1	1	1	1	1	1	5	1	1	1	1	1	1	1
28/71	6	1	1	1	1	1	1	1	7	1	1	1	1	1	1	1	7	1	1	1	1	1	1	1
32/81	8	1	1	1	1	1	1	1	9	1	1	1	1	1	1	1	9	1	1	1	1	1	1	1
36/91	10	1	1	1	1	1	1	1	11	2	1	1	2	1	2	1	11	2	1	1	2	1	2	1
40/102	12	2	1	1	2	1	2	1	13	2	1	1	2	1	2	1	13	2	1	1	2	1	2	1
44/112	14	2	1	1	2	1	2	2	15	2	1	1	1	1	2	2	15	2	1	1	2	1	2	2
48/122	14	2	1	1	2	1	2	2	15	2	1	1	1	1	2	2	15	2	1	1	2	1	2	2

Sizes in/cm	A	B	C	D	E	F	G	H	A	B	C	D	E	F	G	H	A	B	C	D	E	F	G	H
					Slipover								Waistcoat								Short top			
24/61	3	1	1	*1	1	1	1	1	4	1	1	1	1	1	1	1	3	1	1	1	1	1	1	1
28/71	4	1	1	1	1	1	1	1	4	1	1	1	1	1	1	1	4	1	1	1	1	1	1	1
32/81	6	1	1	1	1	1	1	1	6	1	1	1	1	1	1	1	6	1	1	1	1	1	1	1
36/91	7	1	1	1	1	1	1	1	7	1	1	1	1	1	1	1	7	1	1	1	1	1	1	1
40/102	8	1	1	1	1	1	1	1	8	1	1	1	1	1	1	1	8	1	1	1	1	1	1	1
44/112	9	1	1	1	1	1	1	1	9	1	1	1	1	1	1	1	9	1	1	1	1	1	1	1
48/122	10	2	1	1	1	1	1	1	10	1	1	1	1	1	1	1	10	2	1	1	1	1	1	1

Zigzag chart placing instructions

Follow basic pattern instructions as given on pages 99-103, working pattern chart thus:

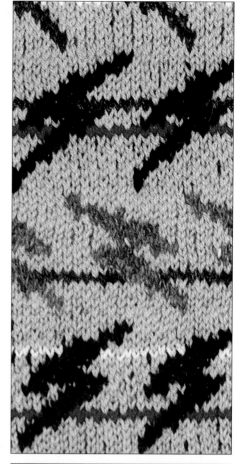

Sizes in/cm	*Work patt across knit rows (odd nos):*	*Work patt across purl rows (even nos):*
Sweater back/front, Jacket back, Cardigan back, Slipover back/front, Short top back/front		
24/61	Work sts (1-14) 6 times.	Work sts (14-1) 6 times.
28/71	Work sts (1-14) 7 times.	Work sts (14-1) 7 times.
32/81	Work sts (1-14) 8 times.	Work sts (14-1) 8 times.
36/91	Work sts (1-14) 9 times.	Work sts (14-1) 9 times.
40/102	Work sts (1-14) 10 times.	Work sts (14-1) 10 times.
44/112	Work sts (1-14) 11 times.	Work sts (14-1) 11 times.
48/122	Work sts (1-14) 12 times.	Work sts (14-1) 12 times.
Sweater sleeves		
24/61	Work sts (1-14) 3 times, then sts (1-2) once.	Work sts (2-1) once, then sts (14-1) 3 times.
28/71	Work sts (1-14) 3 times, then sts (1-6) once.	Work sts (6-1) once, then sts (14-1) 3 times.
32/81	Work sts (1-14) 3 times, then sts (1-10) once.	Work sts (10-1) once, then sts (14-1) 3 times.
36/91	Work sts (1-14) 4 times, then sts (1-8) once.	Work sts (8-1) once, then sts (14-1) 4 times.
40/102	Work sts (1-14) 5 times, then sts (1-2) once.	Work sts (2-1) once, then sts (14-1) 5 times.
44/112	Work sts (1-14) 5 times, then sts (1-6) once.	Work sts (6-1) once, then sts (14-1) 5 times.
48/122	Work sts (1-14) 5 times, then sts (1-6) once.	Work sts (6-1) once, then sts (14-1) 5 times.
Jacket fronts, Cardigan fronts		
24/61	Work sts (1-14) twice, then sts (1-10) once.	Work sts (10-1) once, then sts (14-1) twice.
28/71	Work sts (1-14) 3 times, then sts (1-2) once.	Work sts (2-1) once, then sts (14-1) 3 times.
32/81	Work sts (1-14) 3 times, then sts (1-10) once.	Work sts (10-1) once, then sts (14-1) 3 times.
36/91	Work sts (1-14) 4 times, then sts (1-4) once.	Work sts (4-1) once, then sts (14-1) 4 times.
40/102	Work sts (1-14) 4 times, then sts (1-10) once.	Work sts (10-1) once, then sts (14-1) 4 times.
44/112	Work sts (1-14) 5 times, then sts (1-2) once.	Work sts (2-1) once, then sts (14-1) 5 times.
48/122	Work sts (1-14) 5 times, then sts (1-10) once.	Work sts (10-1) once, then sts (14-1) 5 times.
Jacket sleeves		
24/61	Work sts (1-14) 5 times, then sts (1-10) once.	Work sts (10-1) once, then sts (14-1) 5 times.
28/71	Work sts (1-14) 5 times, then sts (1-12) once.	Work sts (12-1) once, then sts (14-1) 5 times.
32/81	Work sts (1-14) 6 times, then sts (1-2) once.	Work sts (2-1) once, then sts (14-1) 6 times.
36/91	Work sts (1-14) 7 times, then sts (1-2) once.	Work sts (2-1) once, then sts (14-1) 7 times.
40/102	Work sts (1-14) 7 times, then sts (1-12) once.	Work sts (12-1) once, then sts (14-1) 7 times.
44/112	Work sts (1-14) 8 times, then sts (1-2) once.	Work sts (2-1) once, then sts (14-1) 8 times.
48/122	Work sts (1-14) 8 times, then sts (1-4) once.	Work sts (4-1) once, then sts (14-1) 8 times.
Cardigan sleeves		
24/61	Work sts (1-14) 4 times.	Work sts (14-1) 4 times.
28/71	Work sts (1-14) 4 times, then sts (1-6) once.	Work sts (6-1) once, then sts (14-1) 4 times.
32/81	Work sts (1-14) 4 times, then sts (1-12) once.	Work sts (12-1) once, then sts (14-1) 4 times.
36/91	Work sts (1-14) 5 times, then sts (1-2) once.	Work sts (2-1) once, then sts (14-1) 5 times.
40/102	Work sts (1-14) 5 times, then sts (1-8) once.	Work sts (8-1) once, then sts (14-1) 5 times.
44/112	Work sts (1-14) 6 times.	Work sts (14-1) 6 times.
48/122	Work sts (1-14) 6 times, then sts (1-6) once.	Work sts (6-1) once, then sts (14-1) 6 times.
Waistcoat fronts		
24/61	Work sts (1-14) twice, then sts (1-13) once.	Work sts (13-1) once, then sts (14-1) twice.
28/71	Work sts (1-14) 3 times, then sts (1-6) once.	Work sts (6-1) once, then sts (14-1) 3 times.
32/81	Work sts (1-14) 3 times, then sts (1-13) once.	Work sts (13-1) once, then sts (14-1) 3 times.
36/91	Work sts (1-14) 4 times, then sts (1-6) once.	Work sts (6-1) once, then sts (14-1) 4 times.
40/102	Work sts (1-14) 4 times, then sts (1-13) once.	Work sts (13-1) once, then sts (14-1) 4 times.
44/112	Work sts (1-14) 5 times, then sts (1-6) once.	Work sts (6-1) once, then sts (14-1) 5 times.
48/122	Work sts (1-14) 5 times, then sts (1-13) once.	Work sts (13-1) once, then sts (14-1) 5 times.

BASIC PATTERNS

4 ply wool

These instructions are for use with the following pattern charts: **Poodle p. 17, Harlequin p. 24, Mouse p. 37, Bavarian flower p. 50, Cherry p. 54, Acorn p. 58, Odeon p. 73, Persian stripe p. 80, Zigzag p. 96.** The yarn used for all the garments photographed is Rowan Botany wool, with the occasional use of Rowan Light Tweed and Rowan Fine Fleck Tweed, however any standard 4 ply yarn may be used instead, as long as the correct tension is obtained.

Six different body shapes may be knitted in 4 ply wool: a sweater, jacket, cardigan, slipover, waistcoat, short top; in any of seven different chest sizes: 24in, 28in, 32in, 36in, 40in, 44in, 48in (61cm, 71cm, 81cm, 91cm, 102cm, 112cm, 122cm). Remember that these chest measurements are the *actual* measurements not the *to fit* measurements, so you must choose a size that allows your desired amount of ease.

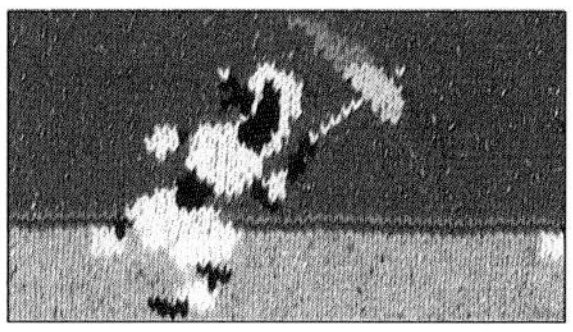

Poodle

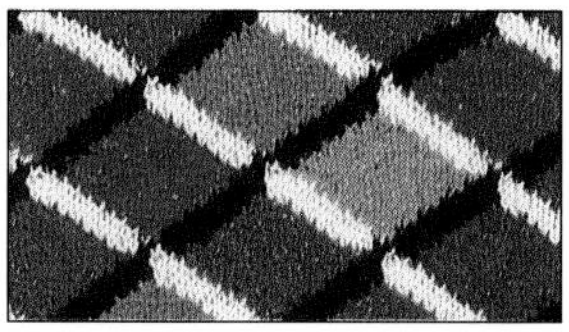

Harlequin

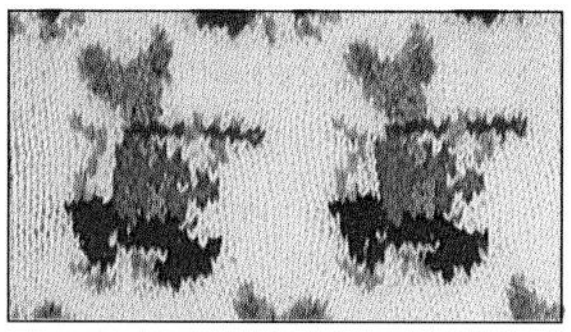

Mouse

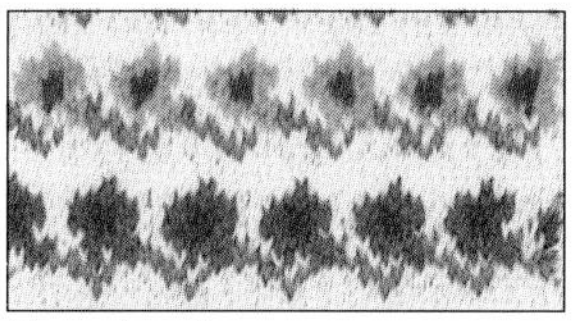

Bavarian flower

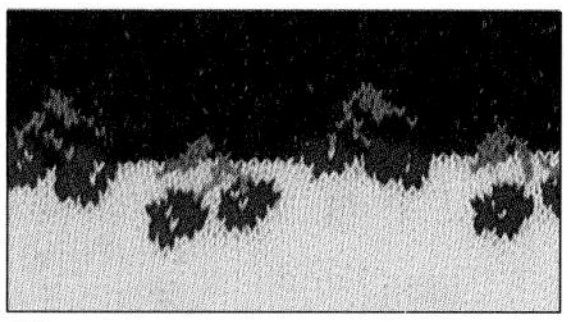

Cherry

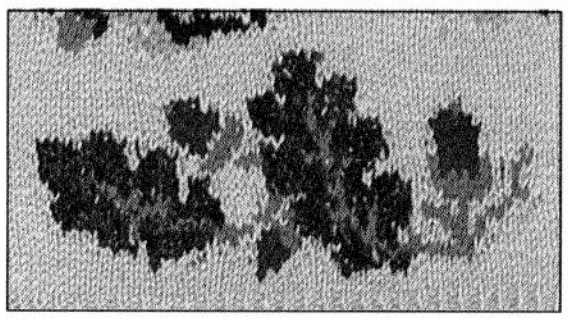

Acorn

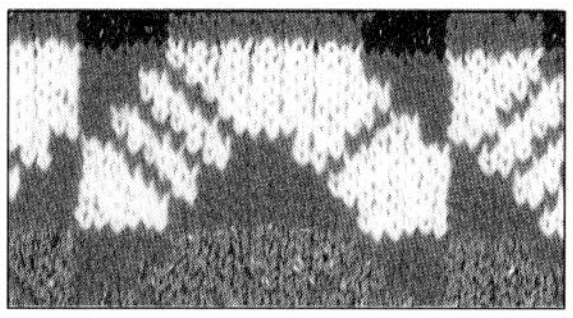

Odeon

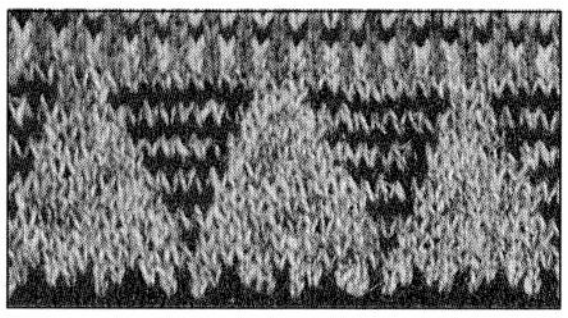

Persian stripe

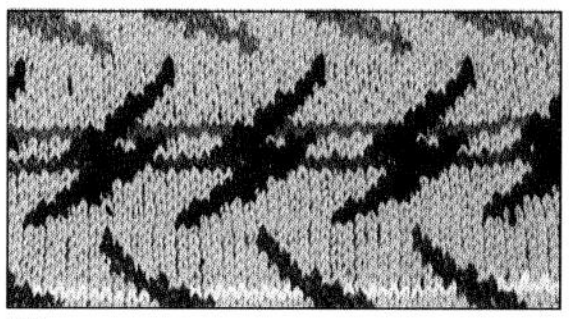

Zigzag

SWEATER

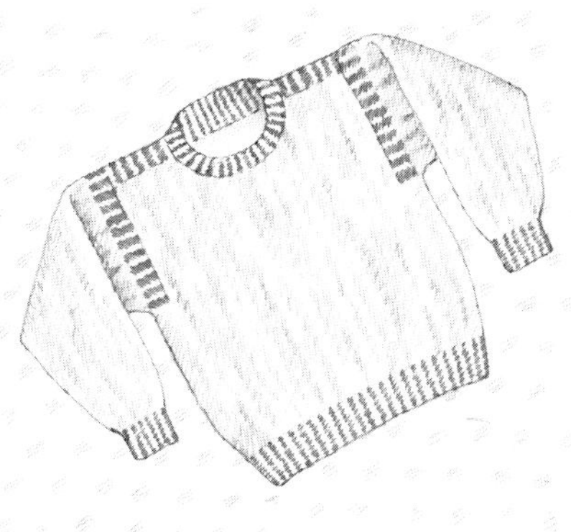

MEASUREMENTS

Actual chest size
24/28/32/36/40/44/48in
61/71/81/91/102/112/122cm

Length to shoulder
14/17$\frac{1}{2}$/21/24/26/27/27$\frac{1}{2}$in
36/44/54/61/67/69/70cm

Sleeve seam
10$\frac{1}{2}$/13/15/19/20/21$\frac{1}{2}$/22$\frac{1}{2}$in
27/33/38/48/51/54/57cm

Tension
28 sts and 28 rows measure 10cm over pattern on 3$\frac{3}{4}$mm needles (or size needed to obtain this tension).

MATERIALS

Yarn
Rowan Botany, or standard 4 ply wool; quantity as stated on your chosen pattern chart page

Needles
Suggested sizes
1 pair 2$\frac{3}{4}$mm (US 2)
1 pair 3$\frac{3}{4}$mm (US 5)

Notions
Sizes 24in and 28in (*61cm and 71cm*) only: 3 buttons

RIBBING

Work ribbing in yarns specified on pattern chart page.

SPECIAL NOTE

The two smallest sizes: 24in and 28in (*61cm and 71cm*) have a buttoned shoulder opening.

BACK

**With 2$\frac{3}{4}$mm needles cast on 80/90/100/112/124/136/146 sts. Work 17/17/17/29/29/29/29 rows k1 p1 rib, always going into the back of every knit stitch to give a twisted effect. Increase 4/8/12/14/16/18/22 sts evenly across last row – 84/98/112/126/140/154/168 sts.
Change to 3$\frac{3}{4}$mm needles and st st beginning with a k row. Work straight in pattern from chosen chart until back measures 9$\frac{1}{2}$/11$\frac{1}{2}$/14/14$\frac{1}{2}$/15$\frac{1}{2}$/16/16$\frac{1}{2}$in (*24/29/36/37/40/41/42cm*) from cast-on edge, ending with a row on wrong side.
Shape armholes Cast off 4/4/4/8/12/13/14 sts at beginning of next 2 rows.** Continue straight until armhole measures 4$\frac{1}{4}$/5$\frac{1}{4}$/6$\frac{1}{4}$/8$\frac{1}{2}$/9$\frac{1}{2}$/10/10in (*11/13/16/21/24/25/25cm*) from start of shaping. Change to yarn for ribbing and with right side facing, knit 1 row in yarn colour for rib, then work 5/5/5/7/7/7/7 rows k1 p1 twisted rib. Cast off loosely in rib right across for sizes 24in/28in (*61/71cm*) only.
Shape shoulders for remaining 5 sizes Cast off 11/12/12/14/15 sts at beginning of next 4 rows, then 11/9/11/12/15 sts at beginning of following 2 rows; leave remaining 38/44/46/48/50 sts on a stitch holder.

FRONT

Work as for back from ** to **. Continue straight in pattern until front measures 2$\frac{1}{4}$/2$\frac{1}{4}$/3$\frac{3}{4}$/5$\frac{1}{4}$/6$\frac{1}{4}$/6$\frac{1}{2}$/6$\frac{3}{4}$in (*6/6/9/13/15/16/17cm*) from start of armhole shaping ending with a row on wrong side.
Divide for neck Next row: Patt 31/38/43/43/45/50/55, cast off 14/14/18/24/26/28/30 sts loosely, patt to end.
Continue on last set of sts decreasing 1 st at neck edge on next 10 rows – 21/28/33/33/35/40/45 sts remain. Work straight until armhole measures 4$\frac{1}{4}$/5$\frac{1}{4}$/6$\frac{1}{4}$/8$\frac{1}{2}$/9$\frac{1}{2}$/10/10in (*11/13/16/21/24/25/25cm*).
Change to yarn for ribbing and with right side facing, knit 1 row, then work twisted rib as on back for 5/5/4/6/6/6/6 rows. Cast off loosely in rib right across for sizes 24in/28in (*61cm/71cm*) only.
Shape shoulder for remaining 5 sizes Cast off 11/12/12/14/15 sts at beginning of next and following alternate row, then 11/9/11/12/15 sts at beginning of following alternate row.
With wrong side facing, join yarn to remaining sts at neck edge. Finish to correspond with first side, reversing shapings.

SLEEVES

With 2$\frac{3}{4}$mm needles cast on 44/48/52/58/64/68/68 sts. Work 17/17/17/25/25/25/25 rows twisted rib, increasing 0/0/0/6/8/8/8 sts evenly across last row. Change to 3$\frac{3}{4}$mm needles and st st beginning with a k row. Work in pattern from chart as for back, *at the same time* shape sides by increasing 1 st at each end of 5th and every following 3rd row until there are 70/84/98/132/146/154/154 sts. Work straight until sleeve measures 9$\frac{3}{4}$/12$\frac{1}{4}$/14$\frac{1}{4}$/17$\frac{1}{2}$/19$\frac{1}{4}$/19$\frac{3}{4}$/21$\frac{3}{4}$in (*24/31/36/44/49/50/55cm*) from cast-on edge. Join in yarn for ribbing and with right side facing, knit 1 row. then work 5/5/5/9/9/9/9 rows twisted rib. Cast off loosely in rib.

NECKBAND

Join right shoulder seam. With 2$\frac{3}{4}$mm needles begin at left shoulder and pick up and k 1 stitch for each row of knitting around front of neck, 34/34/38/44/46/48/50 sts across back of neck. Work 8/8/8/12/12/12/12 rows twisted rib. Cast off loosely in rib.
Left shoulder opening for sizes 24/28in (*61/71cm*) only With 2$\frac{3}{4}$mm needles pick up and k 28/34 sts across left front shoulder and up side of neckband. Work 1 row twisted rib. Make 3 buttonholes in next row: rib 5/7, (cast off 2, rib 7/9) twice, cast off 2, rib 3/3.
Next row: Work in rib, casting on two sts over those cast off.
Work 2 rows rib; cast off loosely in rib.
Underlap With 2$\frac{3}{4}$mm needles and right side facing, pick up and k 28/34 sts down side of neckband and along left back shoulder. Work 5 rows twisted rib; cast off loosely in rib.

FINISHING

Sizes 24/28in (*61/71cm*): Lap buttonhole band of shoulder opening over underlap to back; catch down double fabric at armhole edge.
Sizes 32/36/40/44/48in (*81/91/102/112/122cm*): Join left shoulder seam.
All sizes: Pin cast-off edge of sleeve top into armhole – the straight sides at top of sleeve to form a neat right-angle at cast-off sts of armhole on back and front. Sew in place on wrong side with narrow back stitch. Join rest of sleeve seam and side seams. Sew on buttons, if applicable.

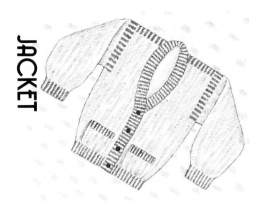

JACKET

MEASUREMENTS
Actual chest size
24/28/32/36/40/44/48in
61/71/81/91/102/112/122cm
Length to shoulder
15½/19/22½/25½/26½/27/27½in
39/48/57/65/67/68/69cm
Sleeve seam
11/13/16/18/20/20½/21½in
28/33/40/45/51/52/55cm
Tension
28 sts and 28 rows measure 10cm over pattern on 3¾mm needles (or size needed to obtain this tension).

MATERIALS
Yarn
Rowan Botany, or standard 4 ply wool; quantity as stated on your chosen pattern chart page
Needles
Suggested sizes
1 pair 2¾mm (US 2)
1 pair 3¾mm (US 5)
Notions
4/4/5/5/5/6/6 buttons

RIBBING & POCKET LININGS
Work ribbing and pocket linings in yarns specified on pattern chart page.

SPECIAL NOTE
When sewing the garment pieces together, the ribbed welts, cuffs, front bands and pocket tops are folded in half to give double thickness.

BACK
With 2¾mm needles, cast on 84/98/112/126/140/154/168 sts. Work 24/32/32/36/36/36/36 rows k1 p1 rib, always going into the back of every knit st to give a twisted effect.
Change to 3¾mm needles and st st beginning with a k row. Work straight in pattern from chosen chart until back measures 11/13/15¾/17¼/17¾/17¾/17¾in (*28/33/40/44/45/45/45cm*) from cast-on edge, ending with a row on wrong side.
Shape armholes Cast off 6/7/8/10/11/12/13 sts at beginning of next 2 rows – 72/84/96/106/118/130/142 sts. Continue straight in patt until armhole measures 6/7½/8½/10/10½/11/11½in (*15/19/22/26/27/28/29cm*) from start of shaping. Cast off right across loosely in rib.

FRONTS
Begin by making two pocket linings. With 3¾mm needles cast on 24/28/32/34/36/38/40 sts. Work 2½/2¾/2¾/4¼/4¼/4¼/4¼in (*6/7/7/11/11/11/11cm*) st st ending with a p row; leave sts on a spare needle.
Left front With 2¾mm needles cast on 36/42/48/56/62/66/74 sts. Work 24/32/32/36/36/36/36 rows twisted rib. Increase 2/2/4/4/4/6/6 sts across last

row – 38/44/52/60/66/72/80 sts.
Change to 3¾mm needles and st st beginning with a k row. Work straight in patt from chart for 2½/2¾/2¾/4¼/4¼/4¼/4¼in (*6/7/7/11/11/11/11cm*) ending with a row on wrong side.
Introduce pocket Next row: Patt 7/8/10/13/15/17/20, slip next 24/28/32/34/36/38/40 sts onto a spare needle and in their place, patt across 24/28/32/34/36/38/40 sts of one pocket lining, patt 7/8/10/13/15/17/20. Continue straight in patt until front measures 10¼/12¼/14½/16¼/16¼/16¼/15¾in (*26/31/37/41/41/41/40cm*) from cast-on edge, ending with a row on wrong side.
Place a marker at front edge to indicate start of front shaping. Continue in patt, shaping front edge by decreasing 1 st at this edge on next and every following 3rd row, 11/13/16/18/20/22/25 times in all. At the same time, when front measures 11/13/15¾/17¼/17¾/17¾/17¾in (*28/33/40/44/45/45/45cm*) from cast-on edge, shape armhole as follows:
Cast off 6/7/8/10/11/12/13 sts at beginning of next row. Keep armhole edge straight but continue to decrease at front edge as before until front decreasings have been done and 21/24/28/32/35/38/42 sts remain. Work straight until front matches back, ending with same patt row.
Change to yarn for ribbing. Knit 1 row, then work 9/9/9/11/11/13/13 rows twisted rib. Cast off in rib, using a bigger needle. Mark centre of side of rib at neck edge with contrast thread to indicate natural shoulderline.
Right front Work as for left, reversing all shapings.

SLEEVES
With 2¾mm needles cast on 66/68/72/84/90/94/96 sts. Work 28/36/36/40/40/40/40 rows twisted rib, increasing 14/14/14/16/20/20/20 sts evenly across last row – 80/82/86/100/110/114/116 sts.
Change to 3¾mm needles and st st beginning with a k row. Work in patt from chart, increasing 1 st at each end of 5th and every following 4th row until there are 92/112/126/148/156/162/170 sts, taking extra sts into patt as they are made.
Work straight until sleeve measures 12¼/14½/17¼/20/21/21½/22½in (*31/37/44/51/53/56/57cm*) from cast-on edge ending with row on wrong side.
Change to yarn for ribbing. Knit 1 row then work 7/9/9/9/9/11/11 rows twisted rib. Cast off loosely in rib.

She wears a striking jacket in the gray version of Zigzag. He looks comfortable in a loose fitting black crew neck Zigzag sweater.

BUTTON BANDS & COLLAR
Join cast-off edges of rib at top of fronts to back to form shoulder seams, leaving 4¾/5/5½/6/7/7½/8½in (*12/13/14/15/18/19/21cm*) free at centre for back of neck. Join side seams on wrong side with narrow backstitch. Turn under half of ribbing at lower edge to wrong side and hem loosely.
The following instructions are for a woman's band, i.e. buttoning right over left. For a man's, reverse instructions, reading left for right and right for left.
Left Beginning at centre back of neck, with 2¾mm needles, pick up and k 15/18/20/21/24/27/29 sts across left side of back of neck, pick up and k 12/12/12/14/14/16/16 sts down side of rib, then pick up and k 1 st for each row of knitting down left front to start of front shaping, then down to lower edge, going through double thickness of ribbing at the welt. Work 23/31/31/35/35/35/35 rows twisted rib; cast off loosely in rib.
Right Work in the same way as for left side. Beginning at lower edge, pick up the same number of sts as on left. Work 5/7/7/9/9/9/9 rows twisted rib. *Make 4/4/5/5/5/6/6 buttonholes in next row beginning first buttonhole after 6 sts have been worked from lower edge, last one 4 sts before start of front shaping and remainder spaced evenly between. Cast off 4 sts for each buttonhole. In next row cast on 4 sts over those cast off.* Work 10/14/14/14/14/14/14 rows rib. Repeat from * to * once more. Work 4/6/6/8/8/8/8 rows twisted rib. Cast off loosely in rib.

POCKET TOPS
With right side facing and 2¾mm needles knit across 24/28/32/34/36/38/40 sts of pocket, increasing 3 sts evenly across. Work 15/15/19/19/19/21/21 rows rib as before; cast off loosely in rib.

FINISHING
Pin cast-off edge of sleeve top into armhole – the straight sides at top of sleeve to form a neat right-angle at cast-off sts of armhole on back and front. Sew in place on wrong side with narrow back-stitch. Join rest of sleeve seam. Join sides of collar at back of neck with a flat seam. Turn left front band in half back to right side and hem neatly in place from lower edge to start of front shaping. Finish right front in the same way to end of last buttonhole. Fold back rest of ribbing to form shawl collar – do not sew down. Fold pocket top in half to right side and hem. Catch down sides of pocket tops and linings. Oversew around double button-holes to strengthen. Sew on buttons.

CARDIGAN

MEASUREMENTS
Actual chest size
24/28/32/36/40/44/48in
61/71/81/91/102/112/122cm
Length to shoulder
14½/17/20/22/23/23½/24in
37/44/51/56/59/60/61cm
Sleeve seam
11/13/16/18/19/19/19½in
28/33/40/45/48/48/49cm
Tension
28 sts and 28 rows measure 10cm over pattern on
3¾mm needles (or size needed to obtain this
tension).

MATERIALS
Yarn
Rowan Botany, or standard 4 ply wool; quantity as
stated on your chosen pattern chart page
Needles
Suggested sizes
1 pair 2¾mm (US 2)
1 pair 3¾mm (US 5)
Notions
6/6/7/7/8/8/8 buttons

RIBBING & POCKET LININGS
Work ribbing and pocket linings in yarns specified
on pattern chart page.

SPECIAL NOTE
When sewing the garment pieces together, the
ribbed welts, cuffs, front bands, neckband and
pocket tops are folded in half to give double
thickness.

BACK
With 2¾mm needles cast on 84/98/112/126/140/
154/168 sts. Work 24/32/32/36/36/36/36 rows k1 p1
rib, always going into the back of every knit st to
give a twisted effect.
Change to 3¾mm needles and st st beginning with
a k row. Work straight in pattern from chosen
chart until back measures 10/12/13¼/15¼/15¼/15¼/
15¼in (25/30/35/39/39/39/39cm) from cast-on edge
ending with a row on wrong side.
Shape armholes Cast off 6/7/8/10/11/12/13 sts at
beginning of next 2 rows – 72/84/96/106/118/130/
142 sts remain. Continue straight in pattern until
armhole measures 6/7/8/8½/9½/10/10½in (15/18/20/
21/24/25/26cm) from start of shaping, ending with
a row on wrong side.
Shape shoulders Cast off 7/8/9/10/12/12/14 sts at
beginning of next 4 rows, then 7/8/10/11/12/14/14
sts at beginning of following 2 rows. Leave remaining 30/36/40/42/48/54/58 sts on a spare needle.

FRONTS
Begin by making two pocket linings. With 3¾mm
needles cast on 20/24/28/30/32/34/36 sts. Work

1¼/1½/1½/2/2/2/2in (3/4/4/5/5/5/5cm) st st ending
with a p row; leave sts on a spare needle.
Left front With 2¾mm needles cast on 38/44/52/60/
66/72/80 sts. Work 24/32/32/36/36/36/36 rows
twisted rib as on back. Change to 3¾mm needles
and st st beginning with a k row. Work straight in
pattern from chart for 1¼/1½/1½/2/2/2/2in (3/4/4/5/
5/5/5cm) ending with a row on wrong side.
Introduce pocket Next row: Patt 9/10/12/15/17/19/
22, slip next 20/24/28/30/32/34/36 sts onto a spare
needle, in their place patt across 20/24/28/30/32/
34/36 sts of one pocket lining, patt to end. Continue straight in patt until front measures 10/12/
13¼/15¼/15¼/15¼/15¼in (25/30/35/39/39/39/39cm)
from cast-on edge, ending with a row on wrong
side.
Shape armhole Cast off 6/7/8/10/11/12/13 sts at
beginning of next row. Continue straight until
armhole measures 3½/3¾/5¼/5¾/5¾/6¾/7¼in (9/10/
12/14/15/17/18cm) from start of shaping, ending
with row on right side.
Shape neck Next row: Cast off 3/4/5/6/7/8/8 sts at
beginning of next row, then dec 1 st at this edge
on following 8/9/11/12/13/14/17 rows. Work
straight until front measures same as back, ending
with same patt row.
Shape shoulder Cast off 7/8/9/10/12/12/14 sts at
beginning of next and following alternate row,
then 7/8/10/12/11/14/14 sts at beginning of following alternate row.
Right front Work as for left reversing all shapings.

SLEEVES
With 2¾mm needles cast on 56/62/68/72/78/84/90
sts. Work 28/36/36/40/40/40/40 rows twisted rib.
Change to 3¾mm needles and st st beginning with
a k row. Work in patt from chart, increasing 1 st at
each end of 5th and every following 4th row until
there are 84/98/112/118/134/140/146 sts, taking
extra sts into patt as they are made. Work straight
until sleeve measures 12¾/14¾/18¼/20½/21¼/21¼/
22in (32/37/46/52/54/54/56cm) from cast-on edge.
Cast off right across.

BUTTON BANDS
Join side seams on wrong side with narrow
backstitch.
The following instructions are for a woman's band,
i.e. buttoning right over left. For a man's, reverse
instructions, reading left for right and right for left.
Left Fold welt in half to wrong side and hem
loosely. With 2¾mm needles, begin at start of neck
shaping and pick up and k 1 st for each stitch of
knitting down to lower edge, going through double
thickness of welt. Work 24/32/32/36/36/36/36 rows
twisted rib; cast off loosely in rib. Fold band in half
to wrong side and hem in place; join short sides at
bottom, and halfway along top.
Right Begin at lower edge and work as for left.
Pick up the same number of sts. Work 5/7/7/9/9/9/
9 rows twisted rib. *Make 6/6/7/7/8/8/8 buttonholes in next row, beginning first buttonhole after
6 sts have been worked from lower edge, last
buttonhole 8 sts from top edge and remainder
spaced evenly between. Cast off 4 sts for each
buttonhole. In the next row cast on 4 sts over
those cast off.* Work 10/14/14/14/14/14/14 rows
twisted rib. Repeat from * to * once more. Work
4/6/6/8/8/8/8 rows rib; cast off loosely in rib. Fold
in half to wrong side and hem; join short sides at
bottom, and halfway along top.

NECKBAND
Join shoulder seams on wrong side with narrow
backstitch. With 2¾mm needles, beginning halfway
across top edge of right front band, pick up and
knit 1 st for each row of knitting along band

*This tiny tot looks sweet in her white Bavarian
flower cardigan. She knows the importance of
flower power.*

(going through double thickness) and up side of
neck to right shoulder, k 30/36/40/42/48/54/58 sts
from back of neck, then 1 st for each st of knitting
down left side of neck to halfway across left front
band. Work 24/32/32/36/36/36/36 rows rib as
before. Cast off loosely in rib.

POCKET TOPS
With right side facing and 2¾mm needles, knit
across 20/24/28/30/32/34/36 sts of pocket, increasing 3 sts evenly across. Work 15/15/19/19/21/21/21
rows twisted rib; cast off in rib.

FINISHING
Fold back welt in half to wrong side and hem. Pin
cast-off edge of sleeve top into armhole – the
straight sides at top of sleeve to form a neat right-
angle at cast-off sts of armhole on back and
front. Sew in place on wrong side with narrow
backstitch. Join rest of sleeve seam. Fold pocket
top in half to right side and hem. Catch down
sides of pocket tops and linings. Fold neckband
in half to wrong side and hem loosely; join short
sides. Oversew around double buttonholes to
strengthen. Sew on buttons.

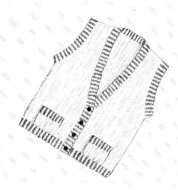
Next row: Purl.
Next row: K2 tog, k to end.
Next row: K2 tog, p to end.
Continue thus, decreasing 1 st at armhole edge on next and every alternate row 1/3/4/5/6/8/10 times more, then keep armhole edge straight. At the same time continue to decrease 1 st at neck edge on every following 3rd row until 19/22/26/29/31/33/36 sts remain. Work straight until front measures same as back to shoulder shaping, ending with a row on wrong side.
Shape shoulder Cast off 10/11/13/14/15/16/18 sts at beginning of next row, then 9/11/13/15/16/17/18 sts at beginning of following alternate row. Leave centre 2 sts on a stitch holder, rejoin yarn to last 36/42/48/54/59/65/70 sts, k to last 2 sts, k2 tog. Finish to correspond with first side, reversing shapings.

MEASUREMENTS
Actual chest size
24/28/32/36/40/44/48in
61/71/81/91/102/112/122cm
Length to shoulder
14/17/21½/23/24½/26/27in
35/43/54/58/62/66/69cm
Tension
28 sts and 28 rows measure 10cm over pattern on 3¾mm needles (or size needed to obtain this tension).

MATERIALS
Yarn
Rowan Botany, or standard 4 ply wool; quantity as stated on your chosen pattern chart page
Needles
Suggested sizes
1 pair 2¾mm (US 2)
1 pair 3¾mm (US 5)

RIBBING
Work ribbing in yarns specified on pattern chart page.

BACK
* *With 2¾mm needles cast on 80/90/100/112/124/136/146 sts. Work 13/17/17/25/25/25/25 rows in k1 p1 rib, always going into the back of every knit stitch to give a twisted effect, increasing across last row as follows: rib 2/1/2/7/6/5/7, (rib twice in next st, rib 18/10/7/6/6/6/5) 4/8/12/14/16/18/22 times, rib 2/1/2/7/6/5/7 – 84/98/112/126/140/154/168 sts.
Change to 3¾mm needles and st st beginning with a k row. Work straight in pattern from chosen chart until back measures 7/8½/12/13/14/15/15½in (18/22/30/33/35/38/39cm) from cast-on edge ending with a row on the wrong side**.
Shape armholes Cast off 5/6/7/8/10/11/13 sts at beginning of next 2 rows, then k2 tog at each end of next and every following alternate row until 66/74/84/94/102/110/116 sts remain. Work straight until back measures 7½/8½/9½/10/10½/11/11½in (18/21/24/25/26/28/29cm) from start of shaping, ending with a row on wrong side.
Shape shoulders Cast off 10/11/13/14/15/16/18 sts at beginning of next 2 rows, then 9/11/13/15/16/17/18 sts at beginning of following 2 rows; leave remaining 28/30/32/36/40/44/44 sts on a spare needle.

FRONT
Work as for back from ** to **.
Shape armholes and neck Cast off 5/6/7/8/10/11/13 sts at beginning of next 2 rows.
Next row: K2 tog, k 34/40/46/52/57/63/68, turn; leave remaining sts on a spare needle.
Next row: Purl.
Next row: K2 tog, k to last 2 sts, k2 tog.

A roomy slipover in the gray Acorn style is fun to knit and looks terrific.

NECKBAND
Join right shoulder seam with narrow backstitch on wrong side. With 2¾mm needles, begin at left shoulder and pick up and k 1 st from each row down left side of neck (an even number) to the centre 2 sts on holder, k these 2 sts and mark with contrast thread, pick up and k 1 st for each row up right side of neck (an even number), k across 28/30/32/36/40/44/44 sts from spare needle at back of neck.
Next row: Work in k1 p1 twisted rib beginning with p1 to within 2 sts of contrast thread at centre front; slip 1, k1, psso, p2, k2 tog, rib to end.
Next row: Rib to within 2 sts of marker, slip 1, k1, psso, k2, k2 tog, rib to end.
Repeat these 2 rows twice more, then first row once. Cast off loosely in rib, taking together 2 sts each side of coloured marker as before.

ARMBANDS
Join left shoulder seam as before. With 2¾mm needles and yarn for ribbing pick up and knit 1 st for each row around armhole. Work 7 rows k1 p1 twisted rib; cast off loosely in rib.

FINISHING
Join side seams.

MEASUREMENTS
Actual chest size
24/28/32/36/40/44/48in
61/71/81/91/102/112/122cm
Length to shoulder
13½/16½/20½/22½/23½/24½/25in
34/42/52/57/59/62/64cm
Tension
28 sts and 28 rows measure 10cm over pattern on 3¾mm needles (or size needed to obtain this tension).

MATERIALS
Yarn
Rowan Botany, or standard 4 ply wool; quantity as stated on your chosen pattern chart page
Needles
Suggested sizes
1 pair 2¾mm (US 2)
1 pair 3¾mm (US 5)
Notions
4/4/5/5/5/5 buttons

RIBBING & POCKET LININGS
Work ribbing and pocket linings in yarns specified on pattern chart page.

BACK
With 2¾mm needles cast on 83/97/111/125/139/153/167 sts. Work 13/13/13/17/17/21/21 rows k1 p1 rib, rows on right side having a k1 at each end. Always work into the back of every knit stitch to give a twisted effect.
Change to 3¾mm needles and continue straight in twisted rib until back measures 7/8½/12/13/13½/14/14in (18/22/30/33/34/36/36cm) from cast-on edge, ending with a row on wrong side.
Shape armholes Cast off 5/6/7/8/9/10/12 sts at beginning of next 2 rows, then decrease 1 st at each end of next and every following alternate row 7 times – 59/71/83/95/107/119/129 sts remain. Continue straight until armhole measures 6½/8/8½/9½/10/10½/11in (16/20/22/24/25/26/28cm) from start of shaping, ending with a row on wrong side.
Shape shoulders Cast off 8/9/11/12/14/16/18 sts at beginning of next 2 rows, then 8/9/10/11/13/16/17 sts at beginning of following 2 rows. Cast off remaining 27/35/41/49/53/55/59 sts. Place a marker at centre back of neck.

FRONTS
Begin by making two pocket linings. With 3¾mm needles cast on 17/19/21/23/25/28/30 sts. Work 2/2/2/2¾/2¾/3¼/3¼in (5/5/5/7/7/8/8cm) in st st ending with a purl row, leave sts on a spare needle.
Left front * *With 2¾mm needles cast on 34/41/48/55/62/69/76 sts. Work 13/13/13/17/17/21/21 rows k1 p1 twisted rib, increasing 7 sts evenly across last row – rib 4, (rib twice in next st, rib 3/4/5/6/7/8/9) 7 times, rib 2 – 41/48/55/62/69/76/83 sts.

Change to 3¾mm needles and st st beginning with a k row. Chosen pattern from chosen chart for 2/2/2/2¾/2¾/3¼/3¼ in (5/5/5/7/7/8/8cm), ending with a row on wrong side.**

Introduce pocket Next row: With right side facing, patt 12/14/17/19/22/24/26, slip next 17/19/21/23/25/28/30 sts onto a stitch holder then patt across 17/19/21/23/25/28/30 sts of one pocket lining in their place, patt 12/15/17/20/22/24/27. Continue straight in patt until front measures 6/7½/10½/11½/12/13/13in (16/19/27/30/31/33/33cm) from cast-on edge. Place marker at front edge.

Shape front edge Next row: With right side facing, patt to last 2 sts, k2 tog. Work 2 rows straight. Next row: P2 tog, patt to end.
Work 2 rows straight. Continue thus decreasing 1 st at front edge on next and every following 3rd row. *At the same time,* when front measures 7/8½/12/13/13½/14/14in (18/22/30/33/34/36/36cm) from cast-on edge, shape armhole. With right side facing cast off 5/6/7/8/9/10/12 sts at beginning of next row, then decrease 1 st at armhole edge on following 7 alternate rows. Keep armhole edge straight but continue to decrease at front edge as before on every 3rd row until 16/18/21/23/27/32/35 sts remain. Work straight until front measures same as back, ending with a row on wrong side.

Shape shoulder Cast off 8/9/11/12/14/16/18 sts at beginning of next row, then 8/9/10/11/13/16/17 sts at beginning of following alternate row.

Right front Work as for left front from ** to **.
Introduce pocket Next row: With right side facing, patt 12/15/17/20/22/24/27, slip next 17/19/21/23/25/28/30 sts onto a stitch holder and in their place, patt across sts of 2nd pocket lining, patt 12/14/17/19/22/24/26. Finish to correspond with left front, reversing all shaping.

BUTTON BANDS

The following instructions are for a woman's band, i.e. buttoning right over left. For a man's, reverse them, reading left for right and right for left. Join shoulder seams with backstitch on wrong side.
Left With right side facing, 2¾mm needles, beginning at centre back of neck, pick up and k 1 st for each cast-off st across to shoulder seam, 1 st for each row down left front to lower edge of welt. Work 7/7/7/9/9/9/9 rows k1 p1 twisted rib. Cast off loosely in rib.
Right In the same way as left front, begin at lower edge and pick up and k 1 st for each row up to shoulder, 1 st for each cast-off st across back of neck to centre. Work 3 rows twisted rib all sizes. Make 4/4/5/5/5/5/5 buttonholes in next row, beginning first hole after 6 sts have been worked from lower edge, last at marker at start of front shaping, and remainder spaced evenly between. Cast off 4 sts for each buttonhole. In next row cast on 4 sts over those previously cast off. Work a further 2/2/2/4/4/4/4 rows rib. Cast off loosely in rib.

ARMBANDS

With right side facing and 2¾mm needles, pick up and k 1 st for each row evenly around armhole. Work 7/7/7/9/9/9/9 rows twisted rib. Cast off loosely in rib.

POCKET TOPS

With right side facing and 2¾mm needles, knit across 17/19/21/23/25/28/30 sts of pocket, increasing 3 sts evenly across. Work 6/6/6/8/8/8/8 rows twisted rib. Cast off in rib.

FINISHING

Join side seams with narrow backstitch, join rib at back of neck. Catch down sides of pocket tops; sew down linings on wrong side. Sew on buttons.

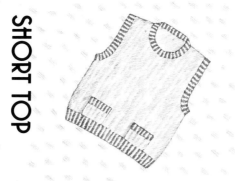

SHORT TOP

MEASUREMENTS
Actual chest size
24/28/32/36/40/44/48in
61/71/81/91/102/112/122cm
Length to shoulder
13/14½/16/17½/19/20/21in
33/36/41/44/48/50/53cm
Tension
28 sts and 28 rows measure 10cm over pattern on 3¾mm needles (or size needed to obtain this tension).

MATERIALS
Yarn
Rowan Botany, or standard 4 ply wool; quantity as stated on your chosen pattern chart page.
Needles
Suggested sizes
1 pair 2¾mm (US 2)
1 pair 3¾mm (US 5)

BACK
**With 2¾mm needles cast on 80/90/100/112/124/136/146 sts. Work 13/13/13/17/17/17/17 rows in k1 p1 rib, always going into the back of every knit stitch to give a twisted effect, increasing across last row as follows: rib 2/1/2/7/6/5/7, (rib twice in next st, rib 18/10/7/6/6/6/5) 4/8/12/14/16/18/22 times, rib 2/1/2/7/6/5/7 – 84/98/112/126/140/154/168 sts.
Change to 3¾mm needles and st st beginning with a k row.** Work straight in pattern from chosen chart until back measures 7/8/9/10/11/11½/12in (18/20/23/25/28/29/30cm) from cast-on edge ending with a row on the wrong side.
Shape armholes Cast off 5/6/7/8/9/10/11 sts at beginning of next 2 rows, then k2 tog at each end of next and every following alternate row until 64/74/84/94/104/114/124 sts remain. Work straight until armhole measures 6/6½/7/7½/8/8½/9in (15/16/18/19/20/21/23cm) from start of shaping, ending with a row on wrong side.
Shape shoulders Cast off 10/11/13/14/16/17/18 sts at beginning of next 2 rows, then 8/11/13/15/16/18/19 sts at beginning of next 2 rows, then 8/11/13/15/16/18/19 sts at beginning of following 2 rows; leave remaining 28/30/32/36/40/44/50 sts on a spare needle.

FRONT
Begin by making two pocket linings. With 3¾mm needles cast on 17/19/21/23/25/28/30 sts. Work ¾/¾/1¼/2/2/2½/2½in (2/2/3/5/5/6/6cm) st st ending with a p row; leave sts on a spare needle.
Work front as for back from ** to **. Continue straight in pattern from chart for ¾/¾/1¼/2/2/2½/2½in (2/2/3/5/5/6/6cm).
Introduce pocket Next row: Right side facing, patt 11/15/19/22/26/28/31 sts, slip next 17/19/21/23/25/28/30 sts onto a spare needle and in their place

patt across 17/19/21/23/25/28/30 sts of one pocket lining, patt 28/30/32/34/38/42/46 sts, slip next 17/19/21/23/25/28/30 sts onto a spare needle, then patt across sts of 2nd pocket lining, patt to end. Work straight until front measures same as back to start of armhole shaping ending with a row on the wrong side.
Shape armholes Cast off 5/6/7/8/9/10/11 sts at beginning of next 2 rows, then k2 tog at each end of next and every alternate row until 64/74/84/94/104/114/124 sts remain. Work straight until front measures 2/2½/3½/4/4¼/4¾/5in (5/6/9/10/11/12/13cm) from start of armhole shaping, ending with a row on the wrong side.
Divide for neck Next row: Patt 25/30/35/39/44/49/53, turn and leave remaining sts on a spare needle. Continue on first set of sts, decreasing 1 st at neck edge on next 4/4/4/7/9/10 rows, then 1 st on following 3/4/5/6/5/5/6 alternate rows, 18/22/26/29/32/35/37 sts remain. Work straight until front measures same as back to shoulder.
Shape shoulder Cast off 10/11/13/14/16/17/18 sts at beginning of next row, then 8/11/13/15/16/18/19 sts at beginning of following alternate row. Leave centre 14/14/14/16/16/16/18 sts on a spare needle. Join yarn to last 25/30/35/39/44/49/53 sts at neck edge. Finish to correspond with first side, reversing shapings.

NECKBAND
Join right shoulder seam with narrow backstitch on wrong side. With 2¾mm needles begin at left shoulder and pick up and k 1 st for each row down left side of neck, k 14/14/14/16/16/16/18 sts from spare needle at centre front, pick up and k 1 st for each row up right side of neck, k across 28/30/32/36/40/44/50 sts across back of neck. Work 8/8/8/12/12/12/12 rows k1 p1 twisted rib, cast off loosely in rib.

ARMBANDS
Join left shoulder seam as before. With 2¾mm needles pick up and knit 1 st for each row around armhole. Work 8/8/8/12/12/12/12 rows k1 p1 twisted rib, cast off loosely in rib.

POCKET TOPS
With 2¾mm needles and right side facing, join ribbing yarn to pocket top sts. Knit 1 row increasing 3 sts evenly across. Work 8/8/8/12/12/12/12 rows k1 p1 twisted rib, cast off in rib.

FINISHING
Join side seams with a narrow backstitch as before. Sew down sides of pocket tops to main work; catch down pocket linings on wrong side.

The Harlequin short top is easy to knit and fun to wear with a short skirt or casual trousers.

4 ply cotton

These instructions are for use with the following pattern charts: **Cowboy p. 20, Flower girl p. 32, Almond blossom p. 62, Splash p. 68, Lightning p. 76, Cube p. 84.** The yarn used for all the garments photographed is Rowan Sea Breeze cotton, however any standard 4 ply cotton may be used, as long as the correct tension is obtained.

Five different body shapes may be knitted in 4 ply cotton: a sweater, cardigan, slipover, waistcoat, short top; in any of seven different chest sizes: 24in, 28in, 32in, 36in, 40in, 44in, 48in (61cm, 71cm, 81cm, 91cm, 102cm, 112cm, 122cm). Remember that these chest measurements are the *actual* measurements not the *to fit* measurements, so you must choose a size that allows your desired amount of ease.

Cowboy

Flower girl

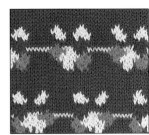
Almond blossom

Splash

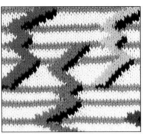
Lightning

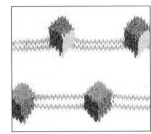
Cube

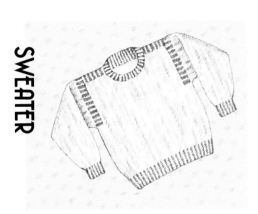

MEASUREMENTS
Actual chest size
24/28/32/36/40/44/48in
61/71/81/91/102/112/122cm
Length to shoulder
14/17/21/24/25½/26½/27in
36/43/54/61/65/67/68cm
Sleeve seam
10½/12½/15/18/20/20½/21½in
27/32/38/46/51/52/54cm
Tension
32 sts and 36 rows measure 10cm over pattern on 3mm needles (or size needed to obtain this tension).

MATERIALS
Yarn
Rowan Sea Breeze cotton or standard 4 ply cotton, quantity as stated on your chosen pattern chart page
Needles
Suggested sizes
1 pair 2¼mm (US 1)
1 pair 3mm (US 3)
Notions
Sizes 24in and 28in (*61cm and 71cm*) only: 3 buttons

RIBBING AND POCKET LININGS
Work ribbing and pocket linings in yarn specified on pattern chart page.

SPECIAL NOTE
The two smallest sizes: 24in and 28in (*61cm and 71cm*) have a buttoned shoulder opening.

BACK
**With 2¼mm needles cast on 90/104/118/132/146/160/174 sts. Work 21/21/21/30/30/30/30 rows in k1 p1 rib, always going into the back of every knit stitch to give a twisted effect. Increase 10/12/14/16/18/20/22 sts evenly across last row – 100/116/132/148/164/180/196 sts.
Change to 3mm needles and st st. Work straight in patt from chosen chart until back measures 8½/10½/13½/15/15½/16/16in (*22/26/35/38/39/40/40cm*) from cast-on edge.
Shape armholes Cast off 6/6/10/10/14/14/16 sts at beginning of next 2 rows**. Continue straight in patt until armhole measures 5/6/7/8/9/9½/10in (*13/15/18/20/23/24/25cm*). Change to yarn for ribbing only. Knit 1 row then work 5/5/5/9/9/9/9 rows twisted rib as before. Cast off right across in rib on sizes 24 and 28.
Shape shoulders for 5 remaining sizes Cast off 15/17/18/21/23 sts loosely at beginning of next 4 rows of twisted rib; cast off remaining 52/60/64/68/72 sts in rib.

FRONT
Work as for back from ** to **. Continue straight until armhole measures 2½/3½/3½/4½/5½/5½/5½in (*6/9/9/11/14/14/14cm*) from start of shaping.
Divide for neck Next row: Patt 35/42/44/50/52/58/62, cast off next 18/20/24/28/32/36/40 sts, patt to end. Continue on last set of sts decreasing 1 st at neck edge on next 11/14/14/16/16/16/16 rows – 24/28/30/34/36/42/46 sts remain. Work straight until armhole measures 5/6/7/8/9/9½/10in (*13/15/17/20/23/24/25cm*) ending with a row on wrong side. Change to yarn for ribbing. Knit 1 row then work 4/4/4/8/8/8/8 rows twisted rib. Cast off for sizes 24 and 28.
Shape shoulder for remaining 5 sizes With wrong side facing, cast off 15/17/18/21/23 sts at beginning of next and following alternate row of twisted rib. Join yarn to remaining sts at neck edge. Finish to correspond with first side, reversing shapings.

SLEEVES
With 2¼mm needles cast on 52/58/60/66/70/72/76 sts. Work 18/18/18/26/26/26/26 rows twisted rib as before. Increase 6/8/8/10/10/10/10 sts evenly across last row – 58/66/68/76/80/82/86 sts. Change to 3mm needles and patt as for back and at the same time shape sides by increasing 1 st at each end of 5th and every following 4th/4th/3rd/3rd/3rd/3rd/3rd row until there are 88/104/120/144/160/168/176 sts, taking extra sts into patt as they are made. Work straight until sleeve measures 10/12/14½/17/19/19½/20½in (*25/30/37/43/48/49/52cm*) from cast-on edge, ending with a row on wrong side. Join in yarn for ribbing. Knit 1 row, then work 5/5/5/9/9/9/9 rows twisted rib; cast off in rib right across.

NECKBAND
Join right shoulder seam. With 2¼mm needles begin at left shoulder and pick up and k 1 st for each row of knitting and 1 st for each cast-off st all around front of neck, k 40/48/52/60/64/68/72 sts from back of neck. Work 5/5/5/8/8/8/8 rows twisted rib. Cast off in rib.
Left shoulder opening For sizes 24/28in (*61/67cm*) only: With 2¼mm needles pick up and k 28/34 sts across left front shoulder and up side of neckband. Work 1 row twisted rib. Make 3 buttonholes in next row thus: Rib 5/7, (cast off 2, rib 7/9) twice, cast off 2, rib 3/3.
Next row: Work in rib, casting on 2 over those cast off. Work 2 rows rib; cast off in rib.

Underlap With 2¼mm needles pick up and k 28/34 sts down side of neckband and along left back shoulder. Work 5 rows twisted rib; cast off in rib.

FINISHING
Sizes 24/28in (*61/71cm*): Lap buttonhole band over underlap to back; catch down double fabric at armhole edge.
Sizes 32/36/40/44/48in (*81/91/102/112/122cm*): Join left shoulder seam.
All sizes: Pin cast-off edge of sleeve top into armholes with sides of sleeve top making a neat right-angle at cast-off edge of armhole on back and front. Join with narrow back stitch. Join rest of sleeve and side seams. Sew on buttons.

SWEATER

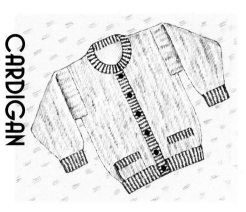

MEASUREMENTS
Actual chest size
24/28/32/36/40/44/48in
61/71/81/91/102/112/122cm
Length to shoulder
14½/17½/20½/22½/23½/24½/25½in
37/44/52/57/59/62/65cm
Sleeve seam
11/13/16/18/20/20½/21½in
28/33/40/45/51/52/54cm
Tension
32 sts and 36 rows measure 10cm over pattern on 3mm needles (or size needed to obtain this tension).

MATERIALS
Yarn
Rowan Sea Breeze cotton or standard 4 ply cotton, quantity as stated on your chosen pattern chart page
Needles
Suggested sizes
1 pair 2¼mm (US 1)
1 pair 3mm (US 3)
Notions
6/6/7/7/8/8/8 buttons

RIBBING AND POCKET LININGS
Work ribbing and pocket linings in yarn specified on pattern chart page.

SPECIAL NOTE
When sewing the garment pieces together, the ribbed welts, cuffs, front bands, neckband and pocket tops are folded in half to give double thickness.

BACK
With 2¼mm needles cast on 100/116/132/148/164/ 180/196 sts. Work 27/36/36/39/39/39/39 rows in k1 p1 rib always going into the back of every knit stitch to give a twisted effect.
Change to 3mm needles and st st. Work straight in patt from chosen chart until back measures 10/ 12¼/14¼/15¾/15¾/15¾/16¼in (25/31/36/40/40/40/ 41cm) from cast-on edge.
Shape armholes Cast off 6/6/10/10/14/14/16 sts at beginning of next 2 rows – 88/104/112/128/136/ 152/164 sts remain. Continue straight until arm-hole measures 6/7/8/8½/9½/10½/11in (15/18/20/21/ 24/27/28cm) from start of shaping.
Shape shoulders Cast off 12/14/15/17/18/21/23 sts at beginning of next 4 rows; leave remaining 40/48/52/60/64/68/72 sts on a spare needle.

FRONTS
Begin by making two pocket linings. With 3mm needles cast on 24/28/32/34/36/38/40 sts. Work 1½/2/2/2½/2½/2½/2½in (4/5/5/6/6/6/6cm) in st st ending with a p row; leave sts on a spare needle.

Left front With 2¼mm needles cast on 42/52/60/68/ 76/84/92 sts. Work 27/36/36/39/39/39/39 rows twisted rib. Change to 3mm needles and work in patt as for back for 1½/2/2/2½/2½/2½/2½in (4/5/5/6 6/6/6cm) ending with a row on wrong side.
Introduce pocket Next row: Patt 10/12/14/17/20/ 23/26 sts, slip next 24/28/32/34/36/38/40 sts onto a spare needle and in their place patt across sts of one pocket lining, patt to end.
Continue straight in patt until front measures same as back to start of armhole shaping, ending with same patt row.
Shape armhole With right side facing, cast off 6/ 6/10/10/14/14/16 sts at beginning of next row.
Continue straight until armhole measures 3¼/3½/ 4¾/5½/6/7/6½in (8/9/12/14/15/18/17cm) from start of shaping, ending with row on right side.
Shape neck Cast off 5/6/7/8/9/11/12 sts at begin-ning of next row, then decrease 1 st at this edge on following 9/12/13/16/17/18 rows – 24/28/30/34/ 36/42/46 sts remain. Work straight until front measures same as back ending with same patt row.
Shape shoulder With right side facing cast off 12/ 14/15/17/18/21/23 sts at beginning of next and following alternate row.
Right front Work as for left, reversing all shapings.

SLEEVES
With 2¼mm needles cast on 52/58/64/66/70/72/76 sts. Work 33/39/39/42/42/45/45 rows twisted rib, increasing 4/6/6/8/8/8/8 sts evenly across last row – 56/64/70/74/78/80/84 sts.
Change to 3mm needles and patt from chart, shaping sides by increasing 1 st at each end of 3rd and every following 4th/4th/ 4th/4th/4th/3rd/ 3rd row until there are 92/108/124/132/148/164/ 172 sts taking extra sts into patt as they are made. Work straight until sleeve measures 12½/15/18/ 20½/22½/23/24in (32/38/46/52/57/58/61cm) from cast-on edge. Cast off right across in rib.

BUTTON BANDS
Join side seams.
Fold welt in half to wrong side and hem loosely. The following instructions are for a woman's band, i.e. buttoning right over left. For a man's, reverse instructions, reading left for right and right for left.
Left With 2¼mm needles begin at top of left front at start of neck shaping and pick up and k 1 st for

each row of knitting down to lower edge going through double thickness of welt. Work 26/35/35/ 38/38/38/38 rows twisted rib as before. Cast off in rib. Fold band in half to wrong side and hem. Join short sides at top and bottom.
Right Work in the same way as for left side. Begin-ning at lower edge pick up and k exactly the same number of sts as on left front. Work 7/9/9/11/11/ 11/11 rows twisted rib. **Make 6/6/7/7/8/8/8 buttonholes in next row beginning first buttonhole after 7 sts have been worked from lower edge, last one to start 9 sts from top edge and remainder spaced evenly between. Cast off 4 sts for each buttonhole. In next row cast on 4 sts over those cast off**. Work 10/14/14/14/14/14/14 rows rib. Repeat from ** to ** once more. Work 5/8/8/9/9/ 9/9 rows twisted rib. Cast off loosely in rib. Fold band in half to wrong side and hem; join sides at top and bottom.

NECKBAND
Join shoulder seams with narrow backstitch. With right side facing and 2¼mm needles, beginning halfway across top of right front band, pick up and k 1 st for each row of knitting along band and up side of neck to shoulder, k 40/48/52/60/64/68/ 72 sts from back of neck, then pick up and k 1 st for each row of knitting as before down left side of neck to halfway across left front band. Work 26/ 35/35/38/38/38 rows twisted rib; cast off loosely in rib.

POCKET TOPS
With 2¼mm needles knit across pocket top sts increasing 3 sts evenly across 27/31/35/37/39/41/ 43 sts. Work 14/14/17/17/20/20/20 rows twisted rib; cast off in rib.

FINISHING
Pin cast-off edge of sleeve top into armhole, the straight sides of sleeve seam forming a neat right-angle at cast-off edges of armhole on back and front. Sew with narrow backstitch. Join rest of sleeve seams. Fold cuff and neckband in half to wrong side and hem; join short sides. Sew down pocket tops. Sew on buttons.

Mum's in a cardigan and her daughter in a matching white Lightning pattern slipover, just right for a summer outing.

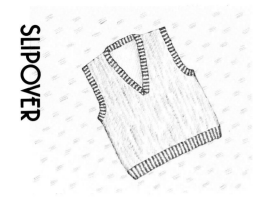

MEASUREMENTS
Actual chest size
24/28/32/36/40/44/48in
61/71/81/91/102/112/122cm
Length to shoulder
14/17/21/22½/24/25½/26½in
35/43/53/57/61/65/67cm
Tension
32 sts and 36 rows measure 10cm over pattern on 3mm needles (or size needed to obtain this tension).

MATERIALS
Yarn
Rowan Sea Breeze cotton or standard 4 ply cotton, quantity as stated on your chosen pattern chart page
Needles
Suggested sizes
1 pair 2¼mm (US 1)
1 pair 3mm (US 3)

RIBBING
Work ribbing in yarn specified on pattern chart page.

BACK
**With 2¼mm needles cast on 92/106/120/134/148/162/176 sts. Work 18/18/21/21/21/27/27 rows in k1, p1 rib, always going into the back of every knit stitch to give a twisted effect. Increase 8/10/12/14/16/18/20 sts evenly across last row – 100/116/132/148/164/180/196 sts.
Change to 3mm needles and st st. Work straight in patt from chosen chart until back measures 7½/9/12/13/14/15/15½in (*19/24/30/33/35/38/39cm*) from cast-on edge**.
Shape armholes Cast off 7/8/9/10/12/14/16 sts at beginning of next 2 rows, then k2 tog at each end of following 6/7/8/8/8/8/8 rows – 74/86/98/112/124/136/148 sts remain. Work straight until back measures 14/17/21/22½/24/25½/26½in (*35/43/53/57/61/65/67cm*) from cast-on edge.
Shape shoulders Cast off 7/9/10/13/15/16/19 sts at beginning of next 2 rows, then 8/8/10/13/14/16/19 sts at beginning of following 2 rows; leave remaining 44/52/58/60/66/72/72 sts on a spare needle.

FRONT
Work as for back from ** to **.
Shape armholes and divide for neck Cast off 7/8/9/10/12/14/16 sts at beginning of next 2 rows.
Next row: K2 tog, patt 37/44/51/58/64/71/76, k2 tog, turn and leave remaining sts on a spare needle.
Next row: Purl.
Next row: K2 tog, patt to end.
Next row: P2 tog, patt to last 2 sts, p2 tog. Continue thus decreasing 1 st at armhole edge on

next 3/4/5/5/5/5/5 rows, then keep armhole edge straight. *At the same time* continue to decrease 1 st at front edge on every following 3rd row from previous decrease until 20/23/26/28/32/35/40 sts remain, then on every following alternate row at this edge until 15/17/20/26/29/32/38 sts remain. Work straight until front measures same as back ending with same patt row on wrong side.
Shape shoulder Cast off 7/9/10/13/15/16/19 sts at beginning of next row, then 8/8/10/13/14/16/19 sts at beginning of following alternate row.
Return to remaining sts, slip centre 2 sts on a safety pin, join yarn to remaining sts, k2 tog, patt to last 2 sts, k2 tog. Finish to correspond with first side, reversing shapings.

NECKBAND
Join right shoulder seam with narrow backstitch on wrong side. With 2¼mm needles and yarn for ribbing begin at left shoulder and pick up and k 1 st for each row of knitting down left side of neck (must be an even number), place marker, k 2 sts from safety pin, place marker, pick up and k 1 st for each row of knitting up right side of neck to shoulder (must be an even number), k 44/52/58/60/66/72/72 sts from spare needle at back of neck.
Row 1: Work in twisted rib beginning with a p1, to within 2 sts of marker, slip 1, k1, psso, p 2 centre sts, k2 tog, rib to end.
Row 2: Rib to within 2 sts of marker, slip 1, k1, psso, k 2 centre sts, k2 tog, rib to end. Repeat these 2 rows 2/2/3/3/3/3/3 times more, then row 1 again. Cast off in rib, taking 2 sts together each side of markers as before.

Wear a Cowboy style slipover and you will certainly be ready for a showdown.

ARMBANDS
Join left shoulder seam as before. With 2¼mm needles and yarn for ribbing pick up and k 1 st for each row of knitting evenly around each armhole. Work 8/8/8/11/11/11/11 rows twisted rib; cast off in rib.

FINISHING
Join side seams.

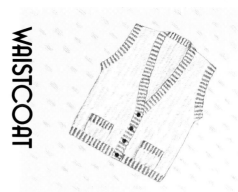

MEASUREMENTS
Actual chest size
24/28/32/36/40/44/48in
61/71/81/91/102/112/122cm
Length to shoulder
13½/16½/20/22/23½/24½/25in
34/42/51/56/59/62/64cm
Tension
32 sts and 36 rows measure 10cm over pattern on 3mm needles (or size needed to obtain this tension).

MATERIALS
Yarn
Rowan Sea Breeze cotton or standard 4 ply cotton, quantity as stated on your chosen pattern chart page
Needles
Suggested sizes
1 pair 2¼mm (US 1)
1 pair 3mm (US 3)
1 pair 3¼mm (US 4)
Notions
4/4/5/5/5/5/5 buttons

RIBBING AND POCKET LININGS
Work ribbing and pocket linings in yarn specified on pattern chart page.

BACK
With 2¼ mm needles cast on 96/112/128/144/160/176/192 sts. Work 15/15/15/21/21/24/24 rows k1 p1 rib, always working into the back of every knit st to give a twisted effect, increasing 1 st at each end of last row – 98/114/130/146/162/178/194 sts.
Change to 3¼mm needles and continue straight in twisted rib until back measures 7/8½/11½/12½/13½/14/14in (*18/22/29/32/34/36/36cm*) from cast-on edge.
Shape armholes Cast off 5/6/7/9/11/13/14 sts at beginning of next 2 rows, then decrease 1 st at each end of next 5/6/7/7/7/7/7 rows – 78/90/102/114/126/138/152 sts remain. Work straight until armhole measures 6½/8/8½/9½/10/10½/11in (*17/20/22/24/25/27/28cm*) from start of shaping.
Shape shoulders Cast off 7/8/10/13/14/16/19 sts at beginning of next 4 rows; cast off remaining sts. Place a marker at centre back of neck.

FRONTS
Begin by making pocket linings. With 3mm needles cast on 20/22/24/26/30/32/34 sts. Work 2/2/2/2¾/2¾/3¼/3¼in (5/5/5/7/7/8/8cm) in st st ending with a p row; leave sts on a spare needle.
Left front With 2¼mm needles cast on 42/50/58/66/74/82/90 sts. Work 15/15/15/21/21/24/24 rows twisted rib increasing 4 sts evenly across – 46/54/62/70/78/86/94 sts.
Change to 3mm needles and work straight in st st in patt from chosen chart for 2/2/2/2¾/2¾/3¼/3¼in

(5/5/5/7/7/8/8cm) ending with a row on wrong side.
Introduce pocket Next row: With right side facing, patt 13/16/19/22/24/27/30, slip next 20/22/24/26/30/32/34 sts onto a spare needle, then patt across 20/22/24/26/30/32/34 sts from one pocket lining in their place, patt 13/16/19/22/24/27/30. Continue straight in patt over all sts until front measures 6/7½/10½/11½/12½/13/13in (15/19/26/29/32/33/33cm) from cast-on edge ending with a row on wrong side.
Shape front edge Next row: Patt to last 2 sts, k2 tog. Place a marker at this edge to indicate start of front shaping. Work 2 rows straight.
Next row: P2 tog, patt to end. Work 2 rows straight. Continue thus decreasing 1 st at front edge on next and every following 3rd row. *At the same time* when front measures 7/8½/11½/12½/13½/14/14in (18/22/29/32/34/36/36cm) from cast-on edge shape armhole. Cast off 5/6/7/9/11/13/14 sts at beginning of next row, then decrease 1 st at this edge on following 5/6/7/7/7/7/7 rows. Now keep armhole edge straight but continue to decrease 1 st at front edge on every 3rd row as before until 14/16/20/26/28/32/38 sts remain. Work a few rows straight until front measures same as back to start of shoulder shaping, ending with a row on wrong side.
Shape shoulder Cast off 7/8/10/13/14/16/19 sts at beginning of next and following alternate row.
Right front Work as for left, reversing all shapings.

BUTTON BANDS
Join shoulder seams with narrow backstitch on wrong side.
The following instructions are for a woman's band, i.e. buttoning right over left. For a man's, reverse instructions, reading left for right and right for left.
Left With right side facing and 2¼mm needles, begin at centre back of neck and pick up and k 1 st for each row evenly across left side of neck to shoulder seam, and down to lower edge of welt. Work 8/8/8/11/11/11/11 rows twisted rib; cast off loosely in rib.
Right In the same way as left front, begin at lower edge and pick up and k exactly the same number of sts as left side up to start of front shaping, up front to right shoulder, and across back of neck to centre. Work 3 rows twisted rib. Make 4/4/5/5/5/5 buttonholes in next row beginning first buttonhole after 7 sts have been worked from lower edge, last buttonhole at marker and remainder spread evenly between. Cast off 3 sts for each buttonhole.
Next row: Work in twisted rib, casting on the same number of sts over those cast off in previous row. Work a further 3/3/3/6/6/6/6 rows twisted rib; cast off loosely in rib.

ARMBANDS
With right side facing and 2¼mm needles, pick up and k 1 st for each row of knitting all around armholes. Work 8/8/8/11/11/11/11 rows twisted rib. Cast off loosely in rib.

POCKET TOPS
With right side facing and 2¼mm needles join yarn to pocket top sts. K 1 row increasing 3 sts evenly across. Work 5/5/5/8/8/8 rows twisted rib; cast off in rib.

FINISHING
Join side seams as before; join rib at centre back of neck. Catch down sides of pocket tops; sew down pocket linings on wrong side. Sew on buttons.

MEASUREMENTS
Actual chest size
24/28/32/36/40/44/48in
61/71/81/91/102/112/122cm)
Length to shoulder
13/14½/16/17½/19/20/21in
33/37/41/44/48/51/53cm
Tension
32 sts and 36 rows measure 10cm over pattern on 3mm needles (or size needed to obtain this tension).

MATERIALS
Yarn
Rowan Sea Breeze cotton or standard 4 ply cotton, quantity as stated on your chosen pattern chart page
Needles
Suggested sizes
1 pair 2¼mm (US 1)
1 pair 3mm (US 3)

RIBBING AND POCKET LININGS
Work ribbing and pocket linings in yarn specified on pattern chart page.

BACK
**With 2¼mm needles cast on 90/104/118/132/146/160/174 sts. Work 12/12/15/15/15/18/18 rows k1 p1 rib, always going into the back of every knit stitch to give a twisted effect.
Next row: Increase as follows: rib (8/7/7/7/7/7/6, rib twice in next st) 10/12/14/16/18/20/22 times, rib 0/8/6/4/2/0/20 – 100/116/132/148/164/180/196 sts.

This geometric Cube patterned waistcoat is as much fun to knit as skipping!

Change to 3mm needles and st st**. Work straight in patt from chosen chart until back measures 6½/7½/8½/9½/10½/11/11½in (16/19/21/24/26/28/29cm) from cast-on edge.
Shape armholes Cast off 6/7/8/9/10/11/12 sts at beginning of next 2 rows then k2 tog at each end of every row until 76/88/100/112/124/136/148 sts remain. Work straight until armhole measures 6½/7/7½/8/8½/9/9½in (17/18/19/20/22/23/24cm) from start of shaping.
Shape shoulders Cast off 7/9/10/12/14/16/18 sts at beginning of next 4 rows; leave remaining 48/52/60/64/68/72/76 sts on a spare needle.

FRONT
Begin by making two pocket linings. With 3mm needles cast on 22/24/26/30/34/34/38 sts. Work 1/1/1/1¼/1¼/1¼/1¼in (2/2/2/3/3/3/3cm) st st ending with a purl row; leave sts on a spare needle. Work front as for back from ** to **. Continue straight in patt for 1/1/1/1¼/1¼/1¼/1¼in (2/2/2/3/3/3/3cm) ending with a row on the wrong side.
Introduce pocket Next row: Right side facing, patt 12/15/18/21/24/28/31, slip next 22/24/26/30/34/34/38 sts onto a spare needle and in their place patt across sts of one pocket lining, patt 32/38/42/46/48/56/58 sts, slip next 22/24/26/30/34/34/38 sts onto a spare needle and in their place patt across sts of 2nd pocket lining, patt 12/15/18/21/24/28/31. Continue straight in patt over all sts until front measures same as back to start of armhole shaping.
Shape armholes Cast off 6/7/8/9/10/11/12 sts at beginning of next 2 rows, then k2 tog at each end of every row until 76/88/100/112/124/136/148 sts remain. Work straight until front measures 2½/2½/3/3/3½/3½/4in (6½/6½/7½/7½/9/9/10cm) from start of armhole shaping.
Divide for neck Next row: Patt 28/34/38/42/46/50/54, turn and leave remaining sts on a spare needle. Continue on first set of sts, decreasing 1 st at neck edge on following 4 rows, then 1 st on following 10/12/14/14/14/14/14 alternate rows, 14/18/20/24/28/32/36 sts remain. Work straight until front measures same as back to start of shoulder shaping.
Shape shoulder Cast off 7/9/10/12/14/16/18 sts loosely at beginning of next and following alternate row. Leave centre 20/20/24/28/32/36/40 sts on a spare needle. Join yarn to last 28/34/38/42/46/50/54 sts at neck edge. Finish to correspond with first side, reversing shapings.

NECKBAND
Join right shoulder seam with narrow backstitch on wrong side. With 2¼mm needles begin at left shoulder and pick up and k 1 st for each row of knitting down left side of neck, k 20/20/24/28/32/36/40 sts from spare needle at centre, pick up and k 1 st for each row up right side of neck, k across 48/52/60/64/68/72/76 sts from back of neck. Work 8/8/8/11/11/11/11 rows k1 p1 twisted rib; cast off in rib.

ARMBANDS
Join left shoulder seam as before. With 2¼mm needles pick up and k 1 st for each row evenly around armhole. Work 8/8/8/11/11/11/11 rows twisted rib; cast off in rib.

FINISHING
Join side seams as before. With 2¼mm needles and right side facing, join yarn for ribbing to pocket top sts. Knit 1 row increasing 3 sts evenly across. Work 5/5/8/8/8/8 rows twisted rib; cast off in rib. Sew down sides of pocket tops to main work; catch down pocket linings on wrong side.

Double knitting wool

These instructions are for use with the following pattern charts: **Chainsaw p. 28, Lavender p. 42, Welsh poppy p. 47, Wandering line p. 88, Obloid p. 92.** The yarn used for all the garments photographed is Rowan Designer DK, with the occasional use of Rowan Fine Cotton Chenille, however any standard double knitting wool may be used, as long as the correct tension is obtained.

Six different body shapes may be knitted in double knitting wool: a sweater, jacket, cardigan, slipover, waistcoat, short top; in any of seven different chest sizes: 24in, 28in, 32in, 36in, 40in, 44in, 48in (61cm, 71cm, 81cm, 91cm, 102cm, 112cm, 122cm). Remember that these chest measurements are the *actual* measurements not the *to fit* measurements, so you must choose a size that allows your desired amount of ease.

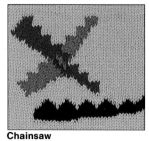
Chainsaw

Lavender

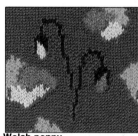
Welsh poppy

Wandering line

Obloid

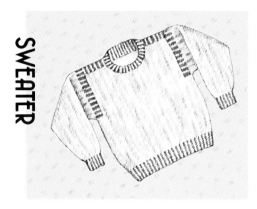

MEASUREMENTS

Actual chest size
24/28/32/36/40/44/48in
61/71/81/91/102/112/122cm

Length to shoulder
14½/17½/20½/24/26/27/27½in
37/44/52/61/67/69/71cm

Sleeve seam
10½/13/15/18/20/20½/22½in
27/33/38/46/51/52/57cm

Tension
23 sts and 30 rows measure 10cm over pattern on 4mm needles (or size needed to obtain this tension).

MATERIALS

Yarn
Rowan Designer DK, or standard double knitting wool, quantity as stated on your chosen pattern chart page

Needles
Suggested sizes
1 pair 3¼mm (US 4)
1 pair 4mm (US 6)

Notions
Sizes 24in and 28in (61cm and 71cm) only: 3 buttons

RIBBING

Work ribbing in yarn specified on pattern chart page.

SPECIAL NOTE

The two smallest sizes: 24in and 28in (61cm and 31cm) have a buttoned shoulder opening.

BACK

**With 3¼mm needles cast on 66/78/88/100/110/122/132 sts. Work 16/16/16/20/20/24/24 rows in k1 p1 rib, always going into the back of every knit stitch to give a twisted effect. Increase 4/3/4/3/4/3/4 sts evenly across last row – 70/81/92/103/114/125/136 sts.

Change to 4mm needles and st st. Work straight in patt from chosen chart until back measures 9/11/13½/14½/15½/16/16½in (23/28/34/37/40/41/42cm) from cast-on edge.

Shape armholes Cast off 5/6/7/8/9/10/11 sts at beginning of next 2 rows – 60/69/78/87/96/105/114 sts.**

Continue straight until armhole measures 4¾/5¾/6¾/8½/9½/10/10in (12/14/17/22/24/25/25cm) from start of armhole shaping, ending with row on wrong side.

Change to yarn for ribbing and knit 1 row, then work 5/5/7/7/7/7/7 rows k1 p1 twisted rib.
Sizes 24in and 28in (61cm and 71cm) only: Cast off right across loosely in rib.

Shape shoulders for remaining 5 sizes Cast off 11/13/14/16/17 sts in rib at beginning of next 2 rib rows, then 11/12/14/15/17 sts at beginning of following 2 rib rows; cast off remaining sts.

FRONT

Work as for back from ** to **. Continue straight in pattern until armhole measures 2½/3½/4¼/6/6¾/7/7in (6/9/11/15/17/18/18cm).

Divide for neck Next row: Patt 23/27/30/34/37/41/44, cast off next 14/15/18/19/22/23/26 sts loosely, patt 23/27/30/34/37/41/44. Continue on last set of sts, decreasing 1 st at neck edge on next 2/3/3/3/3/3/3 rows, then 1 st at this edge on following 5/5/5/6/6/7/7 alternate rows – 16/19/22/25/28/31/34 sts remain. Work straight until armhole measures same as back ending with row on right side.
Change to yarn for ribbing and purl 1 row, then work 5/5/7/7/7/7/7 rows twisted rib.
Sizes 24/28in (61/71cm) cast off right across in rib.
Shape shoulder for remaining 5 sizes Cast off 11/13/14/16/17 sts in rib at beginning of next rib row, then 11/12/14/15/17 sts at beginning of following alternate rib row. With wrong side facing,

join to remaining sts at neck edge. Finish to correspond with first side reversing shapings.

SLEEVES

With 3¼mm needles cast on 39/41/45/51/55/59/61 sts. Work 14/18/18/18/22/22/26 rows twisted rib, increasing 4/4/4/4/6/6/2 sts evenly across last row. Change to 4mm needles and patt from chart and shape sides by increasing 1 st at each end of 3rd and every following 5th/5th/4th/4th/4th/4th/4th row until there are 63/73/89/109/119/125/127 sts, taking extra sts into patt as they are made. Work straight until sleeve measures 9¾/12¼/14/17/19/19½/21½in (25/30/36/43/48/49/55cm) from cast-on edge, ending with row on wrong side.
Change to yarn for ribbing and k 1 row, then work 5/5/7/7/7/7/7 rows twisted rib. Cast off right across in rib.

NECKBAND

Join right shoulder seam. With 3¼mm needles begin at left shoulder and pick up and k 1 st for each row of knitting all around neck. Work 5/5/7/7/7/7/7 rows twisted rib. Cast off in rib.

Left shoulder opening for sizes 24/28in (61/71cm) only With 3¼mm needles pick up and k 22/24 sts across left front shoulder and up side of neck ribbing. Work 1 row in twisted rib. Make 3 buttonholes in next row thus: Rib 3/5, (cast off 2, rib 5/5) twice, cast off 2, rib 3/5.
Next row: Work in rib, casting on 2 over those cast off. Work a further 2 rows rib; cast off.
Underlap With 3¼mm needles pick up and k 22/24 sts down side of neck rib and along back of left shoulder. Work 5 rows twisted rib; cast off in rib.

FINISHING

Sizes 24/28in (61/71cm): Lap buttonhole band of shoulder opening over underlap to back; catch down double fabric at armhole edge.
Sizes 32/36/40/44/48in (81/91/102/112/122cm): Join left shoulder seam.
All sizes: Pin cast-off edge of sleeve top into armhole – the straight sides at top of sleeve to form a neat right-angle at cast-off sts of armhole on back and front; join with narrow backstitch. Join rest of sleeve and side seams. Sew on buttons if applicable.

SWEATER

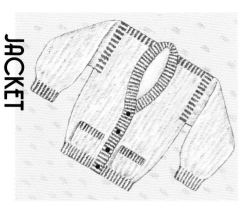

JACKET

MEASUREMENTS
Actual chest size
24/28/32/36/40/44/48in
61/71/81/91/102/112/122cm
Length to shoulder
15½/18/21½/24/25/26/27in
39/46/54/61/63/66/69cm
Sleeve seam
11¼/14/16½/19/20/21½/22in
29/36/42/49/52/56/57cm
Tension
23 sts and 30 rows measure 10cm over pattern on 4mm needles (or size needed to obtain this tension).

MATERIALS
Yarn
Rowan Designer DK, or standard double knitting wool, quantity as stated on your chosen pattern chart page
Needles
Suggested sizes
1 pair 3¼mm (US 4)
1 pair 4mm (US 6)
Notions
4/4/5/5/6/6/6 buttons

RIBBING AND POCKET LININGS
Work ribbing and pocket linings in yarn specified on pattern chart page.

BACK
With 3¼mm needles cast on 70/81/92/103/114/125/136 sts. Work 12/16/16/18/18/22/22 rows in k1 p1 rib, always going into the back of every knit stitch to give a twisted effect.
Change to 4mm needles and st st. Work straight in patt from chosen chart until back measures 9½/11/13½/15/15½/16/16½in (24/26/34/38/39/41/42cm) from cast-on edge.
Shape armholes Cast off 5/6/7/8/9/10/11 sts at beginning of next 2 rows – 60/69/78/87/96/105/114 sts. Continue straight in patt until armhole measures 6/7/8/9/9½/10/10½in (15/18/20/23/24/25/27cm) from start of shaping. Cast off right across in rib, using a bigger needle.

FRONTS
Begin by making two pocket linings. With 4mm needles cast on 18/20/20/22/24/28/30 sts. Work 2/2¾/2¾/3½/3½/4/4in (5/7/7/9/9/10/10cm) st st ending with a p row; leave sts on a spare needle.
Left front With 3¼mm needles cast on 34/40/46/52/58/64/70 sts. Work 12/16/16/18/18/22/22 rows twisted rib.
Change to 4mm needles and work straight in patt from chart for 2/2¾/2¾/3½/3½/4/4in (5/7/7/9/9/10/10cm) ending with a row on wrong side.
Introduce pocket Next row: Patt 8/10/13/15/17/18/20 sts, slip next 18/20/20/22/24/28/30 sts onto a

spare needle and in their place, patt across sts of one pocket lining, patt 8/10/13/15/17/18/20. Continue straight in patt until front measures 9/10½/13/14½/15/15½/16in (23/26/33/37/38/39/40cm) from cast-on edge, ending with a row on wrong side. Place a marker at front edge to indicate start of front shaping (A). Continue in patt, shaping front edge by decreasing 1 st at this edge on next and every following 3rd row, 11/14/17/19/21/23/25 times in all. *At the same time* when front measures 9½/11/13½/15/15½/16/16½in (24/26/34/38/39/41/42cm) from cast-on edge, ending with a row on wrong side, shape armhole thus:
Shape armhole Cast off 5/6/7/8/9/10/11 sts at beginning of next row. Keeping armhole edge straight continue to decrease 1 st at front edge on every 3rd row as before until front decreases have been done and 18/20/22/25/28/31/34 sts remain. Work straight until front measures same as back ending with a row on wrong side.
Change to 3¼mm needles and yarn for ribbing. Knit 1 row, then work 9/9/9/11/11/13/13 rows k1 p1 twisted rib. Cast off in rib using a bigger needle. Mark 4th/4th/4th/5th/5th/6th/6th row of rib at neck edge with contrast thread to indicate natural shoulder line.
Right front Work as for left, reversing all shapings.

SLEEVES
With 3¼mm needles, cast on 41/43/47/51/55/59/63 sts. Work 14/14/14/18/18/22/22 rows twisted rib. Change to 4mm needles and patt from chart, shaping sides by increasing 1 st at each end of 3rd and every following 4th row until there are 73/85/97/109/115/123/129 sts, taking extra sts into patt as they are made.
Work a few rows straight until sleeve measures 10½/13¼/15½/18/18¾/20¼/20¾in (27/34/40/46/48/52/54cm) from cast-on edge, ending with a row on wrong side. Change to yarn for ribbing and k 1 row, then work 5/7/7/7/9/9/9 rows twisted rib. Cast off right across in rib.

BUTTON BANDS AND COLLAR
Join cast-off edges of rib at top of fronts to back to form shoulder seams, leaving centre 24/29/34/37/40/43/46 cast-off sts of centre back free for back of neck. The natural shoulder line is indicated by the markers (B) each side of neck.
The following instructions are for a woman's band, i.e. buttoning right over left. For a man's, reverse instructions, reading left for right and right for left.
Left With 3¼mm needles cast on 20/23/25/29/30/34/35 sts. Work 1 row twisted rib, place a coloured marker at end of this row to indicate natural shoulder line (B)**. Continue in twisted rib, casting on 7/7/8/8/8/8/8 sts at beginning of next and following 5/6/6/7/8/8/9 alternate rows, then 11/11/12/12/8/12/8 sts at beginning of following alternate row – 73/83/93/105/110/118/123 sts.
Next row: Work in twisted rib.
Take hold of left front and on to same needle pick up and k 1 st for each row from contrast marker A at start of front shaping to cast-on edge.** Work a further 12/14/14/16/18/18/20 rows twisted rib over all sts. Cast off in rib.
Right With 3¼mm needles cast on 20/23/25/29/30/34/35 sts. Work 2 rows twisted rib. Continue as for left side from ** to **. Continue as follows: Work 7/9/9/11/13/13/15 rows rib over all sts.
Next row: Make 4/4/5/5/6/6/6 buttonholes beginning first buttonhole after 4 sts have been worked from lower edge, last buttonhole 4 sts from top edge and remainder spaced evenly between. Cast off 3 sts for each buttonhole.
Next row: Work in rib, casting on 3 sts over those cast off.

Work a further 3 rows in rib; cast off in rib.

POCKET TOPS
With 3¼mm needles k across 18/20/20/22/24/28/30 sts of pocket top increasing 3 sts evenly across row. Work 5/7/7/7/9/9/9 rows twisted rib. Cast off in rib.

FINISHING
Pin cast-off edge of sleeve top into armhole – the straight sides at top of sleeve to form a neat right-angle at cast-off sts of armhole on back and front. Sew in place on wrong side with narrow backstitch. Join rest of sleeve seam. Join collar at back of neck with edge to edge seam on under-side. Join shaped edge of collar from centre back of neck, alongside rib at shoulder matching con-trast markers (B), and down left front to start of front edge shaping, with edge to edge seam. Join right side to match. Join sides of pocket tops to main work; catch down pocket linings. Fold back shawl collar and press lightly. Sew on buttons.

If you like the sophisticated city look, try making the black fleck and pink style Wandering line jacket.

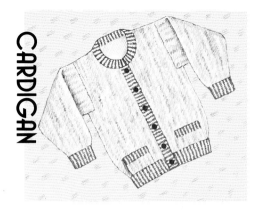

CARDIGAN

MEASUREMENTS
Actual chest size
24/28/32/36/40/44/48in
61/71/81/91/102/112/122cm
Length to shoulder
14½/17½/20½/23/23½/24½/25in
37/45/52/58/60/62/63cm
Sleeve seam
11/13½/16/18/19/19/19½in
28/33/40/46/48/48/49cm
Tension
23 sts and 30 rows measure 10cm over pattern on 4mm needles (or size needed to obtain this tension).

MATERIALS
Yarn
Rowan Designer DK, or standard double knitting wool, quantity as stated on your chosen pattern chart page
Needles
Suggested sizes
1 pair 3¼mm (US 4)
1 pair 4mm (US 6)
Notions
6/6/7/7/7/8/8 buttons

RIBBING AND POCKET LININGS
Make ribbing and pocket linings in yarn specified on pattern chart page.

BACK
With 3¼mm needles cast on 70/81/92/103/114/125/136 sts. Work 14/18/18/22/22/26/26 rows in k1 p1 rib, always going into the back of every knit stitch to give a twisted effect.
Change to 4mm needles and st st. Work straight in patt from chosen chart until back measures 8½/10½/12½/14½/14½/14½/14½in (22/27/32/37/37/37/37cm) from cast-on edge.
Shape armholes Cast off 5/6/7/8/9/10/11 sts at beginning of next 2 rows – 60/69/78/87/96/105/114 sts. Continue straight in patt until armhole measures 6/7/8/8½/9/10/10½in (15/18/20/21/23/25/26cm) from start of shaping ending with a row on wrong side.
Shape shoulders Cast off 8/10/11/13/14/16/17 sts at beginning of next 2 rows, then 8/9/11/12/14/15/17 sts at beginning of following 2 rows; leave remaining sts on a spare needle.

FRONTS
Begin by making two pocket linings. With 4mm needles cast on 18/20/20/22/24/28/30 sts. Work 1¼/1½/1½/2/2/2/2in (3/4/4/5/5/5/5cm) st st ending with a p row; leave sts on a spare needle.
Left front With 3¼mm needles cast on 34/40/46/52/58/64/70 sts. Work 14/18/18/22/22/26/26 rows k1 p1 twisted rib.
Change to 4mm needles and work straight in patt

from chart for 1¼/1½/1½/2/2/2/2in (3/4/4/5/5/5/5cm) ending with a row on wrong side.
Introduce pocket Next row: Patt 8/10/13/15/17/18/20 sts, slip next 18/20/20/22/24/28/30 sts onto a spare needle and in their place patt across 18/20/20/22/24/28/30 sts of one pocket lining, patt 8/10/13/15/17/18/20. Continue straight in patt until front measures 8½/10½/12½/14½/14½/14½/14½in (22/27/32/37/37/37/37cm) from cast-on edge.
Shape armhole Cast off 5/6/7/8/9/10/11 sts at beginning of next row. Continue straight in patt for 3½/4/4¾/5¼/5½/6½/6¾in (9/10/12/14/15/16/18cm) ending with row on right side.
Shape neck Cast off 3/4/5/6/6/7/7 sts at beginning of next row, then decrease 1 st at this edge on following 10/11/12/13/15/16/17 rows. Work straight until front measures same as back ending with same patt row and ending with a row on wrong side.
Shape shoulder Cast off 8/10/11/13/14/16/17 sts at beginning of next row then 8/9/11/12/14/15/17 sts at beginning of following alternate row.
Right front Work as for left front reversing all shapings.

SLEEVES
With 3¼mm needles cast on 35/37/41/47/51/55/59 sts. Work 14/18/18/22/22/22/26 rows twisted rib, increase 2 sts evenly across last row – 37/39/43/49/53/57/61 sts.
Change to 4mm needles and st st. Work in patt from chart, shaping sides by increasing 1 st at each end of 3rd and every following 4th row until there are 67/79/89/97/103/113/119 sts, taking extra sts into patt as they are made. Work straight until sleeve measures 11/13½/16/18/20/20½/22½in (28/33/40/46/51/52/57cm) from cast-on edge. Cast off right across using a bigger needle.

BUTTON BANDS
The following instructions are for a woman's band, i.e. buttoning right over left. For a man's, reverse instructions, reading left for right and right for left.
Left With 3¼mm needles begin at cast-off edge of neck shaping and pick up and k 1 st for each row down left front to lower edge. Work 7/7/9/9/9/9/9 rows twisted rib. Cast off in rib.
Right Begin at lower edge and pick up same number of sts up to start of neck shaping as for left band. Work 3 rows twisted rib. Make 6/6/7/7/7/8/8 buttonholes in next row beginning first buttonhole after 4 sts have been worked from lower edge, last buttonhole 4 sts from top edge and remainder spaced evenly between. Cast off 3 sts for each buttonhole.
Next row: Work in rib, casting on sts to replace those cast off in previous row. Work a further 2/2/4/4/4/4/4 rows rib; cast off in rib.

NECKBAND
Join shoulder seams with narrow backstitch.
With 3¼mm needles beginning halfway across top edge of right front band, pick up and k 1 st for each row of knitting along ribbed border and up side of neck to shoulder, k 28/31/34/37/40/43/46 sts from back of neck, pick up and k 1 st for each row of knitting down left side of neck and along to halfway across top edge of left front band. Work 7/7/9/9/9/9/9 rows twisted rib; cast off in rib.

POCKET TOPS
With 3¼mm needles k across pocket top sts increasing 2 sts in centre. Work 5/7/7/7/7/7/7 rows twisted rib. Cast off in rib.

FINISHING
Pin cast-off edge of sleeve top into armhole – the straight sides at top of sleeve to form a neat right-angle at cast-off sts of armhole on back and front. Sew in place on wrong side with narrow backstitch. Join rest of sleeve and side seams. Catch down sides of pocket tops; sew sides of pocket linings to main work. Sew on buttons.

An old fashioned design can look great. Our picture shows a cardigan in the Lavender style; this is the silver variation, but it will be a golden possession.

SLIPOVER

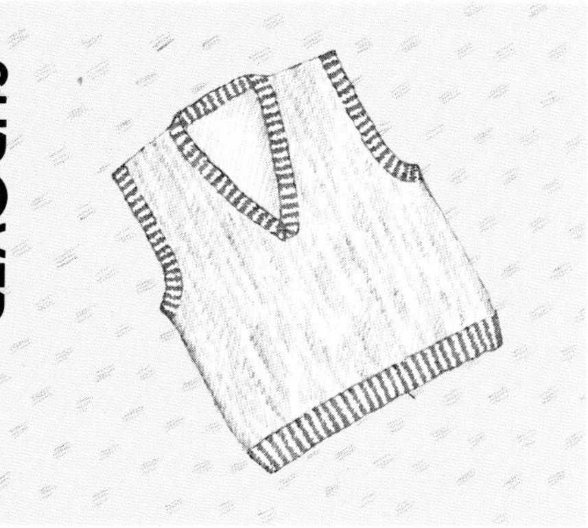

MEASUREMENTS
Actual chest size
24/28/32/36/40/44/48in
61/71/81/91/102/112/122cm
Length to shoulder
14/17/21½/23/24½/26/27in
36/43/55/58/62/66/69cm
Tension
23 sts and 30 rows measure 10cm over pattern on 4mm needles (or size needed to obtain this tension).

MATERIALS
Yarn
Rowan Designer DK, or standard double knitting wool, quantity as stated on your chosen pattern chart page
Needles
Suggested sizes
1 pair 3¼mm (US 4)
1 pair 4mm (US 6)

RIBBING
Work ribbing in yarn specified on pattern chart page.

BACK
With 3¼mm needles cast on 66/77/88/99/110/121/132 sts. Work 16/16/16/20/20/24/24 rows k1 p1 rib always going into the back of every knit stitch to give a twisted effect. Increase 4 sts evenly across last row – 70/81/92/103/114/125/136 sts. Change to 4mm needles and st st. Work straight in pattern from chosen chart until back measures 7/8½/12/13/14/15/15½in (*18/22/30/33/35/38/39cm*) from cast-on edge.
Shape armholes Cast off 6/7/8/10/11/12/13 sts at beginning of next 2 rows, then k2 tog at each end of next and following 4/6/7/7/7/7/8 alternate rows – 48/53/60/67/76/85/92 sts remain. Work straight until armhole measures 7/8½/9½/10/10½/11/11½in (*18/22/24/25/27/28/29cm*), ending with a row on wrong side.
Shape shoulders Cast off 7/8/9/10/11/13/14 sts at beginning of next 2 rows, then 6/7/8/9/10/11/13 sts at beginning of following 2 rows; leave remaining 22/23/26/29/34/37/38 sts on a spare needle.

FRONT
Work as for back from ** to **.
Shape armholes and neck Cast off 6/7/8/10/11/12/13 sts at beginning of next 2 rows.
Next row: K2 tog, k 24/29/33/37/41/46/50, k2 tog, turn and leave remaining sts on a spare needle.
Next row: Purl.
Next row: K2 tog, pattern to end.
Next row: Purl.
Continue thus decreasing 1 st at armhole edge on next and following 2/4/5/5/5/5/5 alternate rows then keep armhole edge straight. *At the same time* decrease 1 st at neck edge on next and every following 4th row until 13/15/17/19/21/24/27 sts remain. Work a few rows straight until front measures same as back, ending with row on wrong side.
Shape shoulder Cast off 7/8/9/10/11/13/14 sts at beginning of next row, then 6/7/8/9/10/11/13 sts at beginning of following alternate row. Return to remaining sts, slip centre 2/1/2/1/2/1/2 sts on a spare needle, join yarn to last 28/33/37/41/45/50/54 sts at neck edge, k2 tog, patt to last 2 sts, k2 tog. Finish to correspond with first side, reversing shapings.

NECKBAND
Join right shoulder seam with narrow backstitch on wrong side. With 3¼mm needles begin at left shoulder and pick up and k one st for each row of knitting down left side of neck (must be an even number), place contrast marker, k 2/1/2/1/2/1/2 sts from holder at front, place marker, pick up and k one st for each row of knitting up right side of neck to shoulder (must be an even number), k 22/23/26/29/34/37/38 sts from spare needle at back.
Row 1: Work in twisted rib beginning with p1 to within 2 sts of contrast thread, slip 1, k1, psso, p 2/1/2/1/2/1/2 centre sts, k2 tog, rib to end.
Row 2: Rib to within 2 sts of marker, slip 1, k1, psso, k 2/1/2/1/2/1/2 centre sts, k2 tog, rib to end.
Repeat these 2 rows once/once/twice/twice/twice/twice/twice more, then row 1 again. Cast off in rib, taking 2 sts together each side of markers as before.

ARMBANDS
Join left shoulder seam. With 3¼mm needles pick up and k one st for each row of knitting around each armhole. Work 5/5/7/7/7/7/7 rows twisted rib. Cast off in rib.

FINISHING
Join side seams.

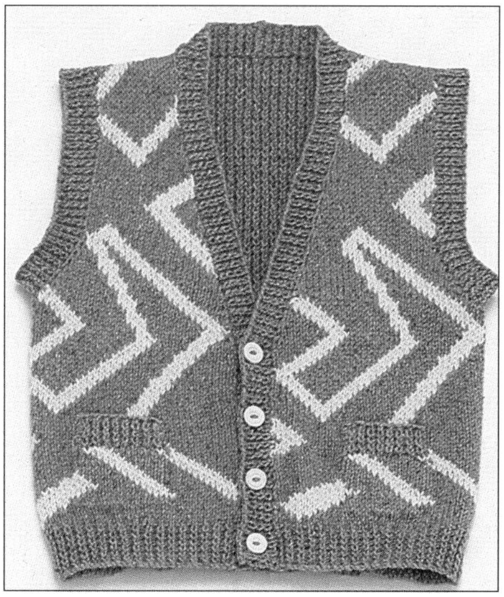

A waistcoat in the Wandering line style is simple to knit. Shown is the gray version but any contrasting colours will look exciting.

WAISTCOAT

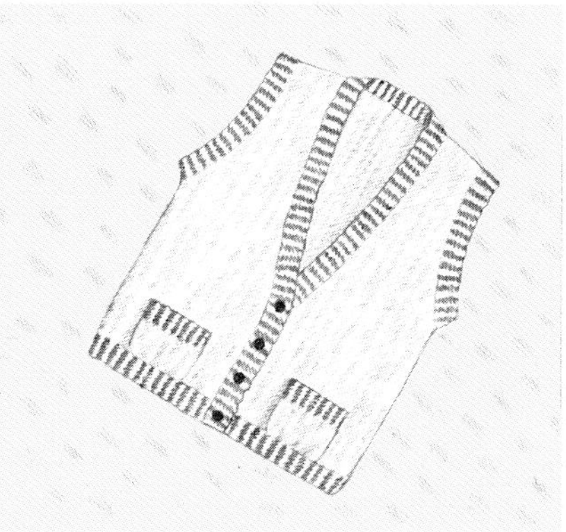

MEASUREMENTS
Actual chest size
24/28/32/36/40/44/48in
61/71/81/91/102/112/122cm)
Length to shoulder
13½/16/19½/22/23½/24½/25½in
34/41/49/56/59/62/65cm
Tension
23 sts and 30 rows measure 10cm over pattern on 4mm needles (or size needed to obtain this tension).

MATERIALS
Yarn
Rowan Designer DK, or standard double knitting wool, quantity as stated on your chosen pattern chart page
Needles
Suggested sizes
1 pair 3¼mm (US 4)
1 pair 4mm (US 6)
Notions
4/4/5/5/5/5/5 buttons

RIBBING AND POCKET LINING
Work ribbing and pocket linings in yarn specified on pattern chart page.

BACK
With 3¼mm needles cast on 81/93/105/117/129/141/153 sts. Work 10/12/12/16/16/20/20 rows k1 p1 rib, always going into the back of every knit st to give a twisted effect.
Change to 4mm needles and continue straight in twisted rib until back measures 7/8½/11½/13/13½/14/14½in (*18/22/29/33/34/36/37cm*) from cast-on edge.
Shape armholes Cast off 4/5/6/7/8/9/10 sts at beginning of next 2 rows then decrease 1 st at each end of next and every following alternate row 6 times – 61/71/81/91/101/111/121 sts remain. Continue straight until armhole measures 6½/7½/8/9/10/10½/11in (*17/19/20/23/25/27/28cm*) from start of shaping.
Shape shoulders Cast off 8/9/11/12/14/15/17 sts at beginning of next 2 rows, then 7/9/10/12/13/15/16 sts at beginning of following 2 rows; leave remaining 31/35/39/43/47/51/55 sts on a spare needle, marking centre stitch with contrast thread.

FRONTS
Begin by making 2 pocket linings. **With 4mm needles cast on 15/15/17/19/19/23/23 sts. Work 1¼/1½/1½/2½/2½/2½/2½in (*3/4/4/6/6/6/6cm*) st st ending with a p row; leave sts on a spare needle.
Left front With 3¼mm needles cast on 33/39/45/51/57/63/69 sts. Work 10/12/12/16/16/20/20 rows twisted rib, increasing 2 sts in centre of last row – 35/41/47/53/59/65/71 sts.
Change to 4mm needles and st st. Work straight in

pattern from chosen chart for 1¼/1½/1½/2½/2½/2½/2½in (*3/4/4/6/6/6/6cm*), ending with a row on wrong side.**

Introduce pocket Next row: Right side facing, patt 10/13/15/17/20/21/24, slip next 15/15/17/19/19/23/23 sts on a spare needle and in their place patt across sts of one pocket lining, patt 10/13/15/17/20/21/24. Work straight in patt until front measures 6¼/7½/10/11/11½/11½/11¾in (*16/19/26/28/29/29/30cm*) from cast-on edge ending with a row on wrong side. Place a marker at front edge.

Shape front Next row: Patt to last 2 sts, k2 tog. Work 3 rows straight. Continue in patt thus decreasing 1 st at front edge on next and every following 4th row. *At the same time* when front measures 7/8½/11½/13/13½/14/14½in (*18/22/29/33/34/36/37cm*) from cast-on edge, shape armhole as follows:

Shape armhole Cast off 4/5/6/7/8/9/10 sts at beginning of next row, then decrease 1 st at armhole edge on following 6 alternate rows. Now keep armhole edge straight but continue to decrease at front edge as before on every 4th row until 13/16/19/22/25/28/31 sts remain. Work a few rows straight until front measures same as back to shoulder shaping ending with row on wrong side.

Shape shoulder Cast off 7/8/10/11/13/14/16 sts at beginning of next row then 6/8/9/11/12/14/15 sts at beginning of following alternate row.

Right front Work as for left front reversing all shapings.

BUTTON BANDS

Join shoulder seams with narrow backstitch on wrong side.

The following instructions are for a woman's band, i.e. buttoning right over left. For a man's, reverse instructions, reading left for right and right for left.

Left With right side facing and 3¼mm needles, begin at centre back of neck, k 15/17/19/21/23/25/27 sts across left half of back of neck, pick up and k 1 st for each row evenly down left front to lower edge. Work 7/7/7/9/9/9/9 rows twisted rib. Cast off in rib.

Right In the same way begin at lower edge and pick up and k the same number of sts as left band up to shoulder, k remaining 16/18/20/22/24/26/28 sts from right half of neck at back. Work 3 rows twisted rib. Make 4/4/5/5/5/5/5 buttonholes in next row, beginning first buttonhole after 4 sts have been worked from lower edge, last buttonhole at marker and remainder spaced evenly between. Cast off 3 sts for each buttonhole.

Next row: Work in twisted rib, casting on 3 over those cast off in previous row. Work a further 2/2/4/4/4/4/4 rows twisted rib; cast off in rib.

ARMBANDS

With 3¼mm needles pick up and k 1 st for each row evenly around each armhole. Work 5/5/5/7/7/7/7 rows twisted rib. Cast off in rib.

POCKET TOPS

With 3¼mm needles k across 15/15/17/19/19/23/23 pocket top sts, increasing 2 sts in centre. Work 5/5/5/7/7/7/7 rows twisted rib, cast off in rib.

FINISHING

Join side seams; join rib at back of neck. Catch down sides of pocket tops; sew linings to main work. Sew on buttons.

SHORT TOP

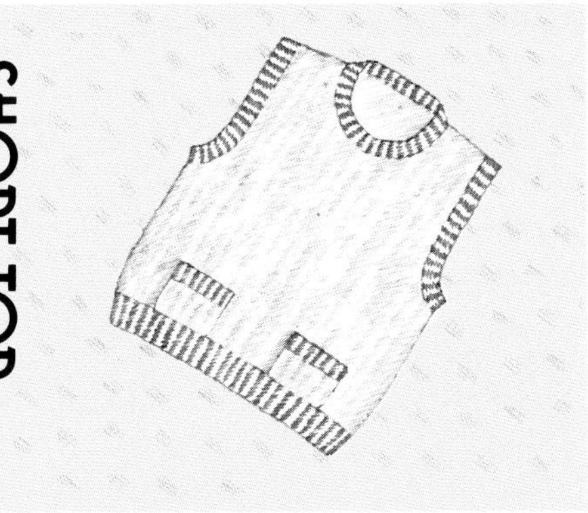

MEASUREMENTS

Actual chest size
24/28/32/36/40/44/48in
61/71/81/91/102/112/122cm

Length to shoulder
13/14½/16/17½/19/20/21in
33/37/40/44/48/51/53cm

Tension
23 sts and 30 rows measure 10cm over pattern on 4mm needles (or size needed to obtain this tension).

MATERIALS

Yarn
Rowan Designer DK, or standard double knitting wool, quantity as stated on your chosen pattern chart page

Needles
Suggested sizes
1 pair 3¼mm (US 4)
1 pair 4mm (US 6)

RIBBING AND POCKET LININGS

Work ribbing and pocket linings in yarn specified on pattern chart page.

BACK

**With 3¼mm needles cast on 70/81/92/103/114/125/136 sts. Work 12/12/12/16/16/16/16 rows in k1 p1 rib, always going into the back of every knit st to give a twisted effect.

Change to 4mm needles and st st.** Work straight in patt from chosen chart until back measures 7/8/9/10/11/11½/12in (*18/20/23/25/28/29/30cm*) from cast-on edge.

Shape armholes Cast off 3/4/4/5/5/6/6 sts at beginning of next 2 rows, then k2 tog at each end of every following alternate row until 54/63/72/81/90/99/108 sts remain. Work straight until armhole measures 6/6½/7/7½/8/8½/9in (*15/16/18/19/20/21/23cm*) from start of shaping, ending with a row on wrong side.

Shape shoulders Cast off 7/9/10/11/12/14/15 sts at beginning of next 2 rows, then 7/8/9/11/12/13/15 sts at beginning of following 2 rows; leave remaining 26/29/34/37/42/45/48 sts on a spare needle.

FRONT

Begin by making 2 pocket linings. With 4mm needles cast on 15/15/17/19/19/23/23 sts. Work 1½/1½/1½/2½/2½/2½/2½in (*4/4/4/6/6/6/6cm*) st st ending with a p row; leave sts on a spare needle.

With 3¼mm needles cast on 70/81/92/103/114/125/136 sts. Work as for back from ** to **. Continue straight in patt from chart for 1½/1½/1½/2½/2½/2½/2½in (*4/4/4/6/6/6/6cm*) ending with a purl row.

Introduce pockets Next row: Right side facing, patt 10/12/14/16/19/20/22, slip next 15/15/17/19/19/23/23 sts onto a spare needle and in their place, patt across 15/15/17/19/19/23/23 sts of one pocket lining, patt 20/27/30/33/38/39/46 sts, slip next 15/15/17/19/19/23/23 sts onto 2nd spare needle, patt across sts of 2nd pocket lining, patt to end.

Work straight until front measures same as back to start of armhole shaping.

Shape armholes Cast off 3/4/4/5/5/6/6 sts at beginning of next 2 rows then k2 tog at each end of every following alternate row until 54/63/72/81/90/99/108 sts remain. Work straight until front measures 2/2¼/3½/4/4¼/4¾/5in (*5/6/9/10/11/12/13cm*) from start of armhole shaping.

Divide for neck Next row: Patt 23/26/28/31/34/37/40, turn and leave remaining sts on a spare needle. Continue on first set of sts decreasing 1 st at neck edge on next 3/3/3/3/4/4/4 rows, then at this edge on following 6 alternate rows – 14/17/19/22/24/27/30 sts remain. Work straight until front measures same as back to start of shoulder shaping, ending with same pattern row.

Shape shoulder Cast off 7/9/10/11/12/14/15 sts at beginning of next row, then 7/8/9/11/12/13/15 sts at beginning of following alternate row. Leave centre 8/11/16/19/22/25/28 sts on a spare needle. Join yarn to last 23/26/28/31/34/37/40 sts at neck edge. Finish to correspond with first side reversing shapings.

NECKBAND

Join right shoulder seam with narrow backstitch on wrong side. With 3¼mm needles begin at left shoulder and pick up and k 1 st for each row down left side of neck, k 8/11/16/19/22/25/28 sts from spare needle at centre front, pick up and k 1 st for each row up right side of neck, k 26/29/34/37/42/45/48 sts from back of neck. Work 5/5/7/7/7/7/7 rows twisted rib; cast off in rib.

ARMBANDS

Join left shoulder seam as before. With 3¼mm needles pick up and k 1 st for each row evenly around each armhole. Work 5/5/7/7/7/7/7 rows twisted rib; cast off in rib.

POCKET TOPS

With 3¼mm needles k across 15/15/17/19/19/23/23 pocket top sts, increasing 2 sts in centre. Work 5/5/7/7/7/7/7 rows twisted rib; cast off in rib.

FINISHING

Join side seams as before. Sew down sides of pocket tops to main work; catch down pocket linings on wrong side.

BASIC TECHNIQUES

The information on the following pages will tell you all you need to know to make the sweaters in the book as well as helping you to design your own patterns.

The instructions are written and illustrated for right-handed knitters. If you are left-handed, reverse any instructions for left and right, or prop the book up in front of a mirror and follow the diagrams in reverse.

CASTING ON

Placing the first row of stitches on the needles is known as "casting on". All further rows are worked into these initial loops. Casting on can be done in a number of ways, but when you are casting on to work a welt in twisted rib, cast on into the back of the stitch.

A slip loop is the first stitch to be made and is the foundation for all the subsequent stitches.

MAKING A SLIP LOOP

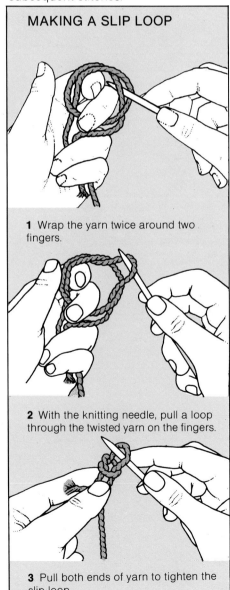

1 Wrap the yarn twice around two fingers.

2 With the knitting needle, pull a loop through the twisted yarn on the fingers.

3 Pull both ends of yarn to tighten the slip loop.

CASTING ON WITH TWO NEEDLES

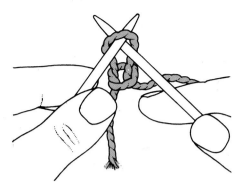

1 With the slip loop on your left-hand needle, insert your right-hand needle through the loop from front to back.

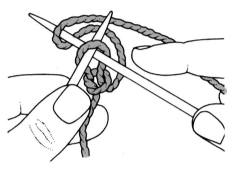

2 Bring the yarn under and over your right-hand needle.

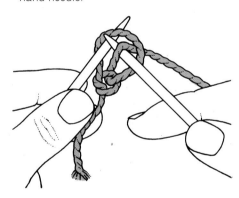

3 Draw up the yarn through the slip loop to make a stitch.

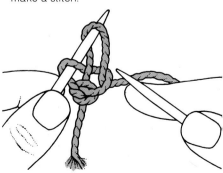

4 Place stitch on left-hand needle. Make more stitches in same way, drawing yarn through last stitch on left-hand needle.

CASTING ON WITH ONE NEEDLE

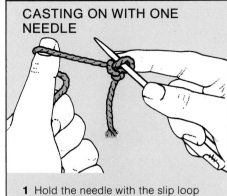

1 Hold the needle with the slip loop in the right hand. Wrap the working end of the yarn around the left thumb and hold it in the left palm, ready to begin casting on.

2 Put the needle through the yarn behind the thumb. Slip the thumb out of the yarn and pull the working end of the yarn to secure the new stitch.

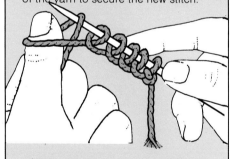

3 Repeat these steps until the required number of stitches has been cast on.

WINDING WOOL

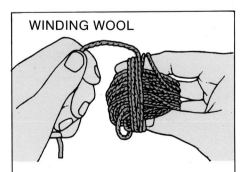

To form a ball with the working end on top, unwrap yarn from a hank and wind tightly over three fingers. Remove the coils, change the position and continue winding to form a ball.

CASTING ON INTO THE BACK OF THE STITCH

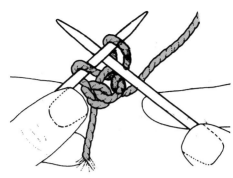

1 Begin by following steps 1 to 4 of casting on with two needles as far as the asterisk. Put the right-hand needle between the slip loop and the first stitch.

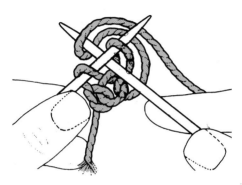

2 Wrap the working yarn under and over the right-hand needle.

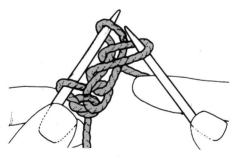

3 Draw the right-hand needle through to form a new stitch.

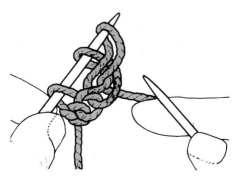

4 Place the new stitch on the left-hand needle. Continue until the required number of stitches has been cast on.

HOLDING NEEDLES AND YARN

The way in which you hold your knitting will affect the tension and evenness of the fabric. Threading the working end of the yarn through the fingers not only makes knitting faster, but also produces a firm, even result.

Holding a yarn in the right hand, use the right forefinger to wrap the yarn over the needles.

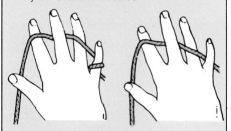

Threading the yarn
Place the working yarn through the fingers of your right hand in either of the ways shown above.

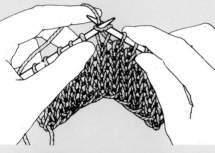

Holding yarn in the left hand
With the working yarn in your left hand, use the left forefinger to position the yarn while you move the right needle to encircle the yarn to form a new loop.

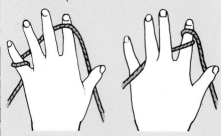

Threading the yarn
Place yarn through fingers of your left hand in either of these ways.

CASTING OFF

When you end a piece of knitting, such as a sleeve, or part of a piece of knitting, such as up to the neck, you must secure all the stitches by "casting off". This is preferably done on a knit row but you can employ the same technique on a purl row. The stitches, whether knit or purl, should be made loosely. With ribbing, you must follow the pattern, and cast off in both knit and purl.

In knit stitch

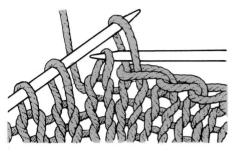

1 Knit the first two stitches and insert the tip of your left-hand needle through the first stitch.

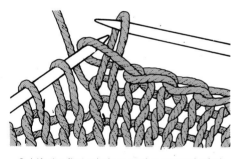

2 Lift the first stitch over the second stitch and discard it. Knit the next stitch and continue to lift the first stitch over the second stitch to the end of the row. Be careful not to knit too tightly. For the last stitch, cut your yarn, slip the end through the stitch and pull the yarn tight to fasten off securely.

In purl stitch

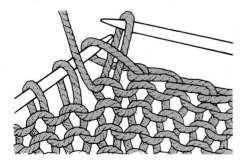

Purl the first two (and all subsequent) stitches and continue as for knit stitch above.

BASIC STITCHES

Knit stitch and purl stitch are the two basic knitting stitches. When every row is knitted back and forth on two needles, garter stitch is formed. When one row is knitted and the next purled, stocking stitch is formed. When working in the round, knitting every row produces stocking stitch. A combination of knit and purl stitches, usually one knit stitch and then one purl stitch, in the same row, is known as ribbing. Ribbing is used on sleeve and body edges to form a neat, stretchable finish. It is usually worked on smaller needles than the body of the garment.

KNIT STITCH (K)

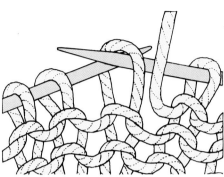

1 With the yarn at the back, insert your right-hand needle from front to back into the first stitch on your left-hand needle.

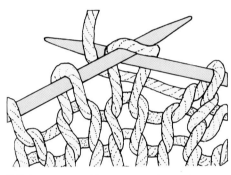

2 Bring your working yarn under and over the point of your right-hand needle.

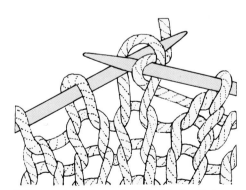

3 Draw a loop through and slide the first stitch off your left-hand needle while the new stitch is retained on your right-hand needle. Continue in this way to the end of the row.

4 To knit the next row, turn the work around so that the back is facing you and the worked stitches are held on the needle in your left hand. Proceed to make stitches as given above, with the initially empty needle held in your right hand.

PURL STITCH (P)

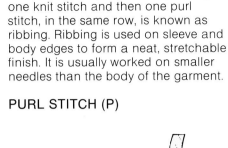

1 With the yarn at the front, insert your right-hand needle from back to front into the first stitch on your left-hand needle.

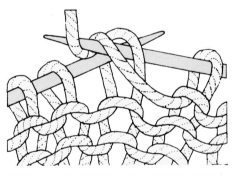

2 Bring your working yarn over and around the point of your right-hand needle.

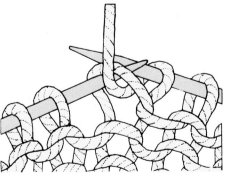

3 Draw a loop through and slide the first stitch off your left-hand needle while the new stitch is retained on your right-hand needle. Continue in this way to the end of the row.

4 To purl the next row, turn the work around so that the back is facing you and the worked stitches are held on the needle in your left hand. Proceed to make stitches as given above, with the initially empty needle held in your right hand.

SINGLE RIBBING

When changing from a knit stitch to a purl stitch bring the yarn to the front. When changing from a purl stitch to a knit stitch bring the yarn to the back. Cast on an odd number of stitches.

Row 1 *Knit 1, purl 1; repeat from * to the last stitch, knit 1.
Row 2 *Purl 1, knit 1; repeat from * to the last stitch, purl 1.
Repeat rows 1 and 2 until the rib is the required length.

DOUBLE RIBBING

When changing from a knit stitch to a purl stitch bring the yarn to the front. When changing from a purl stitch to a knit stitch bring the yarn to the back. Cast on a multiple of 4 stitches, plus 2.

Row 1 *Knit 2, purl 2; repeat from * to the last 2 sts, knit 2.
Row 2 *Purl 2, knit 2; repeat from * to the last 2 sts, purl 2.
Repeat rows 1 and 2 until the rib is the required length.

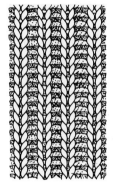 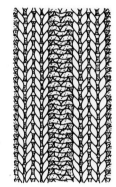

Single rib   **Double rib**

TWISTED RIBBING

This is worked in almost the same way as ordinary ribbing, except that the right-hand needle is put into the *back* of the knit stitch instead of the front.

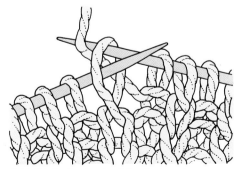

1 Knit into the back of the first and every knit stitch.

2 Purl in the ordinary way.

3 Work back across the following rows in the same way, beginning every row with a knit stitch, unless instructed otherwise in the pattern.

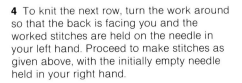

TENSION

At the beginning of every pattern is a tension measurement, such as *28 sts and 28 rows measure 10cm over pattern on 3¾mm needles.*

Basically this tension measurement tells you how large the stitches are on the garment, so that you can match the size and thus produce a garment of the correct size. However since one stitch is too small to be measured accurately, the tension measurement states how many stitches (and rows) there are over ten centimetres. Unless you match the tension exactly, your garment will not be the correct size.

Four factors affect the tension measurement: needle size, stitch pattern, yarn and you, the knitter. The combination of these things determines the size of the stitch.

Needle size

Larger needles produce larger stitches and smaller needles produce smaller stitches. The needle size given in the tension measurement should only be used as a guide – you have to match the *tension* exactly, not the *needle size*.

Stitch pattern

Different stitch patterns produce different tensions, even when the needle size, yarn and knitter are the same. Therefore you must check your tension each time you embark on a new pattern, using the stitch pattern specified.

Yarn

Patterns worked in finer yarns have more stitches and rows to the centimetre than those worked in thicker yarns. It is very important to check your tension when substituting a different yarn, or when patterns give yarn types, rather than brand names.

The knitter

Even when using identical yarn, needles and stitch pattern, two knitters may not produce knitting at the same tension, because individual knitters knit at different tensions. The tension measurement given in the pattern is that produced by the designer of the garment. It is imperative that this tension is matched, however it should *not* be done by deliberately knitting more tightly or more loosely, but by changing to a larger or smaller needle size. If larger or smaller needles are used in the pattern for other parts of the garment, such as the rib, these must be adjusted accordingly.

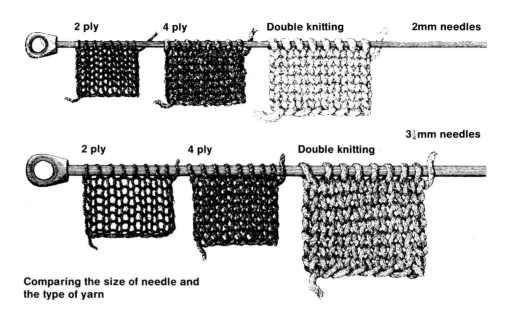

Comparing the size of needle and the type of yarn

MAKING A TENSION SAMPLE

1 Using the same yarn, needles and stitch pattern called for in the pattern instructions, knit a sample slightly larger than 10cm square.

2 Block the sample as the finished garment would be blocked.

3 Place the sample the right way up on a flat surface, being careful not to stretch it.

4 To measure the number of stitches, place a rigid ruler horizontally across the bottom of a row of stitches. Use pins to mark the beginning and end of a 10cm measurement. Count the number of stitches between the pins, including any half stitches. This gives you the figure for the stitch tension of the sample.

5 To measure the number of rows, place a rigid ruler vertically along one side of a column of stitches. Using pins, mark out a 10cm measurement. Count the number of rows between the pins to give the figure for the row tension of the sample.

6 If you produce fewer stitches and rows than given in the tension measurement then your knitting is too loose and you should make another tension sample using smaller needles.

7 If you produce more stitches and rows than given in the tension measurement then your knitting is too tight and you should make another tension sample using larger needles.

8 Repeat the process on different sized needles until you match the number of stitches and rows given in the tension measurement. As a general rule, changing the needles one size larger or one size smaller makes a difference of one stitch every five centimetres.

9 Changing your needle size is normally sufficient to adjust the dimensions. However, occasionally it is impossible to match both stitch and row tension. In such cases use a needle size so that you have the correct *stitch* tension, and work more or fewer rows to adjust the length.

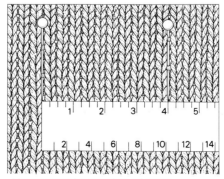

Measuring the number of rows

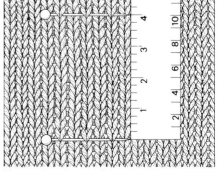

Measuring the number of stitches

CORRECTING MISTAKES

Occasionally you may drop a stitch – especially if you leave off working in the middle of a row – or make a mistake. The techniques given below show how to rectify such problems.

Picking up a dropped knit stitch

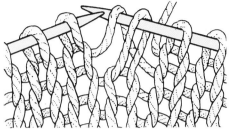

1 Pick up both the stitch and strand on your right-hand needle, inserting the needle from front to back.

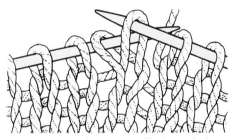

2 Insert your left-hand needle through the stitch only, from back to front. With your right-hand needle only, pull the strand through the stitch to make the extra stitch. (Drop the stitch from your left-hand needle.)

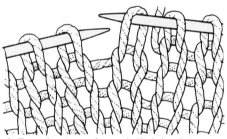

3 Transfer the re-formed stitch back to your left-hand needle, so that it untwists and faces the correct way. It is now ready for knitting again.

Picking up a dropped purl stitch

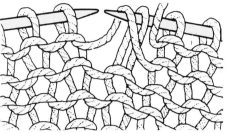

1 Pick up both the stitch and strand on your right-hand needle, inserting the needle from back to front.

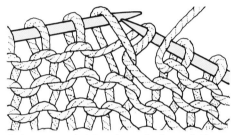

2 Insert your left-hand needle through the stitch only, from front to back. With your right-hand needle only, pull the strand through the stitch to make the extra stitch. (Drop the stitch from your left-hand needle.)

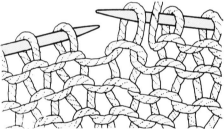

3 Transfer the re-formed stitch back to your left-hand needle, so that it untwists and faces the correct way. It is now ready for purling again.

PICKING UP STITCHES

Occasionally you will come across instructions telling you to pick up a certain number of stitches. Sometimes you have to do this along a straight edge, at other times you have to pick up around a curve.

The number of stitches you pick up does not necessarily correspond with the number of rows in the edge along which you are picking up stitches.

For a stronger, neater finish, pick up stitches from the last line of knitting before the cast-off edge or side selvedge.

Always pick up stitches with right side of work facing you.

To space stitches neatly on a curved edge, divide the edge into small sections by placing pins at regular intervals along it. Divide the number of stitches needed by the number of sections, then pick up this number from each section.

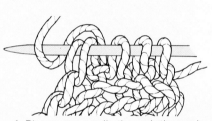

1 Place your needle through the work one stitch in from the edge and bring the yarn around as if knitting the stitch.

2 Pull the yarn through the stitch from the main work, to make a stitch.

LADDERS

If a dropped stitch is left, it can unravel downwards and form a "ladder". In such a case it is easiest to use a crochet hook to pick up the stitches in pattern. If you make a mistake in your knitting, you may have to "unpick" a stitch, in which case a ladder may result. Pick up one dropped stitch at a time, securing any others with a safety pin to prevent further unravelling. Whichever row is being worked, turn the fabric so the knit side is facing you.

Insert a crochet hook through the front of the dropped stitch. Hook up one strand and pull it through the stitch to form a new stitch one row up. Continue in this way to the top of the ladder, and then slip the last stitch from the crochet hook on to the needle.

UNPICKING MISTAKES

Knit row   **Purl row**

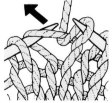 

Holding the stitch on your right-hand needle insert your left-hand needle into the row below and undo the stitch. Repeat undoing until the error has been reached.

INCREASING AND DECREASING

In order to shape knitting, you have to add (increase) or take away (decrease) stitches. Increasing and decreasing techniques are also used for certain stitch patterns, such as bobbles and lace fabrics.

Stitches can be added at the outer edges of the piece you are knitting, such as sleeve edges, or they can be added evenly across the row to give slight fullness, such as across a front or back in the last row of ribbing. There are several ways of increasing, the method shown is the most common.

There are two ways to lose stitches for shaping and these are to knit or purl two stitches together (k2 tog or p2 tog) at the beginning, end or any given point in a row, or to use the slip stitch method (sl 1). Knitting stitches together is the simpler method, but slipping stitches produces a more decorative effect on a garment. Decreases are always visible and have a definite angled slant. It is important to pair decreases so that the direction of slant for the decreases is balanced.

INCREASING IN A KNIT ROW

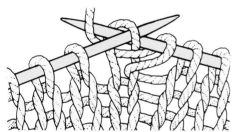

Knit into the front of the stitch in the usual way. Without discarding the stitch on your left-hand needle, knit into the back of it, making two stitches.

INCREASING IN A PURL ROW

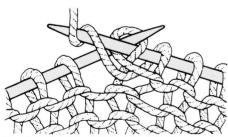

Purl into the front of the stitch in the usual way. Without discarding the stitch on your left-hand needle, purl into the back of it, making two stitches.

INCREASING AT ENDS OF ROWS

When increasing at the beginning or end of knit or purl rows, use the same technique as illustrated above, but work twice into the first or last stitch in the row.

SLIP STITCH DECREASE

Abbreviated as sl 1, k1 psso (slip one, knit one, pass slip stitch over), the decrease forms a slant to the left on

In a knit row

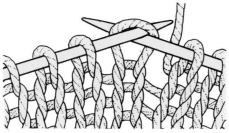

1 Insert your right-hand needle "knitwise" and lift off the first stitch from your left-hand needle.

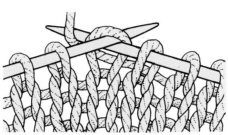

2 Leave the stitch on the needle and knit the next stitch on your left-hand needle in the usual way.

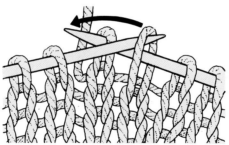

3 Using the point of your left-hand needle, bring the slipped stitch off your right-hand needle, over the knitted stitch.

KNITTING STITCHES TOGETHER

Abbreviated as k2 tog or p2 tog, the decrease forms a slant to the right if

In a knit row (k2 tog)

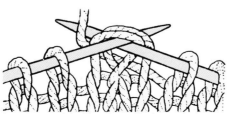

Insert your right-hand needle through the front of the first two stitches on your left-hand needle. Knit them together as a single stitch.

the front of the knitting. A slant to the right is formed on the front if it is made on the purl row – sl 1, p1, psso (slip one, purl one, pass slip stitch over).

In a purl row

1 Insert your right-hand needle "purlwise" and lift off the first stitch from your left-hand needle.

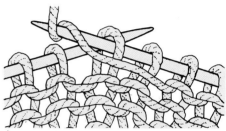

2 Leave the stitch on the needle and purl into the next stitch on your left-hand needle in the usual way.

3 Using the point of your left-hand needle, bring the slipped stitch off your right-hand needle, over the purled stitch.

the stitches are knitted together through the front, and a slant to the left if knitted together through the back.

In a purl row (p2 tog)

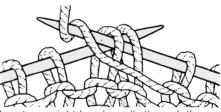

Insert your right-hand needle through the front of the first two stitches on your left-hand needle. Purl them together as a single stitch.

WORKING FROM CHARTS

All the designs in this book are given in chart form, so reading the charts correctly is essential to the successful working of the patterns. The pattern charts take the form of a black outline on a gray grid, with the different areas labelled A, B, C, etc. to correspond with the yarns. Each square on the chart represents one stitch, and each row of squares on the chart represents one row, or part of one row. The rows are numbered with odd numbers (knit rows) on the right side of the chart and even numbers (purl rows) on the left side of the chart. Stitches are numbered across the bottom. The charts are worked from bottom to top.

POSITIONING OF CHARTS

Full instructions as to how many times the pattern chart should be repeated across a garment piece, i.e. the positioning of the chart, are given alongside each chart.

Because there are so many shape and size variations for each chart, the pattern repeat of the chart (i.e. the total number of stitches across the bottom of the chart) does not usually fit exactly into each garment piece. For the majority of pattern charts this does not matter, since many of the designs are abstract and not meant to be symmetrical. For these charts, for every garment piece, you must always start your first knit row at the bottom right-hand corner of the chart (stitch 1, row 1).

However some of the larger, figurative charts have to be positioned centrally on garment pieces to ensure the design is balanced. For these charts, usually just for the back and fronts, you start your first knit row *not* at the bottom right-hand corner of the chart, instead you work part of the left of the chart first, work the required number of pattern repeats, then work part of the right of the chart. Full instructions are given with each pattern chart stating where each pattern chart should be started for each garment piece. Examples of the two ways of working pattern charts, either starting from stitch 1 or starting elsewhere for charts that need to be positioned, are given opposite.

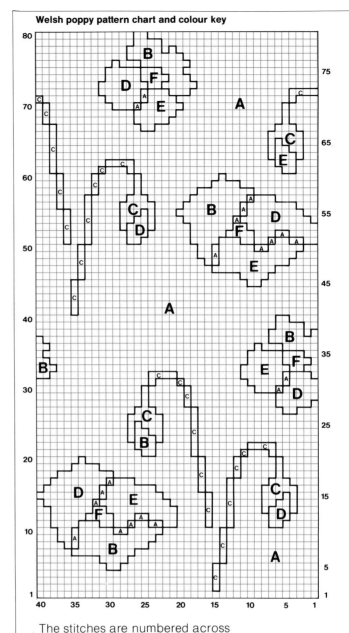

Welsh poppy pattern chart and colour key

KEY	Yellow variation
A	**Violet carmine** DDK 118
B	**Yellow** DDK 13
C	**Olive green** DDK 407
D	**Mustard** FF 14F
E	**Jonquil** B 6
F	**Moss green** DDK 605

The stitches are numbered across the bottom of the pattern chart and the rows are numbered up the side. Information stating which basic pattern instructions can be used, the method of knitting, and the yarn to use for ribbings and pocket linings appears with each chart.

TAKING EXTRA STITCHES INTO THE PATTERN

When you are working a shaped piece such as a sleeve, the side edges are shaped as you progress. Normally the stitches are increased at the side edge, and the extra stitches so made must be taken into the pattern. To do this you treat the new stitch in the same way as you would work the next stitch in the row. So if, for example, your row finished with stitch 16 of a 16 stitch pattern repeat, and you increased on stitch 16, you would work the new stitch in the same way as stitch 1 of the pattern chart.

WHERE TO START

Acorn (below) is an example of a pattern chart worked *from stitch 1*. If you were working the back of the size 44in (112cm) sweater, on knit rows work sts 1-53 three times. For purl rows you have to work back the other way, so work sts 53-1 three times. However, if you were working the back of the size 36in (91cm) sweater, on knit rows work sts 1-53 twice, then sts 1-20 once. For purl rows work sts 20-1 once, then sts 53-1 twice.

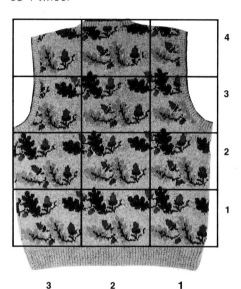

On this size garment the pattern repeats three times horizontally and four times vertically.

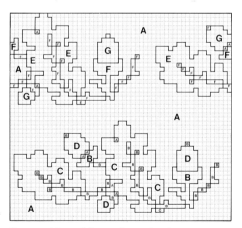

One working of the pattern chart

Poodle is an example of a pattern chart *that has to be positioned*. If you were working the back of the size 32in (81cm) sweater, on knit rows work sts 35-45 once, then sts 1-45 twice, then sts 1-12 once. In these cases instructions are also provided so that the fronts of the cardigan, jacket and waistcoat have a complete pattern repeat at both front edges.

MULTI-COLOURED KNITTING

Since most of the sweaters featured in this book are multi-coloured, there are several techniques you need to know about in order to successfully complete one of these sweaters.

There are basically two different ways of working multi-coloured garments: intarsia, and so called "Fair Isle" knitting. The intarsia method is used when knitting isolated blocks of colour, and produces a single thickness of fabric since yarns are not carried across the back of the knitting. Harlequin is knitted in this way.

The "Fair Isle" method is used when two or three colours are worked repeatedly across a row, and the yarn not in use is carried across the back of the work. Odeon and Persian stripe are worked in this way. There are two different ways of carrying the yarn across the back of the work: stranding and weaving; full details are given overleaf.

Many of Sasha's garments are knitted using a combination of both intarsia and Fair Isle, so that individual motifs are knitted using the Fair Isle method – i.e. the yarn is carried across the back of the work but only in isolated areas. Mouse is an example of this technique, which we have called "individual motif" knitting. Details are given with each pattern as to the correct method to use. It is important to follow this since the yarn quantities given are based on particular methods, and the Fair Isle method takes more yarn. More information about Fair Isle and intarsia is given overleaf.

SWISS DARNING

Although this is, strictly speaking, an embroidery stitch, it is a very useful technique to know about in order to cover up small mistakes in multi-colour knitting, or add small details such as eyes. Swiss darning involves neatly sewing over the required stitches in the correct yarn. It is most successful when worked over small areas. Full details on how to Swiss darn are given overleaf.

Reverse of garment worked in Fair Isle method

Reverse of garment worked in intarsia method

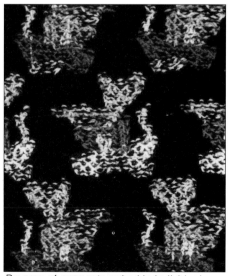

Reverse of garment worked in individual motif method

FAIR ISLE

Several of the designs in this book are all-over designs (i.e. Persian Stripe, Bavarian Flower, and Odeon), and when knitting these, the "Fair Isle" method should be used.

In Fair Isle knitting, two or more colours of yarn are worked repeatedly in the same row. The yarn that is *not* being used must be carried across the back of the knitting, ready for use when called for by the pattern chart. The way this is done can greatly influence the tension of the knitting so it must be done correctly. The two ways of carrying the yarn not in use across the back of the knitting are: stranding and weaving (see opposite).

Stranding yarn means just leaving the yarn not being used in a strand across the back of the work; weaving involves knitting so that the yarn not being used is woven into the knitting.

The strands at the back of the work must be loose enough to allow the natural "give" of knitted fabric. Every time you change colour, gently but firmly pull back the last ten or so stitches on the right-hand needle so your knitting is slightly stretched.

ADDING NEW YARN AT THE BEGINNING OF A ROW

This is the way in which you should join in the yarn if you are working striped rib, either for the welts and cuffs or when working an entire back in striped rib. It is best to carry the yarns not in use up the sides of the work until they are required again. When you have finished using a particular colour of yarn, darn the end of the yarn neatly into the work.

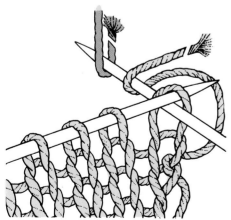

1 Insert right-hand needle through first stitch on left-hand needle and wrap the old, and then the new yarn over it. Knit (or purl) the stitch using both yarns.

INTARSIA

In order to work isolated blocks of colour, a separate ball, or length of yarn, is used for each separate colour. Any number of colours may be used in a row. Plastic bobbins, such as those shown below, can be purchased from yarn stores or made from stiff card, and are useful for keeping the working yarns separate.

In order to avoid gaps when working in intarsia it is very important to secure the colour changeover points. When you move from one colour to the next firmly twist the yarns around each other where they meet on the wrong side.

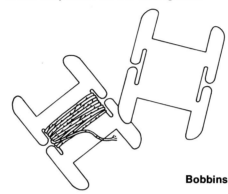

Bobbins

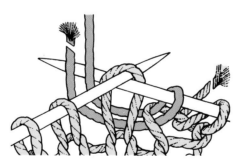

2 Leaving the old yarn at the back, knit (or purl) the next two stitches using the double length of the new yarn.

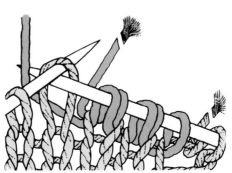

3 Discard the short end of the new yarn and continue to knit as usual. On the following row treat the three double stitches as single stitches.

ADDING NEW YARN IN THE MIDDLE OF A ROW

This method is not recommended when a colour is repeated across the row and up several rows, so it is not suitable when carrying yarn across the back of the work. In these cases you should add yarn at the beginning of a row. However it is suitable for working a small area of stitches in one colour, i.e. intarsia work.

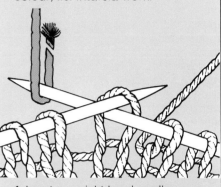

1 Insert your right-hand needle through the first stitch on your left-hand needle. Wrap the new yarn over, and knit (or purl) the stitch with the new yarn. Leave the old yarn at the back of the work.

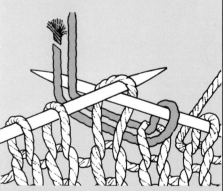

2 Knit (or purl) the next two stitches using the double length of new yarn.

3 Discard the short end of the new yarn and continue to knit as usual. On the following row, treat the two double stitches as single stitches.

CARRYING YARN ACROSS THE BACK OF THE WORK

The two following methods – stranding and weaving – are the most suitable for carrying the different colours across the rows, and both avoid holes appearing as you introduce a new colour. Weaving is the most effective, as it leaves the back of the work neat and hard-wearing, whereas stranding leaves loose yarns at the back which are easily pulled. Whether stranding or weaving try to keep your tension as close as you can to the tension given in the pattern. You may find you prefer to mix the two techniques, stranding those yarns which appear infrequently and weaving those which recur often. As a general guide, strand yarn over two to five stitches, weave yarn when it has to be carried over more than five stitches.

STRANDING YARN

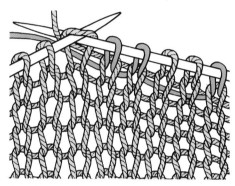

In a knit row

With both yarns at the back of the work, knit the required number of stitches with yarn A (in this case two), and then drop it to the back. Pick up yarn B and knit the required number of stitches and then drop it to the back. Both yarns should be stranded loosely along the back of the work.

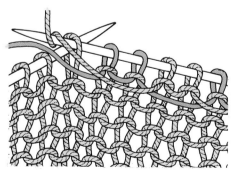

In a purl row

With both yarns at the front of the work, purl the required number of stitches with yarn A (in this case two), and then drop it. Pick up yarn B and purl the required number of stitches and then drop it. Both yarns should be stranded loosely along the front (side facing you).

WEAVING YARN

In a knit row

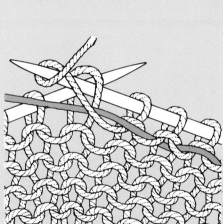

1 Hold yarn A in your right hand and yarn B in your left hand to the back of the work.

2 Knit one stitch with yarn A and, at the same time, bring yarn B below yarn A. When yarn B is being used weave yarn A as above.

In a purl row

1 Hold yarn A in your right hand and yarn B in your left hand to the front of the work.

2 Purl one stitch with yarn A but this time bring yarn B below yarn A. When yarn B is being used, weave yarn A as above.

CHECKING YOUR TECHNIQUE

To prevent the different yarns getting tangled, the strands must be caught up in the back of the work, but not so as they interfere with the pattern or produce undesired effects.

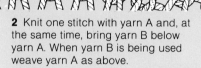

If you have worked weaving correctly, the yarns will cross evenly and remain at the same depth. A "smocking" effect means that you have pulled the yarns too tightly. It is better for the yarns to be woven too loosely than too tightly.

If you have worked stranding correctly, the yarns will be running evenly across the back of the work at the same tension as the knitting. Puckering indicates that you have pulled the yarns too tightly.

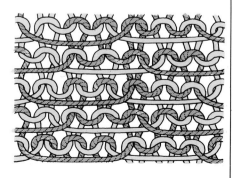

FINISHING

When you have finished all the knitting there are still several things that remain to be done before your garment is ready to be worn: blocking, pressing and sewing together.

The blocking and pressing instructions given below are for cotton and wool garments, if you have used any other yarns refer to your ball band for special instructions.

BLOCKING

Basically this just involves pinning each garment piece (or the finished garment if it is made in one piece) out on a flat surface, to the correct measurements. This pulls all the stitches into place and makes it easier to sew the pieces together. If you omit this stage, your garment will not have a professional finish.

The blocking surface can be a blanket, folded in half, or foam, covered with light-weight cotton fabric such as sheeting or gingham. Using gingham makes the process easier, since it provides straight lines and right angles to work with.

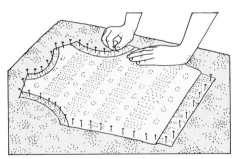

Lay the piece of knitting wrong side up on the blocking surface and gently coax it into the right shape and size. Using rustless pins, pin the knitting to the surface, spacing the pins 1-1½in (2-3cm) apart. Be careful not to stretch or distort the fabric.

PRESSING

After blocking, the garment pieces are pressed while they are pinned in position. Use a warm iron and a clean, absorbent, damp cloth on wool and cotton. Lay the iron on the fabric and lift up, do not move it over the surface. Do not press too heavily as this will flatten the knitting. Do not remove any of the pins until the piece has cooled and dried completely.

SWISS DARNING

This technique imitates knitting. It works up quickly and produces a slightly raised design as it covers, or

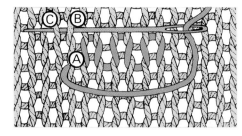

1 Secure the embroidery yarn at the back of the work and bring your needle out to the front of the work at A. Insert the needle at B, under the base of the stitch above, and bring it out at C.

duplicates, the knitted stitch. Use it to cover mistakes or to add small details or decoration at the finishing stage of your garment.

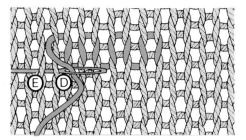

2 Insert the needle at D and emerge at E ready to embroider the next stitch.

SEWING TOGETHER

Sewing together is a most important part of making knitted garments. None of the techniques are particularly

Mattress stitch

This is the most versatile stitch. It provides a strong, invisible seam, the only real disadvantage being that it is bulky on the underside. However, it is well-suited to raglan-sleeve seams, side

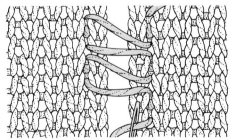

1 Place the two seam edges side by side, right side up. Thread the needle and stitch through two stitchbars, one stitch in from the edge on one side.

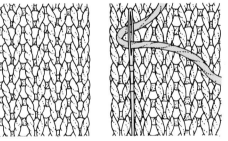

3 Without pulling the stitches taut, pick up the next two stitchbars on the first side. Then pick up the next two stitchbars on the other side, and so on.

difficult, and time and care spent on them will achieve professional looking results. Here are the various stitches you will need, and their uses.

seams, and seams that join two pieces of patterned knitting. This is because it is sewn with the right side facing, so you can match the pattern as you go. You will need a tapestry needle and some yarn.

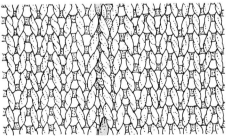

2 Pick up the two stitchbars one stitch in on the other side.

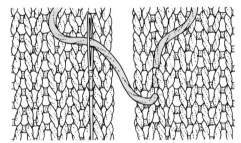

4 When the thread is zigzagged across the two seam edges about five times pull it taut – the seam will be pulled together. Continue picking up the next two stitchbars on each side in turn, pulling the thread taut after about every five stitches until the seam is complete.

Grafting

This is another seam that, if well done, is both invisible and firm. It is often used for shoulder seams or at any time when a flat seam is required. You will need a tapestry needle which you thread with the yarn remaining from the last stitch. Be sure to leave enough yarn on the work to cover the intended seam length, times three.

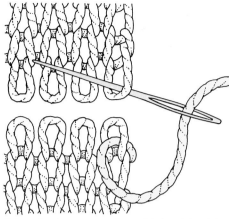

1 Lay the two seam edges side by side, right side up. Bring the needle back through the loop of the first stitch, then take the needle through the first loop on the other side.

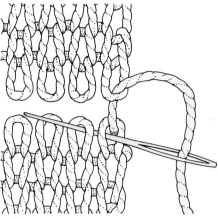

2 Stitch the needle back down through the first loop on the first side, and through the second loop on the same side.

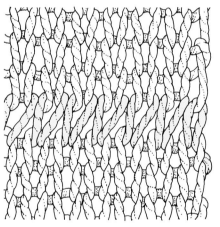

3 Take the needle through the first and second loops on the other side.

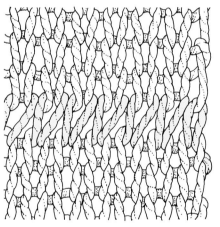

4 Repeat across the row, keeping the tension as close as you can to the tension of the two pieces you are joining.

Edge to edge seam

This produces an almost invisible seam, forms no ridge, and is the best seam to use when a hard edge must be avoided, such as joining a ribbed neckband. It is useful for joining patterned knitting, but it is not as strong as a mattress stitch seam.

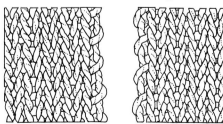

1 Place the pieces to be joined edge to edge with the heads of the knit stitches locking together. Match the pattern pieces carefully row for row and stitch for stitch.

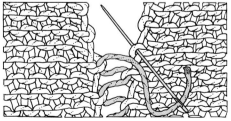

2 Using the same yarn and sewing at the same tension as the knitting, sew into the head of each stitch alternately.

Backstitch

Backstitch provides a quick, satisfactory seam for many purposes, as well as being a technique that most people already know. However, it is difficult to get as neat a finish as with either mattress stitch or by grafting and it is not suitable for garments made from heavier weight yarns. When you sew through both pieces of knitting check that the stitches are in line with each other. Use a tapestry needle and yarn to match the knitting.

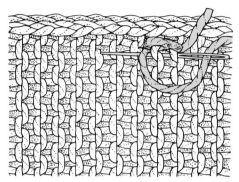

1 Lay the two pieces you are joining with right sides together. With the needle threaded, sew three small stitches one on top of the other at the beginning of the seam.

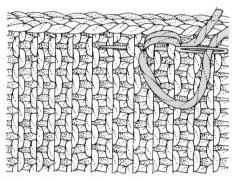

2 Insert the needle into the back of the first stitch and take it out one stitch along.

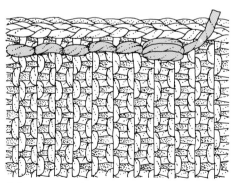

3 Repeat the process all along the seam, keeping the tension constant and the stitches as tight as you can without puckering or distorting the knitting.

WEIGHTS

ounces	1	2	3	4	5	6	7	8	9	10	11	12	13	14	15	16	17	18	19	20
grams	28	57	85	113	142	170	198	227	255	283	312	340	369	397	425	454	482	510	539	567

Please note that these conversions are approximate to the nearest gram.

grams	25	50	75	100	125	150	175	200	225	250	275	300	325	350	375	400	425	450	475	500
ounces	1	$1\frac{3}{4}$	$2\frac{3}{4}$	$3\frac{1}{2}$	$4\frac{1}{2}$	$5\frac{1}{4}$	$6\frac{1}{4}$	7	8	$8\frac{3}{4}$	$9\frac{3}{4}$	$10\frac{1}{2}$	$11\frac{1}{2}$	$12\frac{1}{4}$	$13\frac{1}{4}$	14	15	$15\frac{3}{4}$	$16\frac{3}{4}$	$17\frac{3}{4}$

Please note that these conversions are approximate to the nearest $\frac{1}{4}$ ounce.

MEASUREMENTS

centimetres	1	2	3	4	5	6	7	8	9	10	11	12	13	14	15	16	17	18	19	20
inches	$\frac{1}{2}$	$\frac{3}{4}$	$1\frac{1}{4}$	$1\frac{1}{2}$	2	$2\frac{1}{4}$	$2\frac{3}{4}$	$3\frac{1}{4}$	$3\frac{1}{2}$	4	$4\frac{1}{4}$	$4\frac{3}{4}$	5	$5\frac{1}{2}$	6	$6\frac{1}{4}$	$6\frac{3}{4}$	7	$7\frac{1}{2}$	$7\frac{3}{4}$
centimetres	21	22	23	24	25	26	27	28	29	30	31	32	33	34	35	36	37	38	39	40
inches	$8\frac{1}{4}$	$8\frac{3}{4}$	9	$9\frac{1}{2}$	$9\frac{3}{4}$	$10\frac{1}{4}$	$10\frac{3}{4}$	11	$11\frac{1}{2}$	$11\frac{3}{4}$	$12\frac{1}{4}$	$12\frac{1}{2}$	13	$13\frac{1}{2}$	$13\frac{3}{4}$	$14\frac{1}{4}$	$14\frac{1}{2}$	15	$15\frac{1}{4}$	$15\frac{3}{4}$

Please note that these conversions are approximate to the nearest $\frac{1}{4}$ inch.

KNITTING NEEDLES

Metric	English	US
2	14	0
$2\frac{1}{4}$	13	1
$2\frac{3}{4}$	12	2
3	11	3
$3\frac{1}{4}$	10	4
$3\frac{3}{4}$	9	5
4	8	6
$4\frac{1}{2}$	7	7
5	6	8
$5\frac{1}{2}$	5	9
6	4	10
$6\frac{1}{2}$	3	—
7	2	$10\frac{1}{2}$
$7\frac{1}{2}$	1	11
8	0	13
9	00	15
(mm)		

WASHING KNITWEAR

After spending a lot of time and trouble hand knitting a sweater it pays to wash it with care and respect. Some yarns are produced that may be safely machine washed, but the majority of yarns should be washed by hand, using pure soap flakes, or a special wool detergent. Wash and rinse thoroughly, in warm water, not hot water.

Before washing a brightly-coloured garment, check that it is colourfast by dipping a small piece of it into the soapy water. Press it out in a white cloth. If it leaves a stain, wash in cold water.

Never leave knitted garments to soak, especially if they are deep-dyed or multi-coloured.

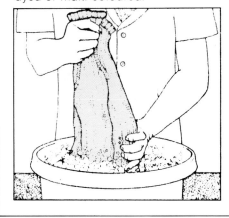

1 Always squeeze the suds into the garment gently and do not rub or felting will occur. Don't leave the garment to soak, but rinse and remove quickly. Make certain the rinse water is clear before removing the garment. Add fabric softener to the last rinse if you wish.

2 Place the garment in a thick towel, white if possible, and roll both up. Place extra towels on top of the garment for extra absorption before rolling up. Press the roll with your hands or "hammer" it with your fists to remove as much water as possible. Repeat this with another towel if the garment is still very wet. Alternatively, put the garment in a pillow-case and give it a fast, short spin in a washing machine. If the yarn is a fine quality wool, the length of the spin must be only a few seconds or the garment may become matted.

3 Finish drying the garment by laying it out flat on another clean towel, away from direct heat. Make sure the knitting is correctly shaped. Store the garment in a drawer; never hang it up as it can be easily pulled out of shape.

ABBREVIATIONS

beg	beginning
dec	decrease
foll	following
g	gram
inc	increase
k	knit
k2 tog	knit two stitches together
()	repeat all the instructions between brackets as many times as indicated
p	purl
patt	pattern
psso	pass slip stitch over
rep from *	repeat all the instructions that follow asterisk
st	stitch
st st	stocking stitch
tog	together
turn	turn the work around at the point indicated, before the end of a row

GLOSSARY OF TERMS

British	North American
cast off	bind off
catch down	tack down
slipover	V-neck vest
stocking stitch	stockinette stitch
Swiss darning	duplicate stitch
tension	gauge
waistcoat	vest
yarn round needle	yarn over

Note: See needle conversion chart, p. 126

YARN QUANTITIES FOR SINGLE-SHADE GARMENTS

You may prefer to make a garment in a single shade; 4 ply wool and double knitting wool give the best results. Below are the approximate quantities of yarn required. If you use a yarn other than Rowan, you must obtain the correct tension given in the basic pattern instructions.

Tweed is not suitable for a single-shade garment.)

4 ply wool
Use 25g hanks of Rowan Botany or Fine Fleck yarn, or standard 4 ply wool. (Light

Sizes in/cm	Sweater	Jacket	Cardigan	Slipover	Waistcoat	Short top
24/61	6	9	7	3	4	3
28/71	7	10	8	4	5	4
32/81	10	14	13	5	6	5
36/91	12	17	15	6	7	6
40/102	14	19	18	8	9	8
44/112	16	21	20	10	10	10
48/122	18	23	22	11	11	11

Double knitting wool
Use 50g balls of Rowan Designer DK, Rowan Fleck DK, or standard double knitting wool.

Sizes in/cm	Sweater	Jacket	Cardigan	Slipover	Waistcoat	Short top
24/61	4	5	4	3	3	3
28/71	6	7	6	4	4	4
32/81	9	10	9	5	5	5
36/91	10	12	10	6	6	6
40/102	12	13	12	6	6	6
44/112	13	14	13	7	7	7
48/122	14	16	14	8	8	8

ACKNOWLEDGMENTS
Dorling Kindersley would like to thank
Sally Powell for design assistance;
The Button Box, Covent Garden, for
supplying all the buttons; and the
following companies for the loan of
clothes and props:
The Fitness Centre, S. Fisher, Hamleys,
The Hat Shop, H & M Hennes, Hobbs,
Betty Jackson, Lyn Lundie, Mulberry,
and Neal Street East.

YARN INFORMATION
The following designs are available in
kit form:

COWBOY p. 18
FLOWER GIRL p. 30
MOUSE p. 34
WELSH POPPY p. 44
ACORN p. 56
SPLASH p. 66
ZIGZAG p. 94

For a list of stockists of Rowan yarns
and kits, please write or telephone:
The Westminster Trading Corporation
5 Northern Boulevard
Amherst, New Hampshire
03031
Telephone (603) 886-5041

KNITTERS
Mrs. Baldwin, Mrs. Bannister, Mrs. Barfoot, Mrs. Bland, Mrs. Bradbury, Mrs. Broda,
Mrs. Bryant, Mrs. Catchpole, Mrs. L. M. Clarke, Mrs. M. Clarke, Mrs. S. Clarke,
Mrs. Collison, Mrs. Cook, Mrs. Downes, Mrs. Edwards, Mrs. A. Ellis, Mrs. W. Ellis,
Mrs. Evans, Mrs. Fields, Mrs. Follis, Mrs. Freeborn, Mrs. Furlong, Mrs. Garland,
Mrs. Gwilliams, Mrs. Hanby, Mrs. Hill, Mrs. Howard, Mrs. Hudson, Mrs. Hyslop,
Mrs. Jarvis, Mrs. J. M. Jones, Mrs. M. Jones, Miss King, Mrs. King, Mrs. Lester,
Mrs. Letts, Mrs. Magigot, Mrs. Mathews, Mrs. Mercer, Mrs. Morgan, Mrs. Naden,
Mrs. Newsam, Mrs. Oliver, Mrs. Pashby, Mrs. Pearce, Mrs. Phillips, Mrs. Prew,
Mrs. Robertson, Mrs. Saxby, Mrs. Shirley, Mrs. Silvester, Mrs. Stanley,
Mrs. Sutherland, Mrs. Thomas, Mrs. Thompson, Mrs. Tidball, Mrs. Turnbull,
Mrs. M. F. Watson, Mrs. R. Watson, Mrs. Weatherstone, Mrs. Webb, Mrs. Williams,
Mrs. Withington, Mrs. Wren, Mrs. Ziontek.

PHOTOGRAPHIC CREDITS
Ursula Steiger model shots, **Douglas Griffins** flat shots
Colin Molyneux photographs of Sasha's family

STYLIST
Victoria Hamilton

HAIR AND MAKE UP
Fliff Lidsey, Lanora at Complections, London School of Make-Up

ILLUSTRATORS
John Hutchinson, Jane Cradock-Watson

TYPESETTING
Chambers Wallace

REPRODUCTION
Hong Kong Graphic Arts